The Psychology of Political Communication

The Psychology of
Political Communication

Edited by Ann N. Crigler

Ann Arbor
THE UNIVERSITY OF MICHIGAN PRESS

1999   1998   1997   1996   4   3   2   1

A CIP catalog record for this book is available from the British Library.

Library of Congress Cataloging-in-Publication Data
The psychology of political communication / edited by Ann N. Crigler.
    p. cm.
   Includes bibliographical references and index.
   ISBN 0-472-10641-4 (hardcover : alk. paper)
   1. Mass media—Political aspects—United States.   2. Mass media—Psychological aspects—United States.   3. Communication—Political aspects—United States.   4. United States—Politics and government—1989–   I. Crigler, Ann N.
P95.82.U6P78   1996
302.23'0973–dc20   96-10324
                        CIP

To Stephen Michael Caine

Contents

Tables

Figures

Acknowledgments

Studies reported in "News, Psychology, and Presidential Politics" are based on articles previously published in the Summer 1991 *Journal of Communication* 41 (3): 6–25, "The Mindscape of the Presidency: *Time* Magazine 1945–1985" by Roderick Hart, D. Smith-Howell, and J. Llewellyn. Reproduced with permission of Oxford University Press. Additional materials were drawn from *Political Communication and Persuasion* 7 (1990): 215–28, "Evolution of Presidential News Coverage" by Roderick Hart, D. Smith-Howell, and J. Llewellyn, published by Taylor and Francis, Inc., Washington, D.C. Reproduced with permission. All rights reserved.

The Gamson chapter is adapted from his *Talking Politics,* New York: Cambridge University Press, 1992. Reprinted with the permission of Cambridge University Press.

"Constructing Public Opinion: The Uses of Fictional and Nonfictional Television in Conversations about the Environment" is a revised version of "Methods, Metaphors, and Media Research: The Uses of Television in Political Conversation" by Michael Delli Carpini and Bruce Williams, published in *Communication Research* 21 (December 1994): 782–812. Reprinted by permission of Sage Publications, Inc.

The Perloff chapter is an enlarged version of a 1993 article on the third-person effect: "Third-Person Effect Research 1983–1992: A Review and Synthesis," *International Journal of Public Opinion Research* 5:167–84. Several sections from that article have been reprinted by permission of Oxford University Press.

The editor is indebted to a number of people whose efforts, advice, and support have made this book possible. The fifteen individual authors have made thoughtful contributions to our understanding of political communication processes. Their timely participation in this project is most appreciated.

A special debt of gratitude is owed to Nelson W. Polsby and the students and staff at the Institute of Governmental Studies at the University of California, Berkeley. They generously shared their ideas, expertise and space while I completed the manuscript.

Many thanks are due to Marion Just, Sherrie Mazingo, Russ Neuman, and Shawn Rosenberg for their constructive comments on parts of the manuscript and for their invaluable encouragement and support. Thanks also to the anonymous reviewers whose very useful suggestions have been incorporated into the manuscript by the editor and authors.

Jody Battles provided many hours of assistance on the final manuscript and bibliography. José Gomez aided with the graphics. My deepest thanks go to the editors and staff at the University of Michigan Press and to Lisa Davis for her diligence and skillful work on the index. I am thankful for their help, which greatly eased the burdens of preparing the text for publication. Whatever errors appear in the final manuscript are, of course, my responsibility.

Finally, I am most grateful for the love and support of my family and friends who were not only understanding and encouraging when I had to spend time on writing and editing, but who were also interested in the substance of political communication.

Introduction: Making Sense of Politics; Constructing Political Messages and Meanings

Ann N. Crigler

Communication is central to the study of politics, political power, and governing. As E. E. Schattschneider argued, political power rests with those who control the arena of debate and the direction of discourse (Schattschneider 1975). This has been true of democratic governments since well before the invention of mass media technologies. However, in a mass media–dominated political arena, such as the United States, the struggle to define issues and disseminate information and opinions favorable to one's own goals is often played out in public with the objective of shifting, harnessing, or tapping into existing popular opinions and beliefs. Political power lies with those who strike the resonant chord, turning the discourse toward or away from particular issues.

The study of political communication focuses on these questions of discourse, analyzing the processes of persuasion, message construction, and interpretation of meaning. In this book the authors take a constructionist approach to political communication, in which all the participants in the communications process—media, officials, and the public—are viewed as actively engaged in constructing messages and meanings. The constructionist approach admits all people to roles of interpretation and issue definition limited only by their interest and attention to the topic.

Constructionism builds on previous research in political communication and attempts to capture the dynamic and interactive process by which elites and individuals give meaning to political events. Constructionism draws on a number of strands in the "media effects" tradition of political communication research, as well as on studies of news making and the psychology of the audience. A brief review of these research approaches is given to show how constructionism has evolved. Constructionism is then defined and differentiated from these other approaches. The chapter concludes with an overview of the remaining chapters.

The Media Effects Tradition

The oldest and dominant approach to the study of political communication focuses on media effects. Researchers in the media effects tradition have concentrated on the impact of media on their audiences by examining the flow of communication and influence from sources, through channels carrying messages to the public. Underlying this approach is the assumption of a one-way causal relationship from media to audience. Roles are defined as either active or passive, with the sources generally described as active and the audience as passive. Later developments in this tradition have refined the model by specifying the conditions and limitations of media effects and have considered feedback from the audience, making the model less unidirectional. These later developments, modifying the unidirectional aspect of media effects, constitute the platform for the constructionist approach. The modified media effects literature is diverse and includes studies of agenda-setting and priming, uses and gratifications, and media systems dependency theory. In addition, constructionism owes a great deal to the study of the construction of messages in the news-making tradition and to the interpretation of meaning in the political cognition perspective. While researchers have been modifying the media effects model, it is still the dominant way of thinking about media and politics.

The Magic Bullet. An assumption of media power pervades everyday language and thinking. American political lore is replete with examples illustrating that mass media affect political outcomes and processes in many ways. William Randolph Hearst, seeking headline stories for his newspapers, is reputed to have been a key factor behind the Spanish-American War. Hitler's propaganda machine was able to mobilize popular German support for the war effort. For those people who watched the 1960 presidential debate on television, John Kennedy's suntanned, smiling countenance seems to have been a decisive factor in his victory over Richard Nixon, who appeared tired and ill. Spiro Agnew claimed that the liberal, Eastern media hounded him from office. Others claim that the media, especially television, catapulted an unknown Georgian from "Jimmy who?" to the White House. The implicit assumption of these examples is that a media message goes out to the public and, like a bullet shot from a gun, penetrates the mind of the audience, where the message lodges in the same condition as it was fired.

The flow of communications. Researchers have been hard-pressed to find more than anecdotal evidence of such "bullet" or "hypodermic" media effects. Harold Lasswell went beyond the simple idea of propaganda and "the big lie" by introducing his now famous flow model of political communication: "who says what, to whom, with what effect" (Lasswell 1964). His definition describes the flow of communication from source through channel to audience with some impact. The messages flow in one direction and the audience is treated as a passive recipient. One of the strengths of this model, however, is that it draws attention to the components and conditions of communication and does not see communication effects as inevitable or monolithic.

Communication and political persuasion. Lasswell's flow theory has been central to the study of persuasion and opinion change. Election campaigns are typically a process of persuasion, in which candidates contend with each other to get their messages across to the public. Campaign advertising can be seen as a classic example of persuasion using the flow model. The source is clearly identified as the candidate, the message is the ad, and the audience is the receiver. The impact of advertising messages on the public has been demonstrated in terms of candidate name recognition and image formation as well as the priority of campaign issues. For example, in the 1988 presidential election, Marjorie Hershey (1989) found that after exposure to the Bush advertising campaign, (along with an independent committee's ads featuring convicted-but-released murderer Willie Horton) "the proportion of respondents saying that George Bush was 'tough enough' on crime and criminals rose from 23% in July to a full 61% in late October, while the proportion saying Dukakis was *not* tough enough rose from 36% to 49%." With evidence of dramatic opinion shifts such as these, it is not surprising that candidates and their staffs spend so much time and money communicating with potential voters and donors. They see communication as central to gaining and maintaining power.

Refinements of Lasswell's flow theory of media effects. Perhaps the most profound refinement of the Lasswellian model was a shift in emphasis from persuasion to agenda priority effects. In their classic study of the 1968 presidential election in Chapel Hill, North Carolina, Maxwell McCombs and Donald Shaw (1972) found that the issues given the most coverage in the press were also the issues identified by the public as "most important" problems. The agenda-setting function of the press suggests to audience members the important topics to think about and for how long to think about them. This power of the press is a resource for officials and others with access to the news media. By directing people's attention toward some issues and away from others, elites may be able to shape public debate.

In a reaffirmation of the McCombs and Shaw agenda-setting thesis, Shanto Iyengar and Donald Kinder (1987a) found that the issues emphasized in the news during an election campaign are the ones that people use to evaluate candidates. Their research expanded upon the agenda-setting model and has indicated that news coverage influences not only which issues people think about, but how they think about them. Iyengar's experiments on political and social problems show that the way in which news stories are framed leads people to attribute responsibility differentially (Iyengar 1992). Moreover, the "causal attributions" that people give for social problems influence their assessments of the president (Iyengar and Kinder 1987a).

The power of the press to influence issue priorities and attributions is enhanced by the public's dependence on the news media for information about subjects beyond their direct experience (Ball-Rokeach 1985). The mass media may be an individual's only source for news about foreign affairs or even about other regions of the country or social classes or cultural groups outside the immediate environment. The priorities and framing of the media presentations can be expected to be more influential when there are no competing sources of information.

Journalists Make News

While much of the research on media effects depends on studies of media content and public reactions, in another approach to political communication, researchers seek to explain the news content by looking at the way news organizations go about their work. These studies examine the construction of news stories through interviews, observation, and participant-observation of journalists. Several researchers have stressed that journalists' values and work patterns contribute to the production of apparently homogeneous news. Gaye Tuchman finds that journalists categorize events in terms of how they happen (e.g., "spot" vs. "continuing" news), giving priority to the most timely news (Tuchman 1973). Herbert Gans, in an observational study of *Time* magazine and CBS News, showed that journalists used certain rules of thumb in "deciding what's news." News about prominent persons, stories that originate in Washington, D.C., crime, and investigations are considered more newsworthy than stories about social trends or about events in foreign countries (Gans 1979). Edward J. Epstein's observation of television news reporting supports Gans's finding about what is newsworthy, but it highlights the organizational and technological constraints on television news gathering that give prominence to events that are most accessible to camera crews (Epstein 1973). In separate studies, Leon Sigal (1973) and Stephen Hess (1981) explain that news organizations' reliance on news "beats" revolves around a relatively small circle of official sources who tend to dominate the news. Timothy Crouse's study of the 1972 presidential campaign, *The Boys on the Bus* (1973), shows that reporters rely not only on a small number of campaign sources but on each other for information. The interactions among reporters, coupled with the pressure to file daily stories from the campaign trail, result in the phenomenon of "pack journalism" and provide a relatively homogeneous version of events.

News making, the process by which a relatively distant, disjointed, and vast political world is condensed and given meaning, is central to the information that is available to the public. In selecting information from the vast panoply of events, journalists present a reality, based on the priorities of newsworthiness. Reporters "construct and reconstruct social reality by establishing the context in which social phenomena are perceived and defined" (Tuchman 1973). W. Lance Bennett (1988) argues that the criteria of news-worthiness result in a construction of reality that is personalized, dramatized, fragmented, and normalized. The news emphasizes conflicts among persons (such as the president and the Speaker of the House) rather than institutions and focuses on the dramatic story elements of events which may not typify reality. By stringing together exciting bits of narrative, reality is fragmented into discrete stories without common motivation or explication. Those explanations that are offered in the press tend to reflect dominant ideologies and official interpretations of events. Therefore the journalists' construction of reality constrains the public's access to information and its understanding of political life.

"Official" Sources Controlling the News

A whole literature has grown up around the process of sources making news. Officials compete with other political actors who seek to present their versions of "reality" in each day's news. In their efforts to prevail in political debate, many researchers find that officials dominate political discourse. Timothy Cook finds that members of Congress are able to control their coverage in news in their home constituencies. Because most local journalists depend upon the member to provide information about congressional action relevant to the constituency, they are generally willing to accept the member's version of events. Members of Congress often find that their press releases are reprinted with only minor editing in local news outlets (Cook 1989).

In a study of critical policy decisions, Martin Linsky (1986) reports that officials who take a proactive approach to managing news appear to be more successful in the political process than those who simply react to external events and news coverage. Officials have various resources at their disposal, including press officers who issue press releases, hold briefings, set up press conferences, and help craft messages to the public. Members of the executive branch have even greater opportunities for controlling news. Samuel Kernell (1986) argues that presidents attempt to control discourse and maximize their power by directly addressing the public through the press. Successful officials utilize press strategies to maximize their effectiveness in office as well as to gain office.

The Active Audience

While research traditions have centered on the roles of journalists and official sources in crafting media messages, other scholars have concentrated on the audience. Researchers have been increasingly impressed that the individual's active role in the communication process is guaranteed by the abundant possibilities of the human mind. Individuals may choose to attend or not to attend to particular messages. Leon Festinger (1957) argues that people select messages that are consonant with their prior beliefs. Jonathan Freedman and David Sears (1965) expanded Festinger's approach to include the individual's selective retention of information that passes through the "perceptual screen". In other words, even if a message is received, it may not be retained.

Individuals also have choices among media channels. What people seek to gain from a medium may affect how they use that channel and its messages. Jay Blumler and Elihu Katz (1974) describe the "uses and gratifications" of media to explain why the same message may affect people differently. People go to the media with different expectations and demands. One person may be seeking an explanation for the latest presidential action, whereas another individual may be searching for some light comedy to ease the tensions of a busy day. A television news story detailing the president's activities may provide useful information to the one viewer, while the other may be amused or bored, depending on the nature of the story. Whether or not one is gratified depends on the uses one expects to make of the media experience.

Political cognition has taken the study of the communication process a step further, focusing on the active role of individuals in making sense of political messages. D. A. Graber, for example, suggests that people process information based on schema for various concepts and objects which they develop over time and out of their own individual experiences (Graber 1988). The more developed the schema, the more likely the individual is to be able to process complex information on the topic. Samuel Popkin further argues that people utilize heuristic "shortcuts" to reason about politics and that even when people do not remember specific information, they may have used that information to modify their thinking about candidates (Popkin 1991). Both authors show how individual cognitive activity "tames the information tide."

Studies of what people learn from political communication show that the audience's interest in the topic makes a difference. W. Russell Neuman, Marion Just and Ann Crigler (1992) find that people are better informed about issues accessible to them in their daily lives and are able to learn more about issues with which they are already familiar. People who are interested in most topics can learn as much as those who are more cognitively skilled but not as interested.

Other researchers emphasize that individuals' political ideologies, interests, and sophistication affect what they comprehend about politics (Neuman 1986; Converse 1964). Neuman points out that many people are unaware of the political world in spite of the plenitude of information channels. He argues that the public can be differentiated based on their level of sophistication in politics. Shawn Rosenberg also differentiates individuals, but he does so according to their level of psychological development. Rosenberg shows that people at higher levels think about politics in more and more complex ways than people at lower levels (Rosenberg 1988). Clearly, these differences in the sophistication and psychological development of individuals affect the meaning they give to political messages.

Constructionism

The constructionist approach builds on past literature in political communication, especially studies of media effects, news making, source control, and political cognition, by recognizing the responsibilities of all the actors in the process of political meaning making: journalists, sources, and individuals. The focus of research, however, moves away from message impact, persuasion, and behavioral change toward an emphasis on how political messages are created and actively interpreted by individuals as well as institutions such as the mass media or government decision makers.

By focusing on how people make sense of a world of political events, personalities, and images, constructionism requires an examination of the process through which political "realities" are shaped and transformed. Many individuals, institutions, and groups share responsibility in this process by controlling, at least to some extent, the nature and scope of political debate, and thus contribute to the construction of political understanding.

Constructionism is not simply an expression of the "active audience" perspective, because all the participants in the communications process—media, officials, and the public—are viewed as engaged in constructing messages and meanings. Unlike the media effects paradigm, constructionism does not overweight the role of the media but includes sources and audiences in the dynamic, interactive process of communication. Literature in the media effects tradition characterizes communication as flowing from sources, through channels, to audiences. Roles are defined as either active or passive, even when applied to members of the audience as in the two-step flow theories with active opinion leaders and passive followers (Katz and Lazarsfeld 1955; Lazarsfeld, Berelson, and McPhee 1954). The constructionist approach acknowledges that all people have the capacity to interpret events and discourse, although the likelihood of actively engaging may be limited by their interest or attention to the topic.

The language of source and audience is not adequate to describe the interpretive process. For example, the Clarence Thomas Supreme Court nomination hearings would be studied very differently by a researcher from the media effects tradition than one taking a constructionist approach. In the effects tradition, the impact of the hearings on the audience's assessment of the Senate, the judicial process, or the problem of sexual harassment might be the focus of the inquiry. A constructionist would ask somewhat different questions.

How did the participants and the media arrange the information and images presented to the public? What picture were they trying to convey? And, how did individuals attending to the coverage understand what was presented? What did they apply from their own experiences to interpret the event? How did the elite participants' anticipation of the public's interpretations and their later sense of the public's interpretation of the hearings affect their actions? Inherent in the constructionist model is the coprocessing of meaning among all the participants.

A constructionist approach places the emphasis of inquiry on political meaning and the process by which people come to make sense of the world of politics. The term *meaning* refers to that which one intends to convey, especially through language, as well as to that which is actually conveyed. These two definitions reflect the process of communication and the key elements of message creation and interpretation. Meaning is one of the major dimensions underlying the field of communication and is common to a number of seemingly conflicting theories, such as "limited effects," critical theory, and semiotics. In an early work on communication effects, Joseph Klapper pointed out why the media had limited power to change opinions. Media impact is constrained by the meaning individuals have already given to political objects, so that meanings are crystallized or reinforced rather than changed by communication (Klapper 1960). Even the major voting studies conducted by University of Michigan researchers dismissed the role of mass media in determining people's vote preferences and argued instead that in the "funnel of causality" stable political beliefs, such as partisanship, shape citizen interpretations and electoral choices (Campbell et al. 1960).

Among critical theorists, interest has been directed to "oppositional reading"—the process in which individuals counter the meanings of messages promulgated by powerful cultural groups and supply their own contrary interpretations to the messages. (See review in Katz 1987.) Semiotics also focuses on interpretation, but it concentrates on the texts of communication. The underlying theory is that "communication is the generation of meaning in messages—whether by the encoder or decoder. Meaning is not an absolute, static concept to be found neatly parceled up in the message. Meaning is an active process . . . " (Fiske 1988).

This moves us to a second characteristic of constructionism. The construction of political meaning is continual and dynamic. Political meaning evolves from an interaction among individuals, the media, and other sources of political information. It is necessary to examine both the creation of the messages presented in the media and the construction of meaning that individuals take from the messages, because they are all part of an integrated process of communicating meaning. The formulation of messages is not an automatic "mirror of reality" presentation of facts or recounting of events. Media messages serve as a primary means for elites to create certain images or to voice or silence particular views, and they serve as a major source of information for a public trying to make sense of the political world. Working with the sources of the news (sometimes cooperatively, other times competitively), journalists convey particular stories to members of the public, who, in turn, give their own meanings to these messages in the context of their own experiences and knowledge. The process of constructing political meaning, then, becomes a dynamic spiral of active interpretations and reinterpretations. The spiral of meaning making takes place within individuals as well as among people, groups, and institutions, within a cultural, social, political, economic, and historical context. Constructing political meaning is both personal and interpersonal, or in Jurgen Habermas's terminology is a subjective and intersubjective process (Habermas [1962] 1989).

To examine the dynamic process of constructing political meaning, it is necessary to consider both the content and the presentation of messages. Issues vary in their salience to members of the public, the media, or political decision makers. For example, the Reagan administration was preoccupied with the importance of what it called the Strategic Defense Initiative (SDI). The media generally paid little attention to this "Star Wars" plan and public interest in the issue was scant indeed (Neuman, Just, and Crigler 1992).

Salience of a topic may be enhanced by the style of presentation. In addition, the style of message presentation affects the interpretations that actors give to the communication. Members of the public, for example, may express meanings that are quite different from those of the media or political elites. Researchers have found that symbolic language may allow a wide array of interpretations to be given to the same message (Mead 1934; Bennett 1975; Edelman 1964, 1988). When communications are condensed, individuals are forced to elaborate the meaning, which they do in light of the cultural context of the message as well as their own experiences and cognitive abilities. Differing interpretations also appear more likely from complex forms of communication, particularly those that combine verbal and nonverbal channels, such as television (Graber 1987b). These complex forms of communication help trigger different aspects of the individual's thoughts and feelings.

The variety of interpretations arises not only from the style of presentation but from the diversity of the participants active in the exchange. Each individual draws upon a unique set of prior experiences to interpret new information. Cognitive structures further constrain the complexity of interpretations that people produce (Rosenberg 1988). Emotions also play a role in the resonance and interpretation of messages (Marcus and Rahn 1990; Sniderman, Brody, and Tetlock 1991).

Constructionism focuses on the generation of meaning. It is pluralistic and dynamic in its approach to the process of communication, taking into account numerous players interacting with one another. In the constructionist view, elites, media professionals and the public actively produce, interpret, and reinterpret messages in the struggle to control political debate. The chapters included in this volume illustrate the richness of interpretations encouraged by the constructionist approach to political communication.

The book is divided into two sections. The first section focuses on the construction of political messages in the media and the roles played by institutions in shaping those messages. These chapters focus on the press, the president, political consultants, campaign staffs, and public opinion. Each author emphasizes the highly interactive dynamic of message construction. The media are one of the powerful purveyors and creators of political information, but control over political debate and influence over policy directions evolve through a struggle of competing players. The news media may work with, in spite of, or, sometimes, against other political actors.

Chapters in the second part of the book take a closer look at individuals and how they construct political meanings from available messages. These chapters clearly highlight the active construction of meaning that individuals contribute to the political process. Data from focus groups, in-depth interviews, and surveys reveal the rich and varied interpretations that citizens create when they draw on their own experiences, perceptions of others' views, and particular media systems.

In the concluding chapter, Doris A. Graber reviews political communication research and suggests that the study of political communication is at a crossroads. Researchers, she argues, can continue to develop the field through "drift," allowing granting agencies and serendipity to set the research agenda, or they can choose a cybernetic approach in which investigators agree on goals and directions and pursue research programmatically. This book offers one possible approach to pursue by focusing on the construction of messages and the interpretation of meaning in the process of political communication.

CHAPTER 1

The Negotiation of Newsworthiness

Timothy E. Cook

Media are an integral part of the political process as they interact with other political actors to construct the news. In this chapter, Cook argues that it is necessary to move beyond a unidirectional flow model of communication that emphasizes political effects on the press or the media's influence on politics. Instead, we must examine the coproduction of news by journalists and sources—the negotiation of newsworthiness. This process of negotiation yields four types of stories running along a continuum from high media control to high source control. Comparing unedited C-SPAN coverage of several presidential events with corresponding stories on the network evening news reveals that neither side dominates the production of stories. White House coverage results from a complex interaction between and an anticipation of reactions by journalists and the president. In all this negotiation of newsworthiness, the public may be overlooked.

Introductory textbooks may not always tell us as much about American politics as we might like, but they provide a decent road map to American political science—or at least to our standard assumptions of what ought to be studied and how. Not only do we have a "textbook presidency" and a "textbook Congress," but political forces that a lay person might expect to encounter are sometimes oddly absent. One of these forces has been the American news media, which, up until the past ten years or so, was peripherally discussed and rarely accorded the status of a key player in contemporary politics. But with American government textbooks going through successive editions, more attention and even chapters have become devoted to the political impact of the news media. Perhaps with the rise of televisual election campaigns, of image-oriented presidencies, of gavel-to-gavel coverage of both houses of Congress, and of the increasingly evident role that journalists have taken for themselves, political science could no longer ignore the media's role and impact.

But there are many ways in which that role can be conceived. In a book devoted to the psychology of political communication, it's worth raising the question: how should political scientists go about studying the role of the news media?

I will propose here that the news media and their personnel may be most productively examined as political actors that deal with, influence, and are influenced by other political actors. Far from an approach of "media and politics" or "press-politics" that implies that the news media, while somehow not part of the political sphere, may affect politics, such an approach emphasizes that the news media are inherently political and that the manner in which they are organized to perform their tasks has political (if often unintended) consequences. In future work, I will develop this model more fully to suggest that reporters and officials do not interact primarily as decontextualized individuals, but as persons-in-roles—roles that have evolved into institutional practices.[1]

For now, however, I will restrict myself to considering the ways in which the news is a *coproduction* involving the significant input both of political actors outside the news media (usually officials) and of media personnel. In line with the constructionist approach that informs this book, the news itself is a construction, born of the ongoing negotiation of newsworthiness.

I should add that none of this requires our expanding the definition of "politics" past its customary use in political science. Indeed, I would go so far as to say that the American news media today are not merely part of politics by "authoritatively allocating values" or by contributing to "the activity by which decisions are arrived at and implemented in and for a community," they are part of *government.*

The Roads Not Taken

Naturally, one might ask: if the news media are so central to politics, why have political scientists overlooked them as objects of study? Some of this neglect was historical accident, but it also reflected the growth of the study of politics within a distinct discipline in the late nineteenth and early twentieth centuries. Ricci (1984), among others, has documented how the study of politics, theretofore an overarching study of the political sciences, evolved into one of several specialized disciplines of social science, imitating the division of the world in the natural sciences. For its proper sphere, political science gravitated toward the governmental; social and economic forces became the purview of related social sciences. The early disputes over how best to carry out a political science were not over the definition of "politics." Both historical comparativists and realists in the late nineteenth century agreed on their focus: the public realm of formal politics. Forces not officially sanctioned were glimpsed only when they intersected with formal processes. Thus, the news media seemed to enter into these processes only in providing information to the mass public. Thus, Woodrow Wilson, in his pathbreaking study *Congressional Government* (1885), referred to the press in decrying how their reporting failed to provide citizens with a clear understanding of how the national legislature operated.[2]

This emphasis on the American press as it intersected with formal institutions and processes may also have seemed unprofitable, insofar as there were and are fewer governmental constraints upon a free press than in other countries. In this context, the American press seemed to be the archetype of an unrestricted and unregulated news media. The disappearance of direct government subsidization of newspapers in the mid–nineteenth century and the rise of the news media as a big business, the liberal libel laws protecting journalists and the relative weakness of regulation all contributed to a portrayal of formal journalistic autonomy that would seem to place the news media outside of political control and thus discourage political scientists from examining the American news media.

As Chaffee and Hochheimer (1982) have nicely shown, the general concern with the news media's impact on politics via public opinion was soon to become further restricted to elections. Social scientists following World War I and the rise of fascism in the 1920s and 1930s were, not surprisingly, preoccupied with the potential of governmental propaganda. Harold Lasswell (1927), the leading student of propaganda in political science, defined it as "the management of collective attitudes by the manipulation of significant symbols," later distinguishing it from education by noting how propaganda aimed at "attitudes that are recognized as controversial within a given community" (1935b, 3). Lasswell's definition suggested that the key place to study media in politics was persuasion that was deliberate, controversial, or manipulative— although the areas that do not fall under this rubric are precisely where media studies have shown considerable influence.

In studying the impact of propaganda, social scientists drew upon expertise in marketing. But to use that knowledge, they needed to find a political decision comparable to those made by consumers selecting a product to purchase. Choosing a candidate fit the bill better than longer-range influences upon attitudes, perceptions, or cognitive frames. These factors came together most powerfully in the work of Paul Lazarsfeld, starting with the 1940 Erie County study, *The People's Choice* (Lazarsfeld, Berelson, and Gaudet 1944), which established the "effects tradition" as the initial paradigm for mass (including political) communication research. As it turns out, by selecting a homogeneous community for their survey, Lazarsfeld and his colleagues were unable to conclude anything but a limited persuasive impact of the news media on the vote. This conclusion was deemed so persuasive that the less sociologically oriented set of election studies from the University of Michigan did not even bother to study the impact of the media; news consumption was regarded only as "vicarious participation in campaign activities available to practically every American" (Campbell, Gurin, and Miller 1954, 30).

Even during the 1950s, not all scholars pointed to limited effects (e.g., cf. Lang and Lang 1959). But the effects paradigm subtly but powerfully foreclosed certain answers by pushing research away from particular questions. Not only did the paradigm highlight only narrow ways to gauge media effects upon the public: in the electoral context via individual voting decisions, more centrally, it directed scholars away from any research that did not fit the larger assumption of the effects tradition: a linear understanding of the communication process, passing from a source who codes the message by a given medium to a receiver who decodes it and acts upon it.

This focus on the flow of communication, thus, emphasized the role of the media in news gathering as "gatekeeping," whereby journalists winnowed out certain news items to come up with the daily news. Research focused on whether messages were received as they were sent and how completely and accurately. The prospect of journalists reformulating and re-creating the news in the day-in-day-out process of news making rather than merely filtering it was not often considered, nor was the occasionally adumbrated possibility that politicians might anticipate the rules of newsworthiness in deciding which messages to provide (for rare exceptions, see Cater 1959; Matthews 1960, chap. 9; and Cohen 1963). Likewise, what members of the audience could do *with* news content for their own purposes was neglected in favor of what the media could do *to* them. Such an understanding was not questioned in the political climate of the 1950s and early 1960s, when the dominance of elitist pluralism implicitly embraced a top-down model of governance.

Since the mid-1960s, of course, the effects tradition has slowly been eroded, first by the expansion of effects to include public agenda setting, and then by the turn to audience studies that stressed the ways in which the public could creatively rework the messages in their own ways for their own purposes. Yet long after its fall, the effects tradition has left a curious hold on political communication studies: a unidirectional model that sees political communication as going from political sources through the news media to the public, which responds and pressures politicians to put forth policy that will then be implemented. In particular, models of political communication have tended to make two unwarranted assumptions: first, if the public is not involved, then by definition the media cannot be said to have exerted influence; second, the media, serving as a conduit of information from others, must not be able to exert an independent influence. The paradigm, even when directly disputed and decried, has continued to limit investigation.

Trouble in Paradigms

Stephen Hess (1986, 103) displayed the first presumption best, when discussing why senators should be expected not to exploit media strategies as part of their legislative work: "Trying to use the media to get legislation through Congress is a Rube Goldberg design based on (A) legislator influencing (B) reporter to get information into (C) news outlet so as to convince (D) voters who will then put pressure on (E) other legislators. Given all of the problems inherent in successfully maneuvering through the maze, no wonder that legislative strategies are usually variations of (A) legislator asking (E) other legislators for their support." Yet, as I have argued elsewhere in greater length (Cook 1989), the American news media can and do directly influence political elites: helping highlight particular issues and alternatives, influence perceptions of public moods, and in other ways shape the context of one legislator asking another for support, with little or no input from the public. It is often forgotten that only once did Ronald Reagan's much-vaunted communication skills succeed in pressuring Congress by mobilizing public opinion (the 1981 tax cut; see West 1988). Reagan's going public at other times might have succeeded to move an otherwise recalcitrant legislature even when public opinion was divided or confused. Far from following Hess's Rube Goldberg scenario, then, Reagan's presidency relied upon setting a context and a tone that raised the stakes of resistance or inaction.

The second presumption is best revealed in John Kingdon's (1984) otherwise estimable study of agenda processes. Kingdon suggests that the essential first step is the definition of problems that are worthy of public consideration and action. In policy realms that are already salient, empirical indicators are deemed most influential; less visible matters require what Kingdon terms "focusing events, crises and symbols" (99). Yet how do policy areas maintain, attain or lose salience? How do occurrences become focusing events, or crises? One flaw in Kingdon's analysis is his neglect of one key actor: the media. He claims that the media are less important than popular wisdom might predict, largely because "the media report what is going on in government, by and large, rather than having an independent effect *on* governmental agendas" (62). Kingdon does point out that the media might be important by allowing communication within policy communities, by magnifying (but not originating) issues, and by influencing public opinion. Yet his main point seems to be that the media have little independent effect upon agenda setting because they are largely passing along information from elsewhere.

Kingdon is partially right. Since journalists must wait for authoritative sources to do or say newsworthy things, their role in agenda setting is fundamentally unlike those of other political actors. Moreover, many studies of journalism reveal the power of sources in suggesting and shaping if not determining the news (e.g., Sigal 1973; Fishman 1980). Yet the literature, largely in sociology, is asymmetrical, with more journalists'-eye views of the process than there are perspectives from the politicians' side.[3] If, as Sigal (1986) has written, "sources make the news," then one has to wonder why these sources complain as much as they do about the coverage they garner.

It is by now well established that the news media do more than reflect—or even than pick and choose from among—what others are doing. The media's selectivity draws upon journalistic criteria for what makes a good news story, and such criteria do not equally favor all issues and all individuals. Far from providing an unfiltered conduit for political sources, journalists enter news making with certain expectations of newsworthy stories, raise their own questions, and rework the responses to establish an angle, find a lead, juxtapose different bits of information, and finish a satisfying account. Even relatively straightforward reporting of quotes can reveal doubts and questions that the sources may have preferred to have remained unasked (Clayman 1990). Moreover, journalists' notions of quality are reinforced within the news organization by superiors and peers who provide far more feedback than does the dimly glimpsed mass audience; such colleagues can work toward counterbalancing the pressure from sources (Darnton 1975; Gans 1979).

Such a conclusion does not mean that the media call the shots in the United States.[4] Instead, the process of news making is the result of what I have elsewhere termed the negotiation of newsworthiness (Cook 1989, 169)—the constant if implicit negotiations between political sources and journalists.[5] Each side controls important resources since news is expected to be both important *and* interesting. Politicians dictate conditions and rules of access and designate certain events and issues as important by providing an arena for them; journalists take this material while deciding whether something is interesting enough to cover and how to craft it into a coherent narrative. Sources likewise craft decisions in anticipation of journalistic definitions, not only reactively when figuring out what questions reporters are likely to pose, but also proactively to gain publicity. Yet if journalists do not consider it newsworthy by their own criteria for judgment, a source's power may not be enough to get it in print or on the air. At other times, sources may provide access to journalists for a particular purpose only to find that they have also unwittingly made themselves available to be questioned on other matters the journalists may find more newsworthy, and even when access is limited, their responses can be easily placed into another and often less favorable context. So whether or not problems and issues can rise to the American political agenda through the media depends not only upon the connection of these issues with powerful "authoritative sources" but also upon journalistic criteria for quality news, which political actors anticipate in deciding what course to pursue.

Any model of the political communication process in the United States must thus be interactive rather than unidirectional from source through medium to public. We cannot make simple interpretations of political effects *on* the news or of the media's effect *on* politics.[6] The two are so intertwined that it is preferable to study the news media's interactions with political actors, including the perspectives from both the political and the journalistic spheres in the process, and the effects that those interactions and negotiations have on the kind of news that appears and the kind of politics and policies that are thereby encouraged.

Consequently, I take a fairly broad approach to "negotiation." Rather than restrict ourselves to a definition that sees negotiation as a form of overt bargaining over precise ways to solve agreed-upon problems, I follow the lead of others who define negotiation more broadly to encompass not just the whole range of interactions but also how the parties to a negotiation learn about each other and anticipate what the actual bargaining will be like (for an overview of this literature in social psychology, see Pruitt and Carnevale 1993). As anthropologist P. H. Gulliver points out: "Throughout the process of interaction, the parties give each other information, directly and indirectly . . . Negotiation is a process of discovery. Discovery leads to some degree of reorganization and adjustment of understanding, expectations and behavior, leading (if successful) eventually to more specific discussion" (1979, 70).

In examining these negotiations, we must not stop with studies of individual journalists interacting with individual politicians. The actions of political actors and of journalists in the United States are contingent upon the roles they occupy within their respective political and social systems and the resultant rewards and sanctions to particular behaviors. Following March and Olsen (1989), among other "new institutionalists," we need to recognize the central part of forms, structures, routines, and established roles as they interact with the everyday practice of these political actors. Individuals within an institution do not act entirely according to a self-interested maximization of goals but according to "a logic of appropriateness" (160). Persons occupy roles that entail particular obligations, and they seek to match up new situations to extant role obligations. In that way, we can begin systematically to study interactions between a variety of political actors outside the media and a variety of journalists, to see the regularities that exist across the board, the variations, and the reasons for such variation.

Are the news media governed by systematized rules, roles, procedures, and structures? Although commonsensically, we think of reporters as individual "authors" of their pieces, news making is a collective process generally more influenced by the routine workings of journalism than by individual attitudes of journalists. Journalists accord high priority to objectivity, impartiality, and balance; so subjective individual opinions and attitudes are important only if and when they are reinforced by the routines of the work that they perform (cf. Lichter, Rothman, and Lichter 1986 and Gans 1985). Deciding what the news media cover by which means and methods are essentially organizational decisions shaped by the canons of responsible journalism and preexisting albeit flexible notions of newsworthiness (see, among others, Epstein 1973; Sigal 1973; Tuchman 1978; Gans 1979; Fishman 1980). And insofar as one's superiors and peers become central judges of one's product, the context of work must crucially influence the content of news (Darnton 1975).

In short, newspersons' decision making is directed by the understanding of what journalism is and what journalists do and constrained by the organizational choices of where to allocate personnel. Since these understandings are widely shared across news outlets,[7] media are more than just organizations; they approach institutional status. This agreement has lasted over time, too, as routines, norms, and values have endured even amid dramatic technological shifts such as the rise of the electronic media. The ideal of impartiality, for example, goes back at least as far as the birth of the penny press in the 1830s, when the search for a large audience necessitated playing down partisanship (Schudson 1978). The current focus of news on events and individual actors within continuing stories rather than analyses of social and political conditions—and indeed, the news emphasis upon reformism to make the system work more efficiently—dates back to the Progressive era's emphasis on cleaning up the system by placing well-qualified individuals in positions of power to administer in a nonpartisan manner. The Progressive era saw professional journalism developed and ensconced, and the terms of journalism and roles of journalists then devised have not significantly shifted, even with the rise of radio and television (Schudson 1978; Gans 1979; Leonard 1986; McGerr 1986).

In short, journalists bring particular conceptions of newsworthiness to bear when they approach their work, conceptions that partake not only of what might be called "production values"—whereby news should be novel, timely, terse, vivid, easily described, colorful, and visualizable—but also what Gans (1979, chap. 2) has called "enduring values," particular understandings of how the world works and of how the world should work. As Gans reminds us, while sources may make themselves *available,* and reporters may be under considerable pressure to report on them in ways that the sources find congenial, they cannot make news unless and until journalists deem the sources to make *suitable* news. Conflict is then built into the system of news making. Above all, for any news medium, whatever the source does must be packaged into a narrative. Not only must the story have protagonists and antagonists in conflict, but the sources' actions must move the story along to a new episode; in the absence of such movement, journalists tend to conclude that "nothing happened" and there is therefore no news (Fishman 1980). We might expect that

sources and journalists would have an interest in cooperation and collaboration, particularly in building a stable exchange relationship whereby journalists
receive information in exchange for the publicity they offer sources. But such
exchanges are fragile, because such an interest is at least partially counterbalanced by the ongoing tension between what the sources and journalists each
wish to get out of the news.

How can we examine the negotiation of newsworthiness in its entirety,
when it involves not only the direct conflicts and bargaining over what information will be provided under what circumstances, but also the ways in which
journalists and political actors learn about and anticipate the other side? Political actors can and do anticipate what is likely to attract journalists when
planning their actions and words; likewise, journalists can and do anticipate
what their sources' reactions will be to the story that they have crafted from the
information that the sources have provided them. Although these processes are
more difficult to approximate than the direct interactions, there are still ways
that scholars can more fully examine the negotiation of newsworthiness. As
one example, I present an exploration of White House media events during the
Bush presidency as they were initially televised by C-SPAN and compare their
construction with the ultimate coverage on the three broadcast networks'
nightly news shows. By so doing, we may begin to build a model of the
negotiation that shows, more fully and complexly, the coproduction of news by
journalists and sources.

Whose News Is the White House News?

How successful are presidents in using the news media to reinforce and enhance their power? There has been no consensual answer to this question.
Some observers have seen the news media as virtual extensions of the White
House, restricted by pack journalism, rarely questioning the agenda and will-
ingly participating in photo opportunities and other media events; particularly
strong portraits emerge from Crouse's (1973) classic participant observation in
the Nixon White House and Hertsgaard's (1988) interviews with White House
officials and reporters in the Reagan administration. Others see an adversarial
news media that consistently contest the president's statements, balance it off
with critics, and report in negative ways about the president, such as Manheim's (1979) study of presidential press conferences, Smoller's (1990) content analysis of the transcripts of television news broadcasts, and Hart's (1987)
examination of the day-after television coverage of presidential State of the
Union messages. Still others see the relationship as variable, most notably in
Grossman and Kumar's (1979, 1981) model of three phases of presidential-
media relations across a term, starting with a consensual alliance, followed by
overt competition and then an agreement to disagree, which they term detente.

I would like to suggest a different model, which emphasizes a division of labor suggested by a plaque on the desk of Larry Speakes when he served as Reagan's chief White House spokesperson: "You don't tell us how to stage the news, and we don't tell you how to cover it." Speakes's plaque was meant to be jocular, but it also suggests a more powerful alternative understanding of the news making process from the White House than is commonly understood.

There are numerous problems with the two sides of the story that emphasize either a pliant or an adversarial White House press corps. The former relies heavily on participant observation and interviews. While Crouse's book may hold true for the White House correspondents themselves, who rely on the president to set their agenda, it does not address the final news product, which might include other perspectives, most notably from Capitol Hill. Hertsgaard's study is even more flawed. By relying so heavily on interviews with both officials and reporters, Hertsgaard cannot get past the intentions and perceptions of those involved to the very process of news making on the spot.

By contrast, others present models of news making suggesting that the bias of television news in favor of conflict and negativity works powerfully against the president's ability to use the media to set the agenda and to persuade other political actors to his point of view. However, each of these studies has problems. Manheim, for instance, judged that it would be to the president's benefit if he were able to focus his attention on a particular agenda item in a news conference, namely that which he announces at the start of the conference; however, not only are those agenda items not always beneficial to the president (e.g., Reagan on the Iran-contra scandal) but presidents often prefer to go on the record on sensitive issues by answering questions from reporters rather than by making a proactive announcement. Hart studied the day-after television coverage of presidential State of the Union messages—but in so doing, he emphasizes a point in time when the "old news" of the president's speech was unlikely to have been viewed as being as important as his opponents' reactions the following day.

Instead of viewing the White House press corps as *either* pliant *or* adversarial, I would propose a model whereby the news is shaped by the negotiation between two sides—here, the president and the White House press corps. The final product in the news story is determined by the resources that the president brings to bear in each case, by the ability of reporters to elicit critical statements from other authoritative sources, and by the journalistic quality of the presidential media event (including production values and importance considerations) in comparison to the other news of the day. Presidents set forth opportunities for reporters that will fulfill their political aims (explicitly and implicitly), but reporters will not take advantage of those opportunities unless they meet the journalistic criteria of drama, conflict, color, and, above all, movement in the standard script of how the process at a news beat operates.[8]

My model thus hypothesizes a division of labor between the White House and the reporters whereby the former has primary control over the visual text (how they stage the news), while the latter have primary control over the verbal text (how they cover the news). The model thereby allows each side an area where it may prevail and feel satisfied at controlling a crucial part of the final product. How beneficial the story is to the president varies, depending on the quality and newsworthiness of the staged product with which the media are provided and the availability (or lack) of alternative authoritative sources to give another point of view.

Methods

Is there a way to see this negotiation of newsworthiness in practice at the White House? I propose a way to study one aspect of this process by studying the presidential media events reported on C-SPAN and recorded by the Public Affairs Video Archives at Purdue University. We can explore how the "raw material" of the presidential media event becomes edited, rearranged, juxtaposed, and broadcast on the nightly network news. In this way, we can see whether and when the president is able to receive favorable news coverage, whether and when his explicit and/or implicit interests set the story for the news, when presidential comments are balanced by critical remarks, either from other sources or from the journalists themselves, and whether and when reporters can use the president's participation in media events to fill out a separate story over which he has little control.

I begin here with the Public Affairs Video Archives compilation, "The Presidency and the Press," which includes eight media events from the first six months of the Bush presidency. This compilation includes a superb range of media events, from a trivial photo opportunity (a meeting with Archbishop Iakovos where the president waxes rhapsodic about the contribution of Greek-Americans to his administration) to a briefing of considerable international consequence (the crisis after the cancellation of the elections in Panama). Likewise, it includes examples of informal photo opportunities (Bush showing off Millie's puppies on the White House lawn), formal occasions (Japanese Prime Minister Takeshita's visit), political speeches (the flag-burning speech at the Iwo Jima memorial) and free-ranging news conferences on subjects of the journalists' choice.[9] Moreover, insofar as Bush experimented with a wider variety of ways to deal with the news media and was respected by the White House press corps for his efforts at outreach (Diamond et al. 1990), we have a more varied sample than we would find with his immediate predecessor or successor.

Thanks to the Vanderbilt Television News Archive, I have collected the stories that appeared the night of the event on the three nightly news broadcasts

TABLE 1.1. Sample of Presidential Media Events and White House News Stories

Presidential Media Event	News Story
February 2, 1989 Formal ceremony Prime Minister Takeshita's visit	CBS (Lesley Stahl report; 2 minutes)[b] Direction/drift of Bush presidency NBC (Brokaw voiceover; 40 seconds) Takeshita visit (intro to Chancellor commentary on Japanese R&D)
March 3, 1989 Photo opportunity; no speech Bush visits Pentagon to show support for Defense Secretary-designate John Tower	CBS (Bob Schieffer; 2 minutes) Status of Tower nomination NBC (Andrea Mitchell; 2:50 minutes) Status of Tower nomination
March 29, 1989 Photo opportunity; banter with press; Bush introduces Millie's pups	ABC (Jennings voiceover; 30 seconds) Millie's pups NBC (Brokaw voiceover; 40 seconds) Millie's pups

April 20, 1989
Rose Garden news conference
   Iran-Contra, assault weapons, first 100
   days
	CBS (Lesley Stahl; 2:20 minutes)
	Bush involvement in Iran-Contra
	NBC (Brokaw intro/outro; 1:40 minutes)
	Iran-Contra/ poll results on Bush

May 11, 1989 News briefing Bush orders 2,000 troops to Panama	ABC (Hume/Collins/Zelnick/Schell; 8:20)[a] Panama and American response CBS (Andrews/Martin/Vasquez; 10:20)[a] NBC (Rabel/Cochran/Francis; 7:40)[a] Panama and American response
June 30, 1989 Speech with audience present Flag-burning amendment	ABC (Brit Hume/Tim O'Brien; 4:10)[a] Flag-burning amendment CBS (Lesley Stahl; 2:20 minutes)[a] Flag-burning amendment NBC (Jim Miklaszewski; 2:20 minutes)[a] Flag-burning amendment

July 18, 1989
Informal briefing in Air Force One on
   returning from Europe trip; new book
   reveals Quayle as candidate
	ABC (Brit Hume; 2:10 minutes)[a]
	Europe/flap over Quayle
	CBS (Lesley Stahl; 2:30 minutes)[b]
	Europe/flap over Quayle

[a]lead story
[b]second story in broadcast

of ABC, CBS and NBC and that indicated having footage of Bush within the story.[10] The eight media events and the sixteen stories that resulted from each one are listed in table 1.1.[11] Seven of the stories were lead stories; two more were second in the evening's flow. Only one of these media events (the Iakovos visit) did not eventuate in any footage on any of the nightly news broadcasts that evening.

I begin by comparing the seven events that received coverage, to judge the amount of visual and verbal content from which reporters could choose and how much of those visuals and sound bites of the president made it into the final news. I presume here that the longer the exposure that the president receives in sound bites and/or visuals, the more beneficial the report to him, insofar as he is able then to get his point of view out in a less mediated way.[12] However, I also compare the amount of content featuring the president himself against that given to the ceremonies themselves (where the president is not visible), to other official sources, to the journalists themselves, and to graphics and file footage generated by the network.

I then compare the stories to the speeches in a more qualitative way. First of all, I suggest the president's explicit and implicit interests in the particular media event and where those interests are included and excluded in the final report. I also examine the aspects of the original news event that are included or excluded from the final story.

Finally, I briefly explore the range of possibilities by noting four different kinds of stories, running along a continuum from high media control to high presidential control: first of all, where the president cedes to the news media his explicit and implicit interests and the visual imagery; second, where his explicit and implicit interests are stymied but where he controls the most powerful visual imagery (the CBS report on the Rose Garden press conference in which Bush discusses new documents in the Oliver North trial); third, where the president cedes the explicit interests but gains both the visual dimension and implicit interests (the flag-burning amendment stories on all three networks); and fourth, a story dominated by the president on all counts (ordering the troops to Panama on all three networks).

Studying the Negotiation of Newsworthiness

Table 1.2 indicates the lengths of the media events when the president was on screen and the lengths of the president's statements within each event. In the photo opportunities, while there was some banter with other participants or reporters, it is generally too indistinct to be easily quantified. The president's visual participation ranges from just over two minutes in the Pentagon visit to Tower to just over twenty minutes in the interview in the Rose Garden. But this variability in visual length masked a similarity in terms of the verbal participa-

TABLE 1.2.   Comparing the Press Events and the News Stories

Event	Length of Pres. Visual (no. of sec.)	Length of Pres. Statement (no. of sec.)		Percent of Story Containing Pres. Visuals (sec. in paren.)		Percent of Story Containing Pres. Soundbites (sec. in paren.)	
Takeshita	389	311	CBS	29.8	(33.6)	2.8	(3.2)
			NBC	70.8	(23.5)	41.6	(13.8)
Tower	130	NA	CBS	5.5	(6.6)	—	
			NBC	11.8	(20.1)	—	
Millie	262	NA	ABC	50.2	(13.8)	—	
			NBC	59.3	(14.7)	8.9	(2.2)
Rose Garden	1203	734	CBS	29.0	(39.5)	15.9	(21.6)
			NBC	16.7	(23.7)	14.3	(20.5)
Panama	724	625	ABC	35.9	(57.4)	17.4	(27.8)
			CBS	22.0	(47.4)	11.6	(25.0)
			NBC	23.3	(54.4)	11.3	(26.3)
Flag-burning	707	643	ABC	7.5	(7.9)	6.5	(6.9)
			CBS	14.7	(21.3)	12.9	(18.7)
			NBC	7.9	(12.4)	7.7	(12.0)
Air Force One	891	747	ABC	59.8	(76.9)	35.8	(46.1)
			CBS	47.8	(70.9)	36.8	(54.5)

NA = Not applicable

tion of the president in most media events (between ten and twelve and a half minutes total).

Of course, out of this total amount, relatively little ended up in the news story. To take one example, covering Bush's impromptu news conference on Air Force One when returning from his European trip, CBS quoted him for a total of 54.5 seconds, almost 37 percent of the total story. Yet that amount, far more than other stories, represented only 7.3 percent of the time that Bush spent talking to reporters in the plane. Bush received consistently more exposure in the visuals than in the sound bites, but in no case did any report include more than 10 percent of the media event on the Public Affairs Video Archive compilation.[13] In sum, presidents and their media advisers must be aware that the vast majority of their appearances and their words will be left conspicuously out of the nightly news broadcast. Journalists have considerable leeway to pick and choose among the president's comments, which enhances their power, even in circumstances of only limited access to one key news maker, as was the case with the return trip from Europe.

Moreover, journalists can and do fill out their reports with other footage. Table 1.3 indicates the lengths of visuals in each story devoted to the president as principal; other political actors; the journalists (including the introduction and/or outro (concluding remarks) by the anchor); distant shots of ceremonies;

TABLE 1.3. Lengths of Visual Shots for Stories from White House (in seconds)

	President	Other Actors	Ceremonies	Journalists	Graphics, File Footage
Panama (ABC)	57.4	22.8	0	53.6	26.2
Flag (ABC)	7.9	40.9	25.7	52.5	14.1
Air Force One (ABC)	76.9	1.9	9.5	40.4	0
Takeshita (CBS)	33.6	40.8	0	30.2	8.1
Rose Garden (CBS)	39.5	37.8	0	28.4	30.5
Panama (CBS)	47.4	42.6	0	76.4	40.4
Flag (CBS)	21.3	36.1	26.6	31.2	29.8
Air Force One (CBS)	70.9	15.9	8.3	32.8	20.3
Rose Garden (NBC)	23.7	0	0	69.1	30.3
Panama (NBC)	54.4	57.0	0	78.3	43.6
Flag (NBC)	12.4	58.9	31.5	40.5	13.1
Total	445.4	354.7	101.6	533.4	256.4

Note: This excludes "tell stories" with anchor voiceover (the two Millie stories and the NBC Takeshita story) and the Tower stories, which were covered by the congressional correspondents in each case.

and easily generated footage, such as graphics, file footage, or stock shots of buildings such as the Democratic party headquarters. In only one media event—the return from his European trip—did Bush dominate the report in comparison to other sources. Across all events, the president received just over a quarter of the airtime (445.4 seconds) of stories from the White House, and the ceremonies in which they participated took up an additional 6 percent (101.6 seconds), which puts the president ahead of other political actors (21 percent, 354.7 seconds) but behind the areas controlled by the reporters, the shots of journalists themselves (31.5 percent, 533.4 seconds) and graphics, file footage and stock shots (15 percent, 256.4 seconds). Thus, journalists tried to find ways to vary and balance the coverage, by showing other actors, by portraying the ceremony around the president, or by the material they have themselves generated.

President Bush did somewhat better if we compare his total sound bites in the White House news stories to the amount of time taken up by the quotes of other sources—executive officials, Democratic politicians, Republican politicians, and nonpartisan experts—as shown in table 1.4. Over half of the airtime taken up by quotes (257 minutes or 53.5 percent) was made up of presidential speech. While executive officials and experts were rarely quoted in these White House news stories, politicians from the opposition party, particularly members of Congress, were much more prominent.

Examining the reports qualitatively rather than quantitatively, the resultant comparisons showed a more complicated picture than the adversarial school (e.g., Manheim, Smoller and Hart) set forth. At times, the presidential

TABLE 1.4.   Total Lengths of Sources' Sound Bites for White House Stories (in seconds)

	President	Executive Official	Member of Congress/ Politician (Dem.)	Member of Congress/ Politician (Rep.)	Expert
Panama (ABC)	27.8	0	12.6	0	0
Flag (ABC)	6.9	0	18.5	0	0
Air Force One (ABC)	46.1	0	0	0	0
Takeshita (CBS)	3.2	4.5	0	0	0
Rose Garden (CBS)	21.6	0	17.8	6.6	0
Panama (CBS)	27.8	0	6.1	33.4	0
Flag (CBS)	18.7	0	16.2	12.2	10.0
Air Force One (CBS)	46.1	12.0	0	0	0
Rose Garden (NBC)	20.5	0	0	0	0
Panama (NBC)	26.3	0	28.3	14.2	0
Flag (NBC)	12.0	0	21.8	0	9.5
Total	257.0	16.5	121.3	66.4	19.5

Note: This is the same subset of stories as in table 1.3.

news event was used as a mere visual backdrop to a completely different—and far more critical—story, most notably in Lesley Stahl's use of the Takeshita visit when she discusses Washingtonians' concern about the "drift" of the Bush presidency after a few weeks in office. At other times, the presidential news event was placed in the less favorable context of a continuing story elsewhere in Washington; thus, the coverage of Bush's trip to the Pentagon on behalf of John Tower was viewed in the context of the script of the congressional consideration of the apparently then-doomed nomination, and Bush's Rose Garden press conference was reported only as an adjunct to coverage of the trial of Oliver North. Yet, the president could make news on his own terms by decisive action, when even the doubts that journalists raised during the event were dispelled by the evening news broadcast, as in the coverage of the American response to the cancellation of the Panama elections; the news adopted the president's definition of the situation as a crisis threatening American safety, with only a few allusions to possible opposition from Latin American countries to an increased American military presence.

Media Domination: Takeshita and Tower

The Takeshita visit is a good example of a formal occasion that apparently lacks overt news value. In its visuals and its spoken sections, it was formulaic and stilted, with "talking heads" rather than vivid action. The event also provided no movement in the continuing story of the relationship between Japan and the United States. Presumably if journalists were to cover any of this event, they had to find creative ways to rework it into a more newsworthy item. The event in its totality unfolded as follows, according to the PAVA tape: Takeshita's vehicle arrived at the front of the White House and he entered; he reemerged with Bush for a photo opportunity, where Bush took one and only one question asking about his health, saying only, "Totally new man. All well. Totally recovered." Later Bush and Takeshita appeared and stiffly read statements of goodwill and friendship.

The three networks chose different strategies. ABC ignored the visit. NBC chose to make it a peg for a story that would otherwise not be considered timely, as a brief introduction by anchor Tom Brokaw and an excerpt from Bush's talk were used to lead into a commentary by John Chancellor on what the United States could learn from Japan's investment in research and development. Most enterprisingly, CBS zeroed in on Bush's off-the-cuff statement on his health and made it into both an example of a "failed event"[14] and part of a separate, larger story on the difficulties the Bush administration was having with some of its appointees. Here is an excerpt from the February 2, 1989, CBS broadcast.

> Dan Rather: President Bush planned to showcase his foreign policy credentials and experience today as he met with Japan's Prime Minister Takeshita. Instead, as CBS White House correspondent Lesley Stahl reports, Mr. Bush was dogged by questions about the ethics of some of his nominees for high office and by questions about his own health.
> Lesley Stahl: President Bush is having trouble getting his message across. Today's well-laid plans highlight the importance of U.S.-Japanese relations with his first foreign visitor, Prime Minister Takeshita, but what was the president asked? How's your health.
> Bush: Totally new man. All well. Totally recovered.
> Stahl: More questions. What about John Tower's personal conduct? The White House spokesman said that the President had confidence in Tower and urges prompt consideration of his nomination. And more questions about other nominees—ethical questions that muddle the central message of President Bush's first thirteen days in office, the importance of ethics in government . . .

This may be an unusually strong example of reportorial initiative in the face of unpromising material. But among the other events and stories, too, there were subtle examples of how a presidential media event can be decontextualized and used to illustrate a different—and less favorable—story occurring elsewhere in Washington.

Bush's visit to the Pentagon to symbolize his continued confidence in his nominee for defense secretary, John Tower, for instance, became a minor part of the continuing story in the Senate, where the nomination appeared to be on the brink of defeat. At the Pentagon, Bush made no statement, except to chide one questioning reporter who, he said, "apparently doesn't know the ground rules." Likewise, the video imagery of Bush's motorcade being greeted by Tower and of Bush and Tower seating themselves was bland and unexceptional. Not only was Bush relegated to only a few seconds of airtime alongside the debate on the Senate floor, but the reporters undercut even this gesture by again portraying it as a contrived and failed event. Bob Schieffer for CBS noted, "The president went to the Pentagon to shift the save-Tower campaign into high gear with a high-profile show of support," and then quoted Vice-President Quayle: "I do believe that in a certain period of time as things go, the numbers keep dwindling." Andrea Mitchell narrated the footage for NBC by saying, "The president of the United States just happened to drop by the Pentagon to see his disputed nominee for the Defense Department at work—a carefully arranged photo opportunity," before turning to the debate on the Senate floor.

Presidential Visuals: The Rose Garden Press Conference

The Rose Garden press conference might have offered more opportunities for stories than these two bland occasions, but the topics considered produced little that could be seen to move any political process along. The conference began with two and a half minutes of colloquy on Bush's reaction to documents recently released in the North trial. After that section, Bush provided no new insight into his policy on assault weapons beyond saying that meetings and discussions were ongoing, explained that his high poll ratings were unimportant, said he had not discussed military aid to the "non-Communist resistance in Cambodia," suggested that his first hundred days in office were characterized by "methodically, pragmatically moving forward," bemoaned the lack of American influence over the civil war in Lebanon, noted how he planned on consulting with Defense Secretary Cheney on the MX missile, said he was unsure what the next step would be in the Middle East peace process, urged an investigation into the explosion on the USS *Iowa,* and noted that a decision had not yet been reached on the attorney general's recommendation to "drug-test people in public housing."

In short, with this laundry list of plans, there is little wonder that the only coverage of this exchange with reporters was in the context of an already newsworthy story, the North trial. But although Bush could not avoid a highly negative story on CBS that suggested the documents had indicated "he had a direct role in the secret deal to help the Contras" and broached "the idea of a cover-up," the story on NBC merely indicated Brokaw noting "new questions about Bush's role" before turning to a clip of Bush's responses to reporters, ending with his "Put it this way: my conscience is clear." Moreover, the visual imagery of both pieces was respectful toward Bush, sitting on the edge of the Rose Garden, with red tulips in the sun behind him and surrounded by attentive reporters.

Most intriguing, the direct negotiation of newsworthiness that often went on during presidential interactions with reporters was entirely left out, even though it represented perhaps the best indication of Bush's intent to stonewall all responses. Take this exchange between President Bush and Lesley Stahl:

> Stahl: Mr. President, when you say your conscience is clear, do you mean that the interpretation that has been made of the documents in this trial, which I gather were made by Mr. North himself, are not entirely accurate?
>
> Bush: I'm not discussing anything about my role in this except to say that everything I've said I'll stand behind.
>
> Stahl: You won't even—since they're sequestered—just give us a—
>
> Bush: I've just told the gentleman that I'm not going to go into that. So, please don't ask me to do that which I've just said I'm not going to do, because you're burning up time.
>
> Stahl: Right. Assault weapons.
>
> Bush: The meter is running through the sand on you. (general hubbub among reporters)
>
> Stahl: Assault weapons.
>
> Bush: And I am now filibustering, so—
>
> Stahl: Sir, can I ask you about assault weapons?
>
> Bush: Oh, no, you've already used up your ticket.
>
> Stahl: No, no, no.
>
> Bush: Go ahead.
>
> Stahl: Assault weapons. (Proceeds to question)[15]

Intriguingly, then, although the final report showed the results of the negotiation of newsworthiness, the express negotiation that occurred during that event (and which Bush won, by moving the discussion to a new issue) is nowhere to be found.

Losing the Battle but Winning the War:
The Iwo Jima Memorial

In other situations, reporters can successfully contest the explicit interest of the president at the same time that the president wins on his implicit interest. The speech that Bush gave at the Iwo Jima memorial to back a constitutional amendment to ban "physical desecration" of the flag was an excellent example of this negotiation. On a cloudless day, with a dramatic setting and with lavish displays of American military personnel and the American flag, the event was, quite literally, picture-perfect. With Democratic and Republican sponsors at his side, each of whom gave a short statement at the beginning of the ceremony, Bush stressed how the issue of protecting the flag was above considerations of partisanship.

All three network broadcasts began their nightly news with the story, and each was quite similar. Each story started with the impressive setting—made in two cases even more powerful by the reporters' opening words that noted the highly contrived nature of the event at the same time that they noted its visual impact:

> It was Reaganesque, using the Iwo Jima memorial as a visually dramatic backdrop for the president to push his constitutional amendment against flag-burning. (Lesley Stahl, CBS)

> President Bush took his campaign for a constitutional amendment to the foot of the World War II memorial, one of America's most powerful patriotic symbols. In a carefully staged event, the White House packed the crowd with servicemen and passed out small American flags. The president pulled out all the emotional stops. (Jim Miklaszewski, NBC)

After a quick sound bite from Bush in all three stories saying that the issue was above politics, each noted that some Democrats were cosponsoring the amendment. But Stahl on CBS and Brit Hume on ABC then explicitly rebutted this characterization by noting that the cosponsors were conservative Democrats and by quoting, first, a spokesperson for the Democratic party, "The heroes of Iwo Jima did not die so that they could become a backdrop for some political photo opportunity," and then Jesse Jackson's dismissal of an amendment when he attended a ceremony for the twenty-fifth anniversary of the 1964 Civil Rights Act later that day. Miklaszewski did not directly quote any critical Democrats but noted continued opposition to the amendment, and all three reports began to wrap up with a sound bite from House Speaker Thomas Foley indicating his agreement that the Supreme Court opinion should be overturned, but by statute instead of by amendment.

These reports thus directly contested Bush's portrayal of the issue as, in his words, "transcending politics and partisanship." But, though the reporters best Bush on his explicit interest by noting the political divisions over flag burning and by pointing out the contrived aspects of the event, they ended up reinforcing Bush's implicit interest, which was to raise the salience of the issue, split the Democratic opposition between Jackson and Foley, and dramatize the potential political power of the flag-burning issue. All three reporters implicitly put pressure on those who would resist the amendment in their closing statements:

> The president obviously feels—and polls say people agree—that freedom of speech should not extend to desecrating the flag. Constitutional scholars may not agree, but no amount of legal scholarship will reelect a politician who gets on the wrong side of this issue. (Brit Hume, ABC)

> But when it comes to the flag, other Democrats remember what happened to Michael Dukakis in the campaign. (Cut to shot of Speaker Foley talking: "There is no partisan difference on this issue." But it has become political. Democrats and Republicans will undoubtedly spend this fourth of July vying over who loves the American flag more. (Lesley Stahl, CBS)

> Even those Democrats that oppose amending the Constitution say there may be no way to stop this patriotic steamroller and predict there will be an amendment out of the Congress by the end of this year, if not this summer. (Jim Miklaszewski, NBC)

Thus, Bush was able to place the issue squarely on the political agenda, as the event led all three networks' broadcasts. The flag-burning speech showed most impressively the unspoken bargain struck by the president and the White House press corps, whereby, as Speakes would have predicted, the president controls the staging of the event while the journalists control the details of the final story. In this way, all actors are somewhat satisfied, the president with his ability to set the agenda, the journalists with their ability to craft a final and somewhat more critical version.

Presidential Domination: Panama and Air Force One

Presidents, however, can dominate nightly news stories as well. Among these media events, two—the briefing on Panama and the impromptu news conference aboard Air Force One as Bush returned from a European trip—were reported in ways favorable to the president's short-term and long-term interests. In each case, the visuals and, by the close of the piece, the reporters' spoken text reinforced Bush's leadership, despite moments where reporters' doubts or agendas briefly resurfaced. Not coincidentally, these stories prominently featured both visuals and sound bites of the president, who was portrayed as not only the initial instigator—as he was in the flag-burning stories—but as the active protagonist throughout.

Bush's decision to send two thousand additional troops to Panama (among other moves) came the day after dramatic film was broadcast showing

Panamanian General Manuel Noriega's "dignity battalions" attacking an opposition demonstration protesting the cancellation of the presidential elections. In Bush's briefing, most of the questions pertained to operational details or to possible bargains with Noriega. The only critical question came from NBC's John Cochran: "Sir, we've been calling around to these Latin American embassies. We find no enthusiasm for the dispatch of American troops there, and the Mexican embassy even said that they warned against intervention. Are you disappointed at the reaction you're getting from Latin America?" Cochran failed to elicit any disappointment on Bush's part. As a result, his question was reflected only by vague unresolved doubts the reporters directly raised in each report about the depth of Latin American commitment to the sending of troops.

> The White House will now try to get the Organization of American States, an institution not known for boldness, to act against Noriega next week. (Brit Hume, ABC)

> The critical test now is whether the Latin American democracies will buy into this notion that two thousand fresh troops represents something other than gunboat diplomacy. (Wyatt Andrews, CBS)

> Bush is sensitive to charges that he is meddling in Panama—sensitive because Latin Americans have long memories of U.S. interventions . . . (Cochran, NBC, speaking over file footage of past American interventions)

However, although these doubts were specifically raised, the broadcasts otherwise were in line with the president's interests. All three reports from the White House prominently showcased congressional leaders endorsing Bush's actions, with the only dissent coming from conservative Republicans on CBS wondering "whether the president had done enough." All three, by replaying the video of the dignity battalions setting upon the opposition candidates, reinforced the gravity of the situation and stressed the conflict as one not within Washington but between the United States and the person of Noriega.

Perhaps most important, the other segments in the flow about Panama built directly on assertions made by Bush. None of the three broadcasts featured a story about any Latin American reaction; however, all three did provide a day-after assessment of Panama that reinforced the perception of a crisis. ABC even went so far as to follow up on claims that Bush made, noting the terms of the 1978 Panama Canal Treaty (the "integrity" of which Bush claimed he was seeking to protect) and providing a profile of Americans in Panama—with anchor Peter Jennings noting, "The number is not inconsiderable"—and their concerns about harassment. Finally, all three featured reports from their

Pentagon correspondents, who provided operational information on "who will go and what they will do," presenting the policy decision as a fait accompli that merely needed to be efficiently implemented.[16]

The impromptu news conference in Air Force One also provided Bush with coverage on his own terms, reinforcing the portrayal of himself as an in-charge world leader in the midst of momentous changes. The two stories (on ABC and CBS) both began with the ceremony of the president's helicopter landing on the White House lawn amid a flag-waving crowd, showing him and Mrs. Bush emerging from the helicopter and quoting some of his prepared remarks, before turning to excerpts from the conversation in Air Force One. To be sure, Stahl asked Bush about a new book on the 1988 presidential campaign that quoted Vice President Quayle's advisors as complaining that he "had the attention span of a child." Both reports referred to Bush's support for Quayle and condemnation of comments that he "found . . . personally offensive," but while dutifully raising doubts, each report quickly dispelled them: Hume on ABC noted in his closer, "The Quayle flap will likely blow over, but the president obviously hopes that the impact of his trip will not," and Stahl on CBS introduced the subject by referring to "only one shadow on the president's mood of exhilaration at the end of this trip." With the exception of a sound bite on CBS from Quayle himself, Bush was the only source quoted in either story, providing him a degree of exposure and control that presidents can achieve, albeit rarely.

Conclusion: The News as Coproduction

To summarize: I argue here that the relationship between president and news media is not characterized either by pliancy or by adversarity, but by an ongoing negotiation of newsworthiness in which neither side is consistently dominant. Moreover, *all* news from the White House contains at least *some* aspect of journalistic cooperation, as it passes along evidence of presidential words, actions, and events, but also contains at least *some* doubt as a way for journalists to distance themselves as autonomous actors. As Blumler and Gurevitch (1981) have nicely pointed out, it is futile to ask whether the relationship is generally collaborative or adversarial; instead, every interaction between officials and reporters partakes both of collaboration and adversarity. Whose interests are best served by this negotiation depends upon the president's ability and willingness to provide journalists with material that they can craft into an interesting and newsworthy story.

We can see this negotiation in process in two ways. One is the direct negotiation preserved on the video record of news conferences and briefings, as presidents and reporters each try to set agendas, as presidents turn aside questions by evasion or even obstinacy and as reporters follow the president's lead or persevere with their own. But the indirect negotiation is at least as important and has been rarely studied. In particular, the complexity of television news gives different advantages to different players. Presidents, who can stage-manage the media event, seem to control the visual content more than the reporters; however, given that reporters can pick and choose among the presidents' statements and mix them in with other evidence of their own choosing, the reverse appears to be true of the spoken text. Yet at times, presidents can obtain a news story that is wholly favorable or wholly unfavorable to their long-term and short-term interests, both explicit and implicit. In particular, when presidents are seen as the decisive protagonist of a newsworthy story of their own—such as ordering troops to Panama or triumphantly returning from Europe—they can override journalists' explicitly stated doubts. But when presidents do not provide journalists with the kind of news event that they need for their stories, as with the Takeshita visit or the trip to the Pentagon to consult with John Tower, they only run the risk of exposure as players in another, less favorable script. Obviously, it is difficult to know which of the four patterns of media/presidential control are dominant, the conditions under which they occur, and the methods each party to the negotiation uses to its own advantage. But the picture of presidential/media relations is, at the very least, a bit more complex than we have traditionally assumed.

This complexity stems from the fact of news being a construction in which both sources and journalists participate. As newsworthiness is negotiated on a daily, continuing basis, the news reflects both the interests of those who are being covered and those who are doing the reporting. But in the process of this negotiation, we must raise some concerns about the quality of this information—and thereby of the public debates and deliberations to which they contribute. After all, in search of favorable coverage, even presidents, who are surely the only sources that can make news on a daily basis and can dictate the terms of access to reporters, must anticipate news values when deciding what issues to discuss and what events to stage, and when, where, and how. Journalists likewise have incentives to begin reporting on the news from the perspective of those they cover, not only because of their close association, but because institutional processes and actions make the best way to sell stories to their superiors and get their product in the news. With officials and journalists working so hard to anticipate each other's reactions in crafting their own, the public may be simply out of the loop.

NOTES

This article draws upon papers presented at the annual meeting of the American Political Science Association in San Francisco, during August 1990, and at the Public Affairs Video Archive conference, "Off the (Video) Record" in Lafayette, Indiana, during

November 1992. Particular thanks to my students at Harvard, Williams, and Yale, with whom I have discussed the Bush media events and news stories in considerable detail. This essay is dedicated to the memory of Douglass Cater, as this work follows his impressive footsteps.

1. I am currently writing a book tentatively entitled *Taking the Fourth Branch Seriously: The Governmental News Media,* under advance contract from the University of Chicago Press.

2. "[T]he utterances of the Press have greater weight and are accorded greater credit, though the Press speaks entirely without authority, than the utterances of Congress, though Congress possesses all authority. The gossip of the street is listened to rather than the words of the law-makers. The editor directs public opinion, the congressman obeys it" (Wilson 1885, 319).

3. Scholars noting this asymmetry include Gans (1983) and Ericson, Baranek, and Chan (1989, chap. 1). Exceptions to this rule include the perspectives from the White House (Grossman and Kumar 1980), the federal agencies (Hess 1984), trial courts (Drechsel 1983), the Supreme Court (Davis 1994), state legislatures (Dyer and Nayman 1978) and the U.S. House of Representatives (Cook 1989).

4. Scholars have occasionally avoided Kingdon's unwillingness to acknowledge media power by going too far in the other direction, arguing media power over politics. Thus, in their otherwise excellent analysis of experimental responses to television news, Iyengar and Kinder (1987) make sweeping conclusions about the independent power of television in politics, while failing to raise the question of how its content is determined. Since political actors help shape the news, the power of television over politicians may not be as vast as these authors imply.

5. A fuller discussion of this position is in Blumler and Gurevitch 1981 and in Cook 1989 (chap. 1). For a good study of this process at work in campaigns, see Arterton 1984.

6. For a similar argument, see Molotch, Protess, and Gordon 1987, esp. 45.

7. This conclusion has been best demonstrated in content analyses of presidential election coverage. See, in particular, Hofstetter 1976, Patterson 1980, and Kerbel 1994.

8. This last point derives from Mark Fishman's (1980) insightful discussion of "phase structures," which suggests that journalists view occurrences at their news beats through an idealized script (e.g., how a bill becomes a law), which is then broken down into separate phases. Newsworthy points are only when the process shifts from one phase to the next, and inaction is thereby ignored. I have adapted Fishman's notion of phase structures for Congress in Cook (1989, 50–52).

9. I should note that this compilation presents a fuller, more thorough understanding of a president's rhetorical activities, at least those aimed at being televised, as compared to standard sources on which we usually rely, such as the *Public Papers of the Presidents.* Of these eight media events, only four (the Takeshita visit, the Rose Garden news conference, the Panama news briefing, and the flag-burning speech) were transcribed for the *Public Papers,* and just as the *Congressional Record* does to the actual floor proceedings in both houses of Congress, these transcriptions considerably clean up the original. In addition to the visual dimension of these media events—especially those, such as photo opportunities, in which the president makes no formal statement—the

compilation gives an excellent indication of the different rhetorical styles and ways in which the president presents himself in various settings. In quantitative terms, too, we can get a sense of the overall amount of presidential communication (both visual and verbal) from which television correspondents can pick and choose in assembling their reports.

10. This may underestimate the number of stories slightly.

11. This total includes multiple and adjacent reports on the same topic. Thus, the ABC, CBS and NBC "stories" on Panama include four different reports, and the story on the flag-burning amendment consists of a report by Brit Hume on the president's speech and an analysis by legal correspondent Tim O'Brien on the constitutional implications. In the analysis that follows, I have examined only the stories that were reported from the White House.

12. This presumption has been borne out by work done by colleagues and myself on news coverage of the 1992 presidential campaign that shows that the length of candidates' quotes in newspaper coverage or of candidates' sound bites in television coverage tended to significantly and positively affect the tone of the overall story (Just et al. 1996).

13. The NBC report on the Tower nomination used, in addition to footage of Bush's motorcade arriving at the Pentagon and being seated at a conference table, an unrelated shot of Bush gamboling manically across the White House lawn to meet his wife, as Andrea Mitchell noted his departure for Camp David.

14. The term *failed event* comes from Adatto (1990).

15. This account is taken directly from the Public Affairs Video Archive compilation, which differs slightly from the version in the *Public Papers of the President,* 1989, vol. 1, p. 450.

16. This is Bob Zelnick's line on ABC. I have suggested elsewhere (Cook 1994) that the division among the three points of Hess's "Golden Triangle"—White House, State Department and Pentagon—produces a complementarity in news reports about foreign affairs that focuses, respectively, on politics, official policy, and operational methods.

CHAPTER 2

News, Psychology, and Presidential Politics

Roderick P. Hart, Deborah Smith-Howell,
and John Llewellyn

This study reports how the American presidency has been rhetorically constructed for the nation's citizens by the mass media between 1945 and 1985. The authors examined 412 Time *magazine articles on the presidency, keying on such matters as how that magazine documented its reportage, which presidential qualities, behaviors, and problems it emphasized, and how* Time *used language strategies to describe and evaluate the presidency. By using a variety of content analytic methods, the authors emphasize four propositions that explain* Time'*s most basic narrative about the presidency. Propositions 1 and 2 focus on the relatively stable themes that characterize* Time'*s coverage throughout the forty years studied, a characterization which emphasizes the political rather than the governmental aspects of the presidency. Propositions 3 and 4 describe the changes in* Time'*s coverage of the presidency that may explain why some citizens have become less interested in politics over the years and why some pundits now portray the presidency as an institution under seige.*

That American politics and the American mass media are intertwined in complex ways has become something of a cliché. Both scholars and laypersons now accept this dictum, even though it becomes labyrinthine when explored even slightly. Some scholars, for example, have argued that American presidents desperately need the mass media when governing an electronic citizenry (Jamieson 1988), while others (Grossman and Kumar 1981; Hart, Jerome, and McComb 1984) see the relationship in reverse, with the mass media feeding upon presidential activities in order to sustain themselves as news organizations (and, perhaps, as entertainment organizations). Yet other scholars have documented the Establishment's dependence on favorable mass media coverage (Turner 1985), while others have featured the media's abilities to advance minority causes and to call into question politics-as-usual (Gitlin 1980). Still other writers have argued that the mass media are now actually determining the government's political agenda (Paletz and Entman 1981), while others (Iyengar and Kinder 1987a) have shown that citizens' categories of evaluation are also greatly affected by what they see and hear in the news. Finally, scholars have shown how the mass media manipulate presidents into changing their daily routines (Hart 1987), while others have concentrated on how presidents selectively leak information to maintain their control over the press (Erickson 1989). In short, while few persons doubt that the press and the presidency have been joined at the hip, we are only now beginning to understand the results of that delicate surgical procedure.

This chapter seeks to establish the broad parameters of presidential news coverage between 1945 and 1985. We hope to expose the reportorial strategies through which the American presidency has been "constructed" for the nation's citizens over time. By conducting a content analysis of *Time* magazine, we hope to establish a suitably comprehensive, and reasonably rigorous, understanding of what the presidency has become during the last four decades. Although no tracing of textual features can establish cause-and-effect relationships, it can shed light on how popular perceptions have been shaped by what the press has said about the president in recent years.

Although there already exists a good deal of research on presidential news coverage, much of the research has been more particularistic than that being reported here. For example, one group of studies has isolated modality differences in presidential reporting, with Paletz and Guthrie (1987) finding, for example, that the *New York Times* describes the president as a policymaker (rather than as a politician) but CBS news reverses that image. K. S. Johnson (1985) contrasted stories about the presidency in the *New York Times* and the *Washington Post* to those in *Time* magazine and found that the latter was more negative in its reportage and more inclined to focus attention on Washington's informal power brokers. Finally, Smoller (1988) observed that televised news emphasizes the personal dimensions of the presidency more than do print sources, although he does not offer hard data to support his speculations. On the basis of these studies, then, *Time* was chosen as an object of study because it had frequently been used in similar studies in the past (e.g., Merrill 1965; Fedler, Meeske, and Hall 1979; Grossman and Kumar 1981; Johnson and Christ 1987), and it nicely split the difference between the sober reporting found in the national newspapers and the more personalized presidency found on the nightly news.

Another set of studies relates personality differences among the presidents to their treatment in the nation's press. In a largely anecdotal study, for example, Fedler, Meeske, and Hall (1979) found that Jimmy Carter received considerably harsher treatment at the hands of the press than did either Lyndon Johnson or Gerald Ford. Orman (1984) reports similar results, but adds that Dwight Eisenhower and John Kennedy received the most favorable news coverage of any of the recent presidents. Both Orman and Streitmatter (1985) document the considerably increased press coverage presidents have received in recent years, with Streitmatter especially noting that "robust, outgoing presidents received 87% more personal news coverage than quiet, reserved presidents" (68). While intriguing, such personality-based studies tend to be of limited value in the absence of genuinely normative information about political reporting. Accordingly in this study, we have analyzed more than four hundred *Time* articles to generate systematic and comparative data about the presidency and the press as institutions.

A third set of studies has examined the role differences bring into play when the press writes about the president. For example, Zeidenstein (1984) has cataloged some of the techniques presidents use to "manage" their mediated images, and Turk (1987) has done an in-depth analysis of one of these techniques: the White House press release. Both studies focus on the use of communication to maintain role status in what has become, in many presidents' eyes, usurpation of their office by the press. The media are quick to respond to such charges. Graber (1987a) notes, for example, that the negative stories the press loves to write reinforce their role as political watchdogs; she argues further that this role, not current events themselves, often best predicts what will be read in the daily newspaper. Although she studied a different medium—national public radio—Larson (1989) agrees, noting that between 1974 and 1983, presidential stories became increasingly negative, perhaps because the press's role as public guardian was severely questioned during the Watergate affair. In focusing so insistently on role, these studies have pointed up an important variable in the political equation. But they have also concentrated on only one or two textual features at a time, a condition we hope to improve upon here by analyzing *Time*'s coverage from several dozen directions simultaneously.

A fourth set of studies examines what might be thought of as narrative differences in political reporting. This has become an increasingly popular, but not always theoretically productive, area of inquiry. Typically, such studies relate media story lines to changes in public opinion on a given matter. Studies by Gustainis (1988), Bormann (1982), and Lule (1988), for example, detail the coverage given to important incidents such as the Tet Offensive in Vietnam, the Iranian hostage release, and the hijacking of the Achille Lauro. Because it is not always easy to determine what master strategies are at work in these isolated incidents, such studies are limited. But they do expose undeniably important features of news coverage, and so the present investigation will be sensitive to narrative features of reportage. It will do so, however, by looking across a wide variety of presidential reportings to find the most general story *Time* tells its readers.

A similar set of studies views political news from an explicitly rhetorical perspective. The rhetorical paradigm (Hart, Jerome, and McComb 1984) presumes that all messages—including news reports—adhere to certain class-bound rules fashioned in response to audience needs and peculiarities. Such a model treats presidential news coverage dramatistically and features such elements as reporters' credibility (Barton and Gregg 1982), audiences' susceptibilities (Smith 1977), news stories' fantasy themes (Bantz 1979), and the "melodramatic imperative" of the mass media industry (Swanson 1977).

The rhetorical approach regards news reportage as just another persuasive text designed to influence the feelings and attitudes of its readers. Naturally, because their approach is message intensive, rhetorical scholars can only estimate how a given text might affect a given audience. Audiences are, after all, fully capable of "resisting" or "subverting" the messages directed at them (see, for example, Fiske 1987). The critic therefore trades the probative "findings" favored by social science approaches for more speculative—but often richer—estimations of suasory potential.

Because previous research has so often employed the case-study method (e.g., Malaney and Buss 1979) or so restricted itself to a particular time period (e.g., Sentor, Reynolds, and Gruenenfelder 1986), the enduring, constitutive factors affecting the presidency have been given short shrift. Too, despite the many fine investigations of election-year reporting (e.g., Graber 1986), there exist comparatively few descriptions of the more regularized, day-to-day, institutional life of the president—how the president relates to Congress, which governmental ceremonies he attends, what political pressure groups he solicits (and is solicited by), how he adjusts to changes in public opinion, and so on.

Although the current study is indebted to the various investigations that have preceded it, it differs from them as well. Procedurally, it casts a broad net, looking for continuities and discontinuities in the basic presidential story line of the years 1945–85. Methodologically, it enters *Time*'s textual corpus in varied ways so that *Time*'s story is treated with the richness a complex story deserves. Conceptually, it borrows from diverse intellectual perspectives in an attempt to make holistic sense out of the press's special relationship to the American presidency. Admittedly, this sense making will be based on the often cumbersome results of formal content analysis. To compensate, we shall quote frequently from *Time*'s pages to capture the nuances of this rather nuanced form of political reporting.

Methods

To see how the presidency has been represented to the American people during the period 1945 through 1985, a stratified random sample of *Time*'s articles on the presidency was constructed. The stratifications completed prior to randomization insured that each of the eight presidents between 1945 and 1985 would be proportionately represented in the sample, resulting in a minimum of ten articles per president per year. The resulting 412 articles were therefore highly diverse in content, representing the broad range of issues reported in the national press during this forty-year period. The articles averaged 43.9 column centimeters in length; their standard deviation of 23.9 column centimeters indicates that cover stories, personality snippets, and traditional news stories were equally well represented in the sample.

The content analyses performed were quite straightforward and required minimal discrimination by the coders. Because nominal data were being gathered in almost all cases, intercoder reliability was at least .83 for all variables and over .90 for most. The texts were treated as follows: After assigning a unique identification number to each article, we recorded the following information: (1) date (with a separate designation of decade); (2) article length (calculated both in column centimeters and in number of paragraphs); (3) president featured; (4) president's party; (5) article's occurrence (first half vs. second half of a presidency); (6) topic: international affairs, domestic affairs (includes all personal profiles of the president), or both (e.g., the "Billygate" affair during the Carter administration); and (7) photos (president depicted alone, president and small group depicted, president and crowd depicted, nonpresidents depicted).

In addition, each information source used by *Time* was recorded, including polls and election returns; other news stories; technical reports; books; speeches or press conferences; memos or press releases; public hearings or legal proceedings; and anonymous (e.g., staff conversations). Finally, the presidential role profiled in each article was categorized as follows: (1) chief legislator: working with Congress to fashion new legislation or to implement existing laws or procedures; (2) commander in chief: planning for military combat or managing resources during wartime; (3) head of party: campaigning for office, settling intraparty squabbles, attending party galas, and the like; (4) chief diplomat: meeting with designated representatives of foreign governments, the international press, or non-U.S. citizens; (5) head of state: signing legislation, presiding over commemorative gatherings, and so forth; (6) private citizen: engaging in family relationships, methods of relaxation, or personal habits; (7) multiple: articles in which no one role received 75 percent or more of that article's textual focus.

In addition to collecting these basic data, a number of more ambitious discriminations were made in the news stories. These included:

Imagery Emphasized. This was a system for capturing *Time*'s overall vision of the current chief executive and the climate of the times. Any article title containing a metaphor was assigned to one of the following categories on a post hoc basis: (*a*) conflictual: images of armed combat ("War of Nerves," "Hostile Congress") or of civilized competition ("Political Horse Race," "Shadowboxing with Republicans"); (*b*) natural: images linking political affairs to bodily processes, plant or animal life, meteorological events, or geographical features such as trees and mountains ("Knee-deep in Alligators," "Gilded Roses,"); (c) physical: images tapping kinetic, thermal, and mechanical realities, including metaphors of motion or transition ("Riding into the Sunrise," "Presidential Odyssey") or physical force ("Opposition Won't Budge," "Reagan and Congress Collide"); (d) transcendent: images comparing political life to mystical events, religious experience, or escapism ("Presidential Magic," "Party in Memphis"); (e) domestic: images of household activities, family relationships, or informal social encounters ("Life with Father," "Guess Who's Coming to Dinner?").

Presidential References. An oblique measure of the existing or presumed relationship between the president and the American people or between the president and the nation's press. Each such presidential allusion was recorded. They ranged from the formal to the informal as follows: (a) disembodied ("the administration"); (b) institutional ("the president" or "President X"); (c) surname ("Mr. X;" "X"); (d) personal (first name; nickname).

Presidential Activities. A measure of the presidential behaviors deemed most worthy of reportage by *Time*. Each president-linked verb was recorded (auxiliary verbs and verb particles having first been removed from consideration) and assigned to one of the following categories: (a) conversational verbs (*declared, conferred, reminded*), (b) exclamatory verbs (*argued, shouted, exulted*), (c) psychological verbs (*thought, felt, hoped*), (d) professional verbs (*signed, initiated, vetoed*), (e) private verbs (*ate, cleaned, slept*), (f) physical verbs (*walked, flew, jogged*), and (g) ceremonial verbs (*laughed, toasted, honored*).

Presidential Qualities and Liabilities. A measure of how *Time* captured a president's personal traits or leadership style. Each president-linked adjective (*careful*) or adjective-derived adverb (*carefully*) was recorded and assigned to one of the following categories: (a) physical states (*handsome, robust, slow, heavy*), (b) social states (*likeable, enjoyable, unpleasant, brusque*), (c) intellectual states (*clever, thoughtful, fickle, irrational*), (d) emotional states (*happy, resilient, dejected, angry*), (e) other (*effective, habitual, partisan, underestimated*).

Presidential Challenges. A measure of the main obstacles confronting the chief executive, including the president's personal difficulties as well as those he addressed on behalf of the American people. For any given paragraph, multiple assignments could be made, if necessary, to the following: (a) material depletion: monetary difficulties, dwindling natural resources, high unemployment rates, and so on; (b) international tension: hostilities confronted by the United States itself (the Vietnam War) or its allies (the Arab-Israeli war) as well as troubling political entanglements (disagreements among NATO members); (*c*) political adversity: problematic rulings of the Supreme Court, contrary votes in Congress, legal prosecution (Watergate), and the like; (*d*) public disfavor: unfavorable characterizations of the president or his programs attributed to the popular press, to opinion polls, or to individual citizens; (*e*) personal inadequacies: arrogance, indecision, impetuosity, chicanery, and so forth; (*f*) fate: factors over which the president had no direct control, including domestic riots, terrorism, political scandals, and a variety of serendipitous events: poor health, a heavy workload, natural disasters, accidents of fortune.[1]

Personalities Featured. A measure of the president's "social world" as envisioned by *Time* whereby each person cited, depicted, or quoted in the articles was assigned to one of the following categories: (*a*) White House regulars: presidential aides (including White House staff, party administrators, and campaign assistants, members of the president's family, and expert commentators (press personnel, polling experts, scholars or authors, and so on); (*b*) Washington officials: members of Congress and other federal office holders (former presidents, members of the Cabinet, heads of federal agencies, titled presidential assistants); (*c*) Washington power brokers: members of the judiciary, military personnel, private leaders (those in the church's hierarchy, union officials, heads of corporations, leaders of organized lobbies, former first ladies), foreign leaders, and celebrities (actors, singers, comedians, professional athletes, historical figures); (*d*) Local constituents: officeholders (mayors, governors, and other elected state officials), private citizens (recorded only when designated by name or when photographed with the president in a small group), and unidentified individuals (any person mentioned or photographed but whose name was not revealed).

Group Reactions. A measure of the political subgroups affecting presidential life. Any paragraph containing a reference to a formally constituted lobby (such as the American Medical Association) or to a more diffuse pressure group (the labor movement) was assigned (on a multiple basis, if necessary) to the following: (*a*) corporate groups (e.g., the National Association of Manufacturers); (*b*) ethnic groups (e.g., Hispanics); (*c*) gender groups (almost exclusively women's organizations); (*d*) religious groups (e.g., evangelicals), (*e*) professional groups (such as the American Bar Association), (*f*) public interest groups (any lobby or social movement not easily included in one of the aforementioned—consumer groups, student protestors, nuclear freeze advocates, for instance).

Popular Reactions. Any paragraph in which "the people," "voters," or "the country" (when treated as a sociological unit) was mentioned was assigned (on a multiple basis, if necessary) to the following: (*a*) behavioral agreement: clapping and cheering at public rallies, favorable "person-on-the-street" interviews, widespread compliance with presidential policies; or (*b*) behavioral disagreement: references to sparse or unenthusiastic crowds at presidential events, outspoken criticism of the president, commentaries on sagging opinion polls, and so on.

When computing virtually all variables, raw totals were divided by length (to control for differences in article size) and multiplied by 100 (to eliminate diminutive numbers). Whenever tests of statistical significance were run, these variables were first converted to Z-scores to eliminate differences in absolute size among the variables. This also made possible the creation of two "master variables": Effort (a summation of all Presidential Activities divided by length) and Embellishment (all Presidential Qualities plus all Presidential Liabilities and the quantity then divided by length). Because it was a paragraph-based measure, an additional master variable, Difficulty (all Presidential Challenges), was computed differently: all challenges were first added and then divided by the number of paragraphs (which had previously been multiplied by six—the maximum number of categories that could be represented) and the quotient multiplied by 100. The statistical tests run on the data gathered were either t-tests or analyses of variance.

Results

Given the large number of content categories used in this study and its sizable database, it seems most parsimonious to discuss the results propositionally rather than variable by variable. With such a procedure, we highlight *Time*'s most basic narrative about the presidency. Propositions 1 and 2 describe the rather invariate themes that characterize *Time*'s coverage throughout the forty years studied, a characterization which reveals a presidency that is less an institution of governance than a trek through the psychic minefields of politics. Propositions 3 and 4 describe the changes in *Time*'s evolving portrait of the presidency, a portrait that may explain why so many citizens have professed increasing disinterest in political matters over the years and why so many pundits now view the presidency as a besieged institution.

PROPOSITION 1. *The U.S. presidency has become a highly reliable site for public drama.*

As shown in table 2.1, *Time* stresses domestic news for the most part (see Topic entry in column 1), although in a considerable number of stories it intertwines domestic and international themes, thereby emphasizing what Burke (1969) would call the "scenic" features of professional politics. That is, when a domestic issue is reflected against an international backdrop (or vice versa), the dramatic register of that issue expands considerably. In an increasingly shrinking world, international matters (e.g., the balance of trade) are having domestic

TABLE 2.1.   Content Features of *Time* Articles on the Presidency, 1945–85
(*N* = 412)

Feature	*N*	Mean per Article	All features (%)	Articles Containing (%)
Topic (*N* = 412)				
Domestic	267	—	64.8	64.8
International	47	—	11.4	11.4
Combined	97	—	23.5	23.5
Role (*N* = 412)				
Chief legislator	93	—	22.6	22.6
Commander in chief	15	—	3.6	3.6
Head of party	56	—	13.6	13.6
Chief diplomat	46	—	11.2	11.2
Head of state	18	—	4.4	4.4
Private citizen	97	—	23.5	23.5
Multiple	87	—	21.1	21.1
Imagery (*N* = 186)				
Conflictual	54	—	29.0	13.1
Natural	35	—	18.8	8.5
Physical	43	—	23.1	10.4
Transcendental	27	—	14.5	6.6
Domestic	27	—	14.5	6.6
Photos (*N* = 487)				
President alone	86	.216	17.6	16.0
President and group	157	.381	32.2	27.2
President and crowd	39	.095	8.0	7.9
Others	205	.498	42.1	30.8
Sources (*N* = 1967)				
Polls/returns	179	.434	9.1	18.0
News stories	442	1.093	22.5	35.0
Technical reports	124	.301	6.3	16.0
Books	54	.131	2.7	5.3
Speeches/conferences	788	1.913	40.0	53.6
Memos	295	.716	15.0	43.5
Hearings	78	.189	4.0	7.8
Anonymous	7	.017	0.3	1.0

consequences while domestic matters (e.g., wheat farming) are affecting world events.

The various professional duties of the American presidency were each well represented (see Role entry in column 1 of table 2.1) in our sample, with *Time*'s collective portrait being that of a chief executive who is warrior, prince, soothsayer, priest, and peasant simultaneously. Many of these roles, of course, are constitutionally designated (e.g., commander in chief and chief diplomat). That the more emergent role of chief legislator now inspires so much coverage may result from the modern presidents' aggressive legislative postures or from *Time*'s special interest in the drama of congressional wrangling (or from both). Without doubt, *Time*'s most preferred presidential role—private citizen—results from the magazine's need to deal with political life on the most human level possible. Stories of churchgoing, ball-throwing, omelet-making chief executives have now become standard for *Time,* and they go a long way toward setting up the Burkean "identification" needed if *Time*'s readers are to respond appreciatively to its coverage.

Almost half of the *Time* articles had metaphors in their titles, suggesting that *Time*'s writers spare no effort when making everyday events emotionally evocative. Thus, Lyndon Johnson's standing in the polls became an "affection gap" (September 23, 1966, 21) and a rather ordinary bit of politicking by Jimmy Carter turned into "Jimmy's Party in Memphis" (December 19, 1978, 22). Not surprisingly, conflict metaphors were the most popular, with *Time* following the long-standing journalistic tradition of treating politics as civilized barbarism. Since the days of Sophocles, stories of human struggle have reliably produced emotional tension in audiences. As if to achieve such effects, *Time* headlined its stories with phrases such as "lines being drawn," "crossfire," and "mission accomplished." Similarly, physical metaphors such as "rolling along" and "plunge into eyewash" are designed to catch readers up in a world beyond the mundane, a world in which movement is always possible (symbolically) no matter how lethargic things may be in the sturdier world of everyday politics.

Table 2.1 also shows that the president is twice as likely to be depicted in the presence of other people as by himself (see Photos entry in column 1), an incidental finding at first blush but one that, on further examination, points up *Time*'s entire view of the presidency: as human rather than ideological, social rather than contemplative, and interactive rather than unilateral. Table 2.1 also shows how heavily *Time* bases its reports on the "live" events staged by presidents (see Sources entry in column 1). Printed information (press reports, technical documents, books, and memos), it appears, has become the resource of the scholar, not the reporter. For their parts, presidents know that their speeches, press conferences, and political rituals will be covered avidly by the press, which is why presidents now spend so much time planning for such symbolically rich occasions (see Hart 1987).

Drama, as countless authorities have observed (see, for example, van Dijk 1988b, 85), requires dialectic, the counterpoising of rival elements. *Time* regularly provides an almost perfect balance between the yea and nay of popular sentiment, a balance that insures the essential tension needed for dramatic encounter (see table 2.2, Popular Reactions entry in column 1). So, for example, a 1961 report on local elections described an exultant John Kennedy: "Kennedy had cause to be pleased. The Democrats scored two big wins—in

TABLE 2.2. Public Involvement Reported in *Time* Articles on the Presidency, 1945–85 (*N* = 412)

Variable	*N*	Mean per Article	Involvement Reported (%)	Articles Containing (%)
Popular reactions (*N* = 653)				
Agreement	338	.820	51.8	35.7
Disagreement	315	.738	48.2	27.7
Group references (*N* = 250)				
Corporate	8	.019	3.2	1.0
Ethnic	55	.133	22.0	5.3
Gender	22	.053	8.8	1.7
Religious	7	.017	2.8	1.0
Professional	115	.279	46.0	9.2
Public Interest	43	.100	17.2	5.8

New York City and New Jersey—where he had personally campaigned for Democratic candidates after former President Eisenhower had intervened for their Republican opponents" (November 17, 1961, 17). The next sentence, however, presents a standard dramatic counterpoint: "But John Kennedy is a political realist. As he looked beyond the major Democratic victories . . . he could see that the Republicans had made disturbing local gains from Buffalo to Louisville, from Toledo to Tucson, often eroding Democratic strongholds."

There are several ways of interpreting this dialectical balance: it inheres in life itself; it inheres in politics; it is a statistical aberration. The latter interpretation seems least likely. Table 2.3, for example, reports similar equivalence between members of the president's party and those in the opposition party, between power brokers inside the White House and those outside it, between members of the president's family and the reporters who haunt them. Each of these pairs contains a natural rivalry that *Time* regularly exploits—often quite artfully.

While each of *Time*'s articles contained some sort of dialectic, its components varied according to the topic being addressed. For example, the domestic articles generated significantly higher Sociability (all Personalities Featured; $F = 3.91, p < .02, df$ 2,408) and Pressure (all Group References; $F = 5.94, p < .01, df$ 2,408) scores than did the international or combined articles. That is, *Time* saw the challenges in domestic politics to be largely interpersonal, with people's activities and opinions dictating symbolic action. Its reporting of the Watergate affair was classic in this regard. Here *Time* calls out the Watergate roll: "White House Counsel J. Fred Buzhardt accepted the committee's subpoena but gave no indication whether it would be honored. . . . Judge William B. Jones ordered all tapes and documents in the milk case to be sealed until

TABLE 2.3.   Personalities Featured in *Time* Articles, 1945–85 (N = 412)

Personalities	Citations (N = 5,785)		Quotations (N = 1,205)		Depictions (N = 586)	
	(N)	(%)	(N)	(%)	(N)	(%)
White House regulars (N = 1,484)						
Presidential aide	843	14.6	186	15.4	79	13.2
Family member	274	4.7	14	1.2	47	7.9
Commentators	367	6.3	246	20.4	30	5.0
D.C. officials (N = 2,310)						
Congress—president's party	400	6.9	93	7.7	45	7.5
Congress—opposition party	343	5.9	67	5.6	24	4.0
Federal officials	1,567	27.1	124	10.3	90	15.1
D.C. power brokers (N = 1,568)						
Member of judiciary	86	1.5	3	0.2	3	0.5
Military personnel	131	2.3	16	1.3	15	2.5
Private leader	446	7.7	162	13.4	32	5.4
Foreign leader	639	11.0	86	7.1	54	9.1
Celebrity	266	4.6	34	2.8	30	5.0
Local constituents (N = 423)						
Government official	206	3.6	36	3.0	25	4.2
Private citizen	201	3.5	95	7.9	95	15.9
Unidentified	16	0.3	43	3.6	17	2.8

presented in court. . . . Barry Goldwater was also asked in the interview whether Watergate might impair the president's power to govern for the next three years" (December 31, 1973, 10–11). It should not be forgotten that focusing on Watergate's personalities was an entirely arbitrary decision. There were, after all, more than enough statutes, laws, principles, and doctrines at stake in that grand fiasco as well. But for *Time* the Watergate story was a people's story because, for *Time,* the American presidency is a people's institution.

Time's international stories were quite different, often describing the president in heroic language. Physical verbs ($F = 4.54, p < .01, df$ 2,408), physical qualities ($F = 4.50, p < .01, df$ 2,408), and physical liabilities ($F = 3.84, p < .02, df$ 2,408) were especially emphasized, ostensibly because the rigors of international travel and the stress of diplomatic negotiations are taxing for chief executives. Given this emphasis, *Time*'s international stories contained the familiar reportorial routines found in domestic tabloids (a phenomenon previously mentioned by news researchers; see, for example, van Dijk 1988a). These routines, in turn, gave *Time*'s reports a decidedly melodramatic cast: "The people of Western Europe had awaited Ike's arrival half in dread, fearful that illness had drained his vitality and transformed a buoyant commander of World War II into a tired old man. But as the President of the U.S. plunged eagerly into a hectic round of private talks and public appearances, fear gave way to reassurance" (December 30, 1957, 20–22). There is also some amount of presidential boosterism in the international articles, with *Time* eschewing discussion of a chief executive's emotional liabilities ($F = 6.15, p < .00, df$ 2,408).

In the combined articles, however, where domestic and international matters were intertwined, *Time* was quite willing to highlight a president's emotional, as well as his intellectual, shortcomings ($F = 4.03, p < .02, df$ 2,408). One of the clearest examples was *Time*'s rebuke of John Kennedy's attempts to plant stories in the press during the Bay of Pigs fiasco. The magazine concluded its article on that affair with the following warning: "By flaunting its taste for news manipulation, the White House had put the press on guard. As if in proof, U.S. dailies [recently] helped build a national cause celebre out of a magazine article in which they detected presidential footprints" (December 14, 1962, 45–46).

To describe reporters as dramatists is not a novel idea, but to find data in support of that notion has been less common. One cannot read *Time* without being struck by what appears to be an attempt to make theater out of presidential life. For their parts, U.S. presidents have been willing for a variety of reasons—some partisan, and many of them personal—to cooperate with such contrivances. They have done so because public figures who become larger than life cannot be critiqued in the terms of everyday life. While drama opens us up to emotional experience, it also separates us from the lived lives of the actors-as-people, thereby giving us a "distant intimacy" with the president. This may not seem problematic. Indeed, some may feel that *Time* and the other news organs do an important social good when using the techniques of dramaturgy to make governance more interesting to people than it would be otherwise. But there is an important difference between drama and democracy, with the former requiring spectators and the latter participants. When fascinating its readers through drama, *Time* might also be fastening them in place. Surely that is a consequence of some magnitude.

PROPOSITION 2. *Time's coverage describes the presidency in "psychological" terms that emphasize the human over the nonhuman and the mental over the physical.*

Numerous authors (Graber 1984; Jamieson 1988) have described the impact of new technologies on how presidents think of and behave in their role. But what of the electorate itself? What roles do citizens have in a media-saturated world and how are they encouraged to think of the forces that decide their political destiny? *Time*'s answer to these questions is consistent: Its presidential story features fewer of the traditional constituents of political life—money, power, legislative leveraging, international entanglements—and more of the sine qua non of modern politics: personality.

Table 2.1 reports that the most popular type of article among the 412 sampled featured the president as a private citizen. This trend held throughout, with no president generating fewer than 15 percent personal profiles and with some (Eisenhower and Nixon) generating more than 30 percent. *Time*'s coverage on July 12, 1962, typified this personal focus. An article on John Kennedy entitled "To the Cape" began in a breathy manner: "The President of the U.S. felt good. Buoyed by his overwhelming reception in Mexico, pleased that things had really gone right with his Trade bill—as indeed they should have—he planned for himself a purposely low-keyed, easy-paced week." The article continued in the same tone, with *Time* commenting generously on the president's private thoughts: "as he looked from his aircraft over the farmlands of Pennsylvania, bright and beautiful in the sunshine, Kennedy mused . . ." (10). These contemplations soon gave way to domestic bliss as the President "packed up Jackie, Caroline, and John Jr. and flew off for Squaw Island on Hyannisport" (11). The article ended with a description of the President driving to the airport to pick up his ailing father and supervising the installation of a heated pool to aid in his father's recovery.

All this chatter is quite unremarkable, which of course is *Time*'s point: the president of the United States is merely a man among men. Table 2.4 reinforces this image in a variety of ways: (1) the president's emotional qualities and liabilities dwarfed their rivals; (2) "psychological verbs" (*thought, felt, hoped*) appeared in almost two-thirds of *Time*'s articles; and (3) the personal and interpersonal (i.e., Public Disfavor) challenges faced by the presidents were stressed more heavily than all other challenges—including monetary short-ages, hurricanes, and nuclear weapons. *Time*'s story is consistent: know your presidency by knowing your president. The magazine projects an integrated presidential personality when the times are good, a disintegrated one when the times are bad, and it finds the force of personality in each major political event.

This emphasis on personality psychology is so consistent (and its man-ifestations so multifaceted) that one senses the presence of an overriding politi-cal model in *Time*. This model includes systemic factors (e.g., economics, demography, and partisanship), but it almost always runs them through psy-chological filters. An example is the way *Time* distinguishes between Democrats and Republicans. Republican presidents are characterized as some-what secluded, with White House insiders being mentioned ($t = 2.59, p < .01$) and quoted ($t = 3.39, p < .01$) more often than they were in Democratic circles. Republicans also seemed besieged, generating a higher Difficulty score (all Challenges; $t = 3.19, p < .01$) than the Democrats and more opposition party mentions ($t = 2.42, p < .01$); moreover, Republicans tended to be the focus of longer ($t = 4.57, p < .01$), and more searching journalistic commentaries.

TABLE 2.4. Descriptions of U.S. Presidents in *Time* Articles, 1945–85 (*N* = 412)

Description	*N*	Mean per article	All Descriptions (%)	Articles Containing (%)
Qualities (*N* = 626)				
Physical	119	.289	19.0	19.4
Social	87	.211	13.9	14.8
Intellectual	117	.284	18.7	19.9
Emotional	218	.529	34.8	32.8
Other	85	.192	13.6	12.4
Liabilities (*N* = 256)				
Physical	54	.131	21.1	10.0
Social	33	.080	12.9	6.8
Intellectual	42	.102	16.4	8.5
Emotional	109	.265	42.6	16.5
Other	18	.044	7.0	3.4
Activities (*N* = 3,981)				
Conversational	1,446	3.311	36.3	71.1
Exclamatory	69	.165	1.7	12.1
Psychological	677	1.643	17.0	66.6
Professional	776	1.883	19.5	64.1
Private	212	.515	5.3	18.7
Physical	424	1.029	10.6	39.8
Ceremonial	377	.915	9.5	35.2
Challenges (*N* = 3,937)				
Material	595	1.444	15.1	54.4
International	845	2.051	21.5	59.5
Political adversity	864	2.097	21.9	58.3
Public disfavor	439	1.066	11.1	41.3
Personal	530	1.286	13.5	43.7
Fate	664	1.612	16.9	61.4

Democratic presidents, in contrast, were depicted as dynamic, generating higher Effort scores (all Activities; t = 3.46, p < .01), stimulating more coverage with their speeches and press conferences (t = 3.35, p < .01), acting more often as family men (see table 2.3; t = 2.59, p < .01), and profiled most commonly with transcendence/entertainment metaphors (22 vs. 5 for the Republicans).

These statistical differences are obviously modest, suggesting only rough trends in *Time*'s coverage. Perhaps more interesting is (1) that there are any such differences at all and (2) that they are drawn along psychological rather than partisan lines. After all, there exist more than enough policy differences between Republicans and Democrats, but these were not what *Time* focused upon when encouraging readers to look inside themselves (and others) for political understanding. An article entitled "A Rallying Round for Reagan" (November 14, 1983, 37, 39) is a case in point. Its subhead contained its thesis:

"His Handling of Lebanon and Grenada Boosts his Standing." The article is awash with psychologized argot ("The armed assault in Grenada threatened to reify his image as a gunslinger"), and human sentiment is equated with military firepower: "the anger and frustration over the Beirut bombing seemed to be counterbalanced by the relatively clean strike in the Caribbean." Descriptions of "bombing," "disaster," and "carnage" are coolly contrasted to the president's "confidence," Congress's "gung-ho support," and the electorate's "positive public mood." *Time*'s choice of quotations was also telling, with one implying that popular emotion can triumph even over death ("Coming on the heels of Beirut and the frustrations over the deaths there, it [Grenada] was something to cheer about") and another implying that the lives of 230 American servicemen pale in comparison to the electoral bottom line: "The most important thing is where attitudes will be three or six months from now." Naturally, *Time* never completely ignores empirical events. Equally, however, it never fails to lace its engaging stories with psychological motifs.

Time's stories feature elite psychology rather than pedestrian psychology. That is, presidents hover well above their fellow citizens: (1) poll results are reported in fewer than 10 percent of the articles (see table 2.1); (2) citizens' explicit reactions are reported in only one-third of *Time*'s essays (table 2.2); (3) formal pressure groups are dismissed almost entirely from presidential life (table 2.2); and (4) while citizens are depicted fairly frequently, they are quoted only half as often and cited even less often (table 2.3). In other words, presidential life is a world of smoke-filled rooms where great persons do great things and where citizens become the backdrop. For that matter, even members of Congress take a backseat (in citations, quotations, and depictions) to the president, his cabinet, and his aides (table 2.3).

In short, *Time* reports a heavily cloistered presidency in which the chief executive's private thoughts—and often his private feelings—are essential political news. Second in importance are the remarks of a shadowy group of professional commentators and private leaders who are quoted three to four times more often than they are depicted (table 2.3). Lay dialectic, in contrast, is almost entirely missing, with the nation's citizens becoming just so many photo opportunities for the president and just so many presidential opportunities for the press. But in dismissing its own readers from the news, *Time* makes recompense by providing colorful, spirited, and humanized portraits of the chief executives themselves. Its "psychological" style removes the fissures between mind and body, between the imagined and the observed. It propels us along gently, making even the most banal events intriguing. *Time*'s writers seem captivated by this so-called psychological model, and they may be captured by it as well. Despite its utility, however, this is only one conceptualization of political life. It behooves citizens, reporters, and scholars alike to examine, and perhaps to worry about, this model and all that it implies.

PROPOSITION 3. *The presidential task has become difficult.*

Numerous scholars (such as Kernell and Jacobson 1987) have determined that media portrayals of the presidency have greatly increased in frequency during the past thirty years. In addition, using databases and methodologies far different from those used here, other scholars (e.g., Smoller 1986) have shown that such coverage has become increasingly negative as well. These two factors—more news, and more bad news in particular—is also borne out in our study of *Time*. This development can be seen in a variety of ways. For example, figure 2.1 reports that the *Time* articles became much longer over the years, with every nook and cranny of the presidency now being scrutinized by *Time*'s reporters. Whereas Harry Truman and Dwight Eisenhower often read self-contained reports about their idyllic fishing trips, more recent essays have gone on at length about Richard Nixon's "Hanging in there at San Clemente," Jerry Ford's "Triple Trouble for a Beleaguered President," or Ronald Reagan's "Budget that will Rarely Budge." Typically, such essays traced the political, economic, moral and intellectual routes of the presidential experience, finding near-disaster at every bend in the road.

Why have *Time*'s articles become so long? For one thing, *Time* and the other news media now posit a multifactored presidency. That is, reporters write as if all presidential activities were interconnected—depicting economic forces as the product of sociological realities, presidential worldviews dictated by the psychology of the age, and international and domestic matters becoming increasingly intertwined. Each *Time* article reintroduces this matrix of variables, thereby transforming the simple news story into the "news essay." An article in May 1978 exemplifies. Stimulated by President Carter's energy policies, the essay sweeps across the history of the modern presidency, combining opinion poll data with SALT talk realities, lurching from New Deal politics to Vietnam and then to Watergate, traversing the globe from Saudi Arabia to Western Europe, and ending with the worry that, "The danger is not so much that we will 'destroy' our Presidents, but that we will destroy ourselves as citizens, by piling on our leaders all our own wants, desires, faults and contradictions" (May 15, 1978, 98). This latter statement is self-reflexively ironic since *Time*'s writers themselves have piled so much data atop Carter's shoulders in this one news report. Because of such layering, *Time*'s essays have indeed grown large. And with so many different dimensions of the presidency now deemed worthy of explication, *Time*'s authors can easily find fault in whichever direction they turn.

Figure 2.1 provides further evidence of modern presidential difficulties, with opinion polls being mentioned with great regularity since the mid-1950s. These findings correspond to the suggestions by Broh (1983), Salwen (1985), and Stovall (1988), who argue that polling data are important not only to

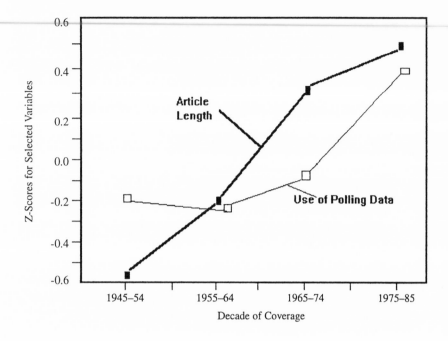

Fig. 2.1. Descriptive changes in *Time*'s presidential coverage

politicians (who use them rhetorically) but also to reporters (who use them metarhetorically). Poll quoting by the latter constantly reinforces the image of an embattled president and also posits an inherently splintered citizenry: blacks vs. whites, old vs. young, Southerners vs. Northerners. As a result, virtually any opinion poll contains bad news for the president, with *Time* using its rhetorical flourishes to determine the exact amount. So, for example, 56 percent of those surveyed were said to constitute "decisive" rejection of Jimmy Carter's plans for the neutron bomb in one instance, and the same bare majority was said to establish a "vote of no confidence" in another case (June 19, 1978, 28). *Time* typically delivers such data in just this oracular style, with statistical overinterpretation being the rule rather than the exception. Minuscule numerical differences constitute a "slide in public esteem" in one news report; a figure of 44 percent of the U.S. electorate is described as a "minority" in another instance; 69 percent of the voters provide "residual strength" in yet another case (June 19, 1978, 28). In short, by reporting polls so often, *Time* virtually ensures maintenance of the political dialectic.

    Figure 2.2 shows that the embattled presidency is described even more

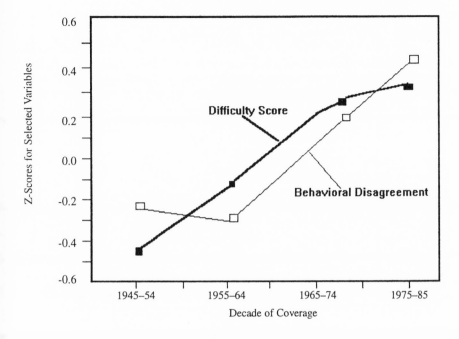

Fig. 2.2. Adversarial changes in *Time*'s presidential coverage

starkly, with presidents Nixon, Ford, Carter, and Reagan associated with significantly more Behavioral Disagreement than their immediate predecessors (t = 4.62, $p < .001$). From a rhetorical standpoint, polling figures can be damaging, but they pale in comparison to a well-wrought narrative describing a dissatisfied citizenry. Nowhere was this clearer than in the case of Richard Nixon. In November 1973, for example, *Time* published an essay entitled "Main Street Revisited: Changing Views on Watergate," which turned out to be a series of deftly edited vignettes describing a troubled people. In Lexington, Virginia, for example, Julie Martin, age forty-six opined: "When you put it all together, it doesn't leave you much room for charity—and I'm a charitable person" (November 12, 1973, 28). Martin's views were echoed by Karen Phillips in Beaver Falls, Pennsylvania, by Patricia Plotkin in Shaker Heights, Ohio, by James Czachowski in Milwaukee, and by another dozen citizens as well. The *Time* article spit forth these opinions in Gatling gun fashion, pausing only when its respondents' remarks were either particularly lyrical or particularly poignant, as were those of Portland's Connie McCready: "Every week you pick up a newspaper you have to say, 'My God.' I feel like I'm standing in the surf, and just as I am hit by one wave, another comes and hits me until I'm reeling. I feel myself drawing inward, pulling in my head like a turtle" (November 12, 1973, 28).

The Watergate affair was clearly an exceptional event in American political life, but Figure 2.2 shows that Behavioral Disagreement continued to rise in the pages of *Time* well after the Nixon administration. Even a supremely popular president, Ronald Reagan, was buffeted by such shirt-sleeved criticism, with the subtitle of one of *Time*'s articles presaging its content: "Trying to Make Amends: Reagan extends a clumsy hand to women, blacks, and the poor" (August 15, 1973, 10–11). In a society of 240 million people, the press can always find such sources of discontent. Increasingly, *Time* has availed itself of those resources.

Figure 2.2 also shows that recent presidents have been bedeviled not just by public opinion but by all political problems, with their Difficulty scores becoming significantly higher ($t = 5.62, p < .001$) than those of the earlier chief executives. One of the most consistent trouble spots for recent presidents has been the presidents themselves. That is, *Time* has found more Personal Inadequacy to comment upon recently than it had before ($t = 3.05, p < .002$). What explains such a change? Perhaps the complications of the age: acid rain, Middle East cartels, nuclear megatonnage, and the Freedom of Information Act. But the rise in Difficulty might also reflect changing reportorial fashion. That is, just as the citizenry has become less monolithic in the eyes of the press, so too has the president's range of responsibility been broadened. With all roads now leading to Washington, it is not surprising to find the same article arguing that New York stock market problems have been occasioned by a Central American uprising, both of which reflect poorly on a vacillating president whose secretary of transportation has just resigned in disgrace. Capturing such breadth leads to increasingly "philosophical" and "psychological" reporting, as *Time*'s writers reach for ever abstract (and ever imprecise) language to survey this expanded presidency. For example, in an article entitled "Where Has All the Power Gone?" *Time* described a Gerald Ford who "seemed further than ever from the Trumanesque image of decisiveness he so admires" (May 24, 1976, 8). Even though the article was quite brief, it covered a considerable range of problems: a postponed test ban treaty, a potentially unconstitutional piece of legislation, an inadequate plan for regulating federal agencies, and uncertain reelection possibilities. In addition, Ford was described as bedeviled by unhappy right-wing Republicans, by dissension within the White House staff, and by an overly aggressive secretary of state (Henry Kissinger). Predictably, these "external" problems were also linked to personal shortcomings in Ford himself, whose reluctance to act contributed to "an aura of confusion and drift" and whose penchant for political barnstorming resulted in his "failure to appear more presidential." *Time* solemnly intoned the results of these presiden-

TABLE 2.5. Changes in Metaphors Used across Time[a]

Metaphor Type	Era	
	1945–65	1966–85
Conflictual	22	32
Natural	17	18
Physical	12	31
Transcendent	9	19
Domestic	12	31
Total	70	116

[a]Use in *Time*'s article titles.

tial miscues: "there is no minimizing Ford's responsibility for the White House blahs."

Table 2.5 indicates that *Time* has increased its metaphorical usage rather dramatically during the last twenty years of our study. At first glance this may seem an incidental trend, signaling little more than changing journalistic styles. A closer examination of the metaphors actually used, however, shows that these images have become not only more plentiful but also considerably darker over the years.

Time's more recent conflict metaphors have been especially dramatic: "The Battle of Bal Harbour," "Nixon Digs in to Fight," "Rebuffs at Home, Flak from Abroad," and "The Making of a Fighting Speech." Conflict metaphors were, of course, used during prior presidencies, but these earlier images were often more oblique (e.g., "Contest of Wills") or more frankly optimistic (e.g., "Mission Accomplished") than those used since. But *Time*'s tale of political woe is not limited to confrontation. In virtually all of the metaphorical families studied, a negative drift is apparent. This is true when examining musical metaphors ("Quiet Interlude" or "Soft Pedal" versus "Carter's Song of Woe" or Reagan's "A Chorus of Demands"), when looking at nautical images ("A Plunge into Eyewash" vs. "Facing a Fresh Gusher of Criticism"), and with kinetic metaphors as well ("Forward Bound" vs. "Budget that will Barely Budge"). The peppy athletic metaphors from the Truman and Eisenhower administrations (e.g., "The Coach" or "Let's Hit the Ball") also became considerably more lugubrious during the Nixon and Ford administrations: "Nixon 1 Senate 0" and "Preparing to Tackle the Domestic Front." Lyndon Johnson's images of domesticity ("Barbecue Politics") became more ominous nine years later ("The Walls Close in on Nixon") and even *Time*'s agricultural metaphors became foreboding: "Country Boy's Faith" and "Acres of Folks" vs. "A Long Way from Spring" and "Sowing Seeds of Real Conflict." Finally, even the very sound of leadership changed between 1952 and 1983: "Zip without Zing" versus "How the Defense Budget Crashed."

In reflecting upon *Time*'s coverage, one is naturally moved to ask: Has life in the White House, in fact, become more onerous in recent years? No doubt, a case could be made that it has, given the threat of nuclear war, increasingly complex geopolitical entanglements, rivalrous domestic factions, and an omnipresent, often voracious media establishment. It could also be argued, however, that none of the recent presidents has had to help the nation recover from a world war (like Harry Truman did), or rebuild corporate and educational infrastructures (like Dwight Eisenhower and John Kennedy did), or mediate severe racial tensions (like Lyndon Johnson did). To suggest, therefore, that *Time*'s increasing negativity about presidential life has been occasioned by empirical events themselves is surely a debatable proposition.

What else could account for it? Several explanations are possible. Culturally, it might be argued that the press has become the captive of the new (perhaps, postmodern) "discourse of disenchantment" also found in other contemporary rhetorical forms—television talk shows, rock lyrics, commercial advertising, short stories, novels, and religious sermonizing. Intellectually, it might be argued that *Time*'s reporters now know more about current political realities, that their stories are not really more negative as much as they are more complex, and that they have simply become more adept at replacing boosterism with discernment in matters political. Rhetorically, it might be argued that *Time*'s reporters have finally mastered political dramaturgy and that the story of the embattled president makes for an intuitively attractive political narrative. But whatever the explanation of *Time*'s reportage, its immediate effect seems clear: The American people are being increasingly invited to think of the presidency as unmanageable. This perception, in turn, could lead to at least three results: lowered expectations of the chief executive, greater sympathy for his difficult task, or increased exasperation with all forms of political life. The societal consequences of all three attitudes are not inconsiderable.

PROPOSITION 4. *The presidency has become institutionalized.*

The evidence for this proposition seems compelling, even though it springs from several different rhetorical patterns and its effects on *Time*'s coverage are sometimes subtle. Perhaps the humblest bit of evidence about institutionalization lies in how *Time* addresses the president. Between 1945 and 1965, for example, the magazine referred significantly more often to "the president" ($t = 8.99, p < .001$) or to presidential first names or nicknames ($t = 6.12, p < .001$) than it did in the second two decades of this study. Correspondingly, as figure 2.3 shows, *Time* steadily increased its use of the more disembodied phrase "the administration." While it is hard to know the political effects of such stylistic alterations, their rhetorical effects are clear enough: *Time* has abandoned its earlier, folksier reportage and replaced it with more objective-sounding, if

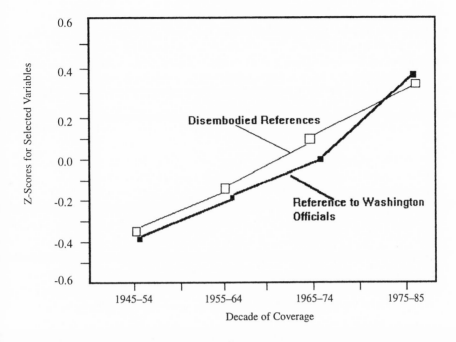

Fig. 2.3. Institutional changes in *Time*'s presidential coverage

more antiseptic, language. Gone is the Luce-inspired "Ike boosting" found in *Time*'s early years. Gone, too, is *Time*'s curious mixture of reporting and editorializing that made it both famous and infamous: "Dwight Eisenhower, among all the politicians in Washington, refused to panic," "during 1958 the President has exercised strong leadership of rare quality," "it took President Eisenhower only twelve hours to have U.S. Marines landing in Lebanon" (October 13, 1958, 19).

Contemporary reporting in *Time* is therefore considerably less promotional. No doubt, this newer style conforms to the dictates of journalistic "professionalism" that have developed over the years. Such a style is typically distanced, equivocal, and politically balanced: "It remains to be seen how these doubts and divisions will be translated back on Capitol Hill. One thing is certain: last year's optimistic faith in Reaganomics is being replaced by skepticism" (March 1, 1982, 15). Such a style also depersonalizes the White House somewhat, making the president seem less figure and more ground. We see this same effect in figure 2.4, which documents *Time*'s increasing disinterest in president-sponsored "news opportunities." No longer do *Time*'s writers merely sit passively at the White House waiting for informational handouts. While

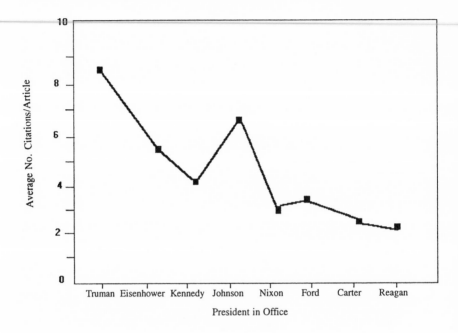

Fig. 2.4. Citations to presidential speeches/news conferences as information sources

they and their colleagues in the press still dog the president wherever he goes, they base less of their reportage on rhetorical events crafted by the chief executive himself. While Hart (1987) has shown that speech making in the White House has increased exponentially over the years (even though formal press conferences have dropped off over that time), *Time* has increasingly refused to become an echo for the president's utterances. This finding takes on special importance when we recall that *Time*'s articles have gotten longer over this same time period, so economies of space cannot account for the magazine's diffidence about such matters.

If presidential articles are not about presidents, what are they about? Increasingly, they are about governmental institutions themselves, about complex patterns of wheeling and dealing, about political deception and intrigue. That is, over the years, *Time* has folded the story of the president into a larger political narrative, detailing fewer of his individual quirks and spending more time on the psychodrama of the nation's capital. This is not to say that *Time*'s presidents are now gray and drab. Far from it. As we have shown in Proposition 2, *Time* specializes in grand psychological motifs. But this is increasingly becoming a relational rather than an individual psychology, with presidential behavior now receiving comparatively less attention than it did earlier. We see

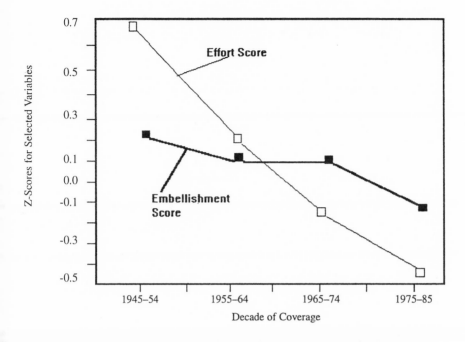

Fig. 2.5. Institutional changes in *Time*'s presidential coverage

this trend evidenced most clearly in figure 2.5, which shows the Embellishment Score (all presidential adjectives) dropping steadily across time and the Effort Score (all presidential verbs) dropping even more precipitously. In other words, *Time* has been offering far fewer characterizations of the chief executive lately; this finding holds true for both Presidential Qualities and Presidential Liabilities. Moreover, *Time* is devoting less space to the president's daily calendar. Comparing its articles for 1945–65 to those published between 1965 and 1985, this trend held true for all six presidential verbs ($p < .02$ in all cases).

Perusal of *Time*'s earlier coverage reveals how stark these changes have been. Notice, for example, how quaint *Time*'s rather breathy, early style sounds to contemporary ears:

> Arriving in Minneapolis next day, the President had a warm greeting for Republican Mayor P. Kenneth Peterson. . . . To 2,000 people who braved the gusty morning chill, Ike then launched into a spirited defense of his Administration and U.S. prestige and ended with a barely disguised appeal for Dick Nixon's election. . . . Ike then flew off to dedicate the new $3,200,000 Hiawatha Interstate Bridge at Red Wing, Minnesota, looked

in briefly at the still-building Eisenhower Library at Abilene, Kansas. . . .
After a day of golf and rest at Palm Springs, California, the President
landed at Treasure Island for his spectacular motorcade through San Francisco. There, before 1,900 dinner guests at the Commonwealth Club, Ike
strode wide and deep into the campaign with an all-but-personal telecast
attacking Jack Kennedy . . . (October 31, 1960, 12)

This is surely a sprightly style. We see here a dynamic chief executive—a doer
as well as a sayer—who carries the American presidency on his back. The
president's every purpose is assessed, his every decision detailed, his every
performance measured for effect. The president stands at the very center of the
political action here, and the political action resides within him as well.

Time has not abandoned the use of verbs and adjectives in recent years,
but it does employ a less hypotactic style when describing the presidency.
What has replaced it? For one thing, *Time* now sketches more people into the
political picture, producing fewer fine-grained portraits of the chief executive
and more landscapes of Washington, D.C., itself, with presidential aides ($t =
4.30$, $p < .001$), federal bureaucrats ($t = 2.62$, $p < .009$), opposition party
members ($t = 2.06, p < .04$), and public interest groups ($t = 2.22, p < .02$) now
being quoted more frequently in the last two decades than in the first two—
minor trends individually but highly suggestive collectively. Also, as we see in
figure 2.3, Washington officials have been referred to with increasing frequency since that time as well.

In other words, the presidential scene is now considerably more crowded
than it was earlier, and political power is more elusive as well, when it can be
found at all. *Time* now describes a government up for grabs, a far cry from the
Great Man Politics that so long dominated it. Gone is the spectacle of the
president on a white steed dominating a panoramic battle scene. In its place we
find Washington politics as guerilla warfare: hand-to-hand combat, snipers
along Connecticut Avenue.

A 1975 article on the Ford administration typifies *Time*'s new style of
presidential coverage. Titled "Further Fallout from the Shake-Up," the article
details the effects of President Ford's changes in his White House staff. The
cast of characters in the article is an ample one, including cabinet members
(Nelson Rockefeller, James Schlesinger, Henry Kissinger), members of Congress (John Stennis, Frank Church, and a half dozen others), federal officials
(George Bush, William Colby), White House staffers (Richard Cheney, Robert
Hartmann, Donald Rumsfeld), and a political columnist (Jerald TerHorst).
Virtually all of these individuals were given speaking parts by *Time*. The
scripts of yet other pressure groups (or "pressure individuals") were ghostwrit-
ten by *Time* itself: Pentagon employees, officials in the Kremlin, the Republican National Committee, China's gerontocracy, and NATO's leaders. The arti-

cle contains seventeen direct quotations, but none is attributed to Ford himself. Regarding content, the article ranges across the political terrain, from domestic affairs to foreign affairs, from inside the White House to inside the Congress, from presidential decision making to presidential campaigning, and from military economics to political philosophy.

Time's increasing emphasis on institutional politics marks the emergence of a more mature reportorial style. By nudging the president offstage a bit, the magazine throws the spotlight on all that remains: Congressional bargaining, White House in-fighting, the influence of political professionals (party officials, media personnel, political consultants), the tortuous process by which legislation is passed, and the thousand other things that make executive politics so complicated and yet so intriguing. Ironically, *Time*'s institutional concerns fly in the face of the electronic media's corresponding personalization of politics. Made-for-TV speeches, on-air interviews with the president, and cozy political advertising (one is reminded of Ronald Reagan's 1984 commercial/ documentary, "Morning in America") feature the president-writ-large. That *Time*'s coverage has moved in quite the opposite direction over the years is a happy eventuality for a nation already dangerously addicted to the politics of personality. In reminding us each week that governance at its best is a systemic matter, *Time* serves us well, even with its empty philosophizing, its even emptier psychologizing, and its myriad reductions. In reminding us, however subliminally, that we are a nation of laws and not of men, *Time* helps to protect the commonweal, at least in some measure.

Conclusion

One cannot know, at present, whether *Time*'s reportorial patterns represent anything larger than themselves. After all, *Time* is but one of many publications, and so the observations noted here—while stark—may not be completely duplicated elsewhere. But since *Time* is not as sober a publication as, say, the *New York Times,* it may be a bit more representative of what passes for popular political information in the United States today. Equally, however, despite its lavish use of color photographs and charts, *Time* is not the *CBS Evening News,* and so it may not completely capture the images of politics the nation's citizens see each night. Despite the shortcomings of our sample, however, the observations noted here are suggestive.

At the risk of being reductionistic, it appears that *Time* magazine (and perhaps much of the rest of the mass media) is eminently comfortable treating the president as a psychic projection rather than as a political actor. By dramatically detailing the mindscape of the presidency, *Time* fosters a model of the office that is becoming increasingly attractive. With each passing election, voting behavior seems better predicted by Nielsen ratings than by Gallup results. With each political debacle (Watergate, the hostage crisis in Iran, the Contra affair), reporters are growing more confident that the psychology of the times, not political infrastructures, determines U.S. power relations. With the enshrining of each Ronald Reagan and the dethroning of each George Bush, voters are being persuaded to prize candidates' psychological profiles more than all other political data available to them. And as these trends take hold, presidents are also reencouraged to exploit the psychological perquisites of the White House and to ignore the empirical, and more nettlesome, institutional and economic forces that also determine governmental outcomes.

During the forty years from 1945 through 1985, *Time* has told us an increasingly unhappy—and increasingly complicated—story of life in the White House. These trends are not incommensurate with lay perceptions of politics. More and more, citizens decry how hard it is to get things done in Washington and how their presidents have failed to deliver for them, perhaps suggesting that the nation's sense of itself as a political entity is eroding.

In any study of this sort, the most pertinent question is this: In reporting on the presidency as it does, does *Time* reflect political reality or create it? Most likely, it does a bit of both. As a mirror, *Time* gives back to its readers what they already feel—that institutional government is difficult and that even with a popular president like Ronald Reagan, political dreams and political realities are often out of sync. In giving the citizenry new examples of what they already know, *Time* does not act transformatively. But in reinforcing our biases, might *Time* actually be undermining American derring-do in politics? By constantly being shown how modest presidential accomplishments really are, will voters come to expect less from their leaders and hence even less from themselves as voters? In telling us that politics is as much a business as business (and often a troubled business at that), does *Time* short-circuit the nation's political imagination? By being so depressingly informative about modern politics, does *Time* contribute to a kind of political truancy on our parts, if not a national malaise? These are not small questions, nor are they answerable ones at the moment. But they are increasingly becoming the questions of the age and, as such, they invite our studied inspection.

NOTES

1. Whenever members of a president's immediate staff were described by *Time* as incompetent or immoral (i.e., the Watergate affair), one-half a numerical assignment was made to both the personal inadequacies category and the fate category on the assumption that most Americans would find such a president neither totally blameworthy nor blameless for the sins of his closest employees.

CHAPTER 3

Constructing Campaign Messages and Public Understanding: The 1990 Wellstone-Boschwitz Senate Race in Minnesota

Dean Alger

Alger focuses on the construction of campaign messages by candidates and the news media. From an insider's perspective, Alger analyzes the active creation of images, issues, and candidates during the 1990 U.S. Senate race in Minnesota, in which an unknown Democratic political science professor defeated the well-financed Republican incumbent. In constructing their strategies, the campaigns recognized the importance of the political temper of the times—the media and the public's mood and abilities to grasp and retain political messages. The candidates constructed advertising messages and made other campaign appearances to take full advantage of media (especially television) and to tap into the citizenry's preconceived ideas about issues, incumbents, and challengers. Many examples are drawn from Minnesota media sources and the Boschwitz and Wellstone campaign organizations to illustrate the interactive dynamic of elections.

The 1990 Wellstone-Boschwitz race was the most celebrated in the nation that year, and mass media communications, especially the political ads for Wellstone, were the most notable element in that campaign. Additionally, some approaches and techniques from those communications were drawn on and became key parts of communications efforts by successful candidates in the 1992 presidential election and in the 1994 elections. Further, the Wellstone-Boschwitz campaign turned out to constitute the leading edge of the dramatic changes in voter responses seen in 1992 and in 1994. Analysis of the communications in the campaign helps deepen our understanding of some prime theoretical points regarding political communications in the 1990s. Because the author was centrally involved in this race (as associate director of communications for the challenger's campaign), this chapter is an opportunity for a more complete analysis than usual of the construction of the candidates' messages and images and how the mass media were used to communicate them.

This chapter begins by reviewing the political climate for the election, along with the more enduring contextual factor of the political culture in Minnesota. The nature of the candidacies of the incumbent and the challenger is then discussed. Next, an analysis is offered of the communications strategies and specific efforts of the campaigns, with particular focus on the political ads, along with a note on relative news coverage. Finally, interviews with key news media people and a pollster provide insights into and evidence on the impact of the campaign communications.

The Electoral Setting: On the Political Climate

Darrell West has pointed out the importance of assessing the setting and context of an election campaign for adequate analysis of the political communications in the campaign (West 1993). The setting for this campaign was crucial. The Reagan years had left a legacy of public concern about "big government," "big spending," and "waste, fraud, and abuse" in government programs. 1990 saw the initial rumblings of deep public dissatisfaction and the electoral earthquakes to come in 1992 and 1994. *Time* magazine described the situation in mid-October: "[P]ublic disgust with congressional pay hikes, the savings-and-loan debacle and the government's inability to devise an acceptable deficit reduction plan erupted into a throw-the-bums-out mood so intense that many lawmakers are afraid to face their constituents. . . . They are scrambling to recast themselves as populist crusaders whose main reason for being in the nation's capital is to fight against its wicked ways." (Barrett 1990, 29) Polls conducted in October found: "Discontent looms large in voters' pre-election mood," with 60 percent of the public "saying they disapprove of the way Congress is doing its job and more than two-thirds saying it is time to replace most members of Congress" (Toner 1990, 6A).

Yet, despite this dissatisfaction, more than 90 percent of House incumbents were successful in reelection and only one Senate incumbent was defeated in 1990. The advantages of incumbency were evident. (The very patterns of news coverage contribute to that advantage, as this analyst has discussed elsewhere [Alger 1991].)

Early in 1990, nearly all in the news media and the political realm considered Republican two-term incumbent Sen. Rudy Boschwitz a shoe-in for reelection. Opinion polls in February 1990 (McGrath 1990a, 1A, 8A) and in early June (McGrath 1990b, 1A, 14A) showed the incumbent with an approval rating or "favorable image" in the 70 percent range. With fellow Senator Durenberger and Governor Perpich in political trouble, the news media regularly labeled Boschwitz "the most popular politician in the state."

Beginning with great success as a businessman, Senator Boschwitz had also established a very folksy, pleasant image, with a down-home plaid shirt as his trademark. In fact, the Director of the Minnesota Poll said Boschwitz seemed "above politics" to much of the public (Daves 1990).

Boschwitz was also a premier fund-raiser. He "raised $4.5 million in the first 18 months of the 1989–90 election cycle, and had $1.15 million in the bank as of June 30." Challengers Paul Wellstone and Jim Nichols combined, on the other hand, had raised "just over $200,000, and had less than $50,000 in cash on hand" by June (Taylor 1990, 2A). Wellstone and Nichols were affiliated with Democratic-Farmer-Labor, or DFL, which is the name of the Democratic party in Minnesota.

Paul Wellstone was a political science professor at Carleton College. Though he had not held public office, he was a longtime activist in Democratic party affairs and in various populist causes. The latter, along with the fact that he cochaired the 1988 Jesse Jackson presidential campaign in Minnesota, made the Boschwitz campaign—and some Democrats—feel he was ripe for portrayal as a leftist, quasi radical who was "out of the mainstream."[1]

However, two key events in Minnesota politics set the scene for the Wellstone-Boschwitz race. First, in October the Minneapolis *Star Tribune* reported claims that the Republican candidate for governor had engaged in inappropriate activities with some teenage girls and a little later splashed allegations of an extramarital affair by that candidate across the front page. Meanwhile, following the first allegations, another Republican candidate started a write-in campaign for governor. Sen. Boschwitz came back to Minnesota to "end the turmoil" in his party—and only succeeded in angering both sides in the party and in getting mixed up in the mud. Second, the incumbent Democratic governor traveled the state brandishing divorce papers of the Republican candidate and accusing him of not making child support payments.

Minnesotans are not used to that kind of scandal and mudslinging, and it clearly had an impact on the political climate in the state. The political culture in Minnesota is a unique one. As the *Almanac of American Politics* put it, Minnesota is "a distinctive commonwealth with high traditions of probity and civic-mindedness" (Barone and Ujifusa 1991, 653); and it has "a vibrant tradition of clean politics" (Barone and Ujifusa 1987, 622). Correspondingly, those political figures who are perceived as dragging politics in Minnesota into the mud are in dangerous territory.

Some Points of Political Communication Theory

As Dalton and Wattenberg have said: "Mountains of survey evidence attest to Americans' declining concern with . . . the role of political parties"(Dalton and Wattenberg 1993, 203). Candidate evaluation has been increasingly focused on as a, if not the, leading determinant of the vote. But as they also note, drawing on several recent works: "Voters may focus on the personal qualities of a candidate to gain important information about characteristics relevant to assessing how the individual will perform in office" (209). Candidates and their advisors are increasingly aware of that, and they construct their campaign messages and images to make best use of these voter inferences.

Five elements of constructionism are particularly relevant. First, as Fenno has discussed, "bonds of trust" are at the core of the candidate-voter relationship, and building or breaking those bonds of trust is a vital part of a campaign's communications efforts. An important part of those bonds are feelings of empathy and a sense of identification of the voter with the candidate (Fenno 1978).

Second, narrative is a prime way to convey those feelings and build—or break—those bonds. Kathleen Hall Jamieson has well expressed a vital function of narrative: A "compelling narrative . . . controls our interpretation of data by offering a plausible, internally coherent story that resonates with the audience while accounting for otherwise discordant or fragmentary information" (Jamieson 1992, 41).

Third, recognizing that the public does not develop a substantial grasp of most issues, political communicators have increasingly sought to join or "dovetail" a message on certain issues with the candidate's character, especially in ads. Often in a narrative and with use of significant symbols, the words, visuals and sounds of ads convey a message about the character of the targeted candidate using an issue as the vehicle (Kern 1989).

Fourth, additional research shows that communications must be constructed with care since the public tends to react negatively to ads that attack on the basis of personal elements, while they see attacks based on issues and performance in office as more legitimate (Johnson-Cartee and Copeland 1991, esp. 11–12). This construction is always a challenge for the challenger: the political reality is that the incumbent's positive image must be brought down and the negatives brought up, without offending the voting public.

Fifth, political communicators have realized the value of "inoculation" ads, which build an image early in the campaign to provide some protection against later attacks. Darrell West has furthered the theoretical understanding of this function, which he calls "defusing": "Candidates often have problematic features. . . . It is in their interest to defuse their shortcomings. They can do this by lowering the overall salience of the topic to the public or by shortening the distance between the candidates to the point where the subject no longer affects the vote." (West 1993, 125–26) For an initially unknown candidate, the prime technique is to build an image through ads and other communications *before* the incumbent's campaign paints the candidate clearly with its own brush.

Bases of a Communications Strategy: Vulnerabilities
of Boschwitz; Wellstone's Image Potential

While the incumbent was seen as a "sure bet" to win, there were a number of vulnerabilities, giving Wellstone some interesting possibilities for image building. First, Boschwitz had the highest approval rating in the state, but a lukewarm feeling thermometer rating of 53 suggested that support for him was wide but not deep or firmly rooted (*Forum* 1990).

Second, Boschwitz's prime strength of a vast amount of money raised for reelection was actually a significant potential vulnerability in Minnesota's political culture. He wound up spending well over $6 million in the campaign—a large chunk of the early money coming from out of state. The vulnerability was reinforced by the fact that in earlier years he had distributed blue stickers to big contributors to put on mail sent to him so the mail would be expedited to him—which looked like special access for the fat cats. Additionally, Boschwitz had written a memo as chair of the Republican Senatorial Campaign Committee for fellow GOP senators up for election in which he advised them to: raise a great deal of money, "don't release your tax returns," avoid debates whenever possible, and do as many parades as possible (with the spouse) and "stop every 100 yards and conspicuously wipe the sweat off your brow." This advice came out in the media (Jackson 1985, 1A) and looked like cynical, manipulative politics, with big money at the core. Could these things be dovetailed with a message on Boschwitz's character to help break his bonds of trust with the public?

Additionally, with a beautiful natural heritage, Minnesotans have very strong feelings about environmental protection. But the incumbent's record on environmental votes was weak, with generally low ratings from the League of Conservation Voters. He also had problems in the children's welfare area, with the Children's Defense Fund giving him some low ratings. Could these problems be used to raise doubts about the incumbent's empathy and caring?

Finally, as the *St. Paul Pioneer Press* editorially observed, Boschwitz had a good constituent service operation, "but was short on legislative achievement" (*St. Paul Pioneer Press* 1990b, 2G). In a state with the legislative legacies of Hubert Humphrey and Walter Mondale, that was also a vulnerability.

Wellstone was a challenger who had not held public office, so there was no voting or other public record to tackle him on—other than the activities that would brand him with the leftist activist label. Additionally, the challenger was unknown to the public—only 20 percent recognized his name as late as May (McGrath 1990b, 14A). This lack of recognition made image building a potential fulcrum of the campaign: what image of Wellstone would the public come to write on the tabula rasa of his candidacy?

Wellstone had considerable potential for positive image building. Wellstone had a classic, warm, close family: his younger son was a high school wrestling champion, his daughter was attractive and vivacious in a nostalgic "coed" style, his older son farmed in Minnesota, his wife had a most pleasant personality, and the family home looked like it was right out of a Norman Rockwell drawing. Wellstone himself was very engaging in interaction with others, which he projected well on television.

The Incumbent's Construction of Campaign Communications

Senator Boschwitz's campaign war chest allowed him the luxury of an early advertising blitz. The Boschwitz strategy involved relatively few "free media" efforts—or "*earned* media" as the campaign appropriately put it—to capture news media attention during the early and middle stages of the campaign (other than some photo opportunities and his tradition of appearing at a booth at the Minnesota State Fair). The campaign complained that Boschwitz's work in the U.S. Senate did not get the attention it should have from Minnesota news media, thus minimizing their "incumbent-Senator-at-work" strategy for that period. Partly due to being in Washington and partly from calculation, he gave few formal speeches (and avoided having to answer questions or attacks). The candidate-controlled ads were the primary means to carry Boschwitz's message through the campaign.

The Boschwitz Ads: The First Wave

The initial Boschwitz communications were a pair of ninety-second TV spots aired in June that had been produced by leading adman Robert Goodman. They began airing during the Democratic state convention so that Boschwitz would have a positive media presence to counter the Democratic activities.

The initial ads were classic first stage advertisements: ID spots, which "trace compact narrative histories of the candidate's life" and establish or reinforce a positive image (Diamond and Bates 1984, 307), but for the Boschwitz campaign there was more involved. Focus groups conducted during the spring revealed that "people like him still, but they were growing fuzzier and fuzzier about *what* they liked" (T. Mason 1991b). So the idea was to reintroduce Senator Boschwitz and prominently show the biographical elements that had impressed people, such as his family's escape from Nazi Germany, his law degree from a major university, and his success as a businessman. The basic message of the "Vision" ad, was "Rudy's life as the American dream." The ad was used in about 90 percent of the TV buy in this phase (Mason 1991b). The keynote of the ad was that "his roots give him a special vision for our future," and it contained images of his family's flight from Nazi oppression, film of the senator's "dramatic" return to Germany in 1990, and the senator in Washington. Noting the dramatic changes in the world in 1989–90, the ad emphasized change, but with reassurance, and suggested that Boschwitz had become a leader on agricultural policy and had "achieved the stature that makes him a world spokesman on the global environment," accompanied by an illustrative picture.[2] The tag line for the first ad was a recognition of the public's displeasure with affairs in Washington, D.C.: "Washington, you see, hasn't changed Rudy Boschwitz, it's Rudy Boschwitz who is changing Washington." (This gave rise to a striking cartoon in the *Star Tribune* on the money issue.)[3]

The second early ad also sought to reintroduce the incumbent, but it targeted key swing voters. The campaign's polling and focus groups showed suburban Twin Cities women tended to think of him as "cold" and not so caring about various types of people and issues. The ad, with a limited airing, portrayed him as a leader in child nutrition programs, suggesting leadership and legislative accomplishment in an area that would appeal to the suburban women.

Boschwitz Ads: the Second Wave

Suburban women continued to top the target list during the second phase of the ad campaign. Five separate ads were aired from mid-September to mid-October. Three of the ads were designed to present a "warm, sympathic image" of Boschwitz, particularly to the suburban women. Two of these ads put him in the midst of children and "spoke" to the issue of governmental action in support of child care; the latter served as a counter to the Democrats' "big government regulation" approach to child care, thus reinforcing a Republican theme. The third, a State Fair ad, was pure feel-good image material with Boschwitz warmly interacting with people in a setting that evokes happy, summery feelings in Minnesotans.

The fourth ad, on senior citizens and what they deserve late in life was an inoculation ad against "Wellstone efforts to play the Social Security card" (Mason 1991b). The fifth ad presented agricultural images, including "Rudy's" relationship with a farmer to reaffirm Boschwitz's base in rural areas and to play to what the campaign staff felt was a prime issue strength. These were all positive ads, with no attack on the challenger, who continued to go unmentioned. With a big lead in the polls, the incumbent did not want to give the challenger any added attention or any extra openings for press conferences. (That didn't work, though; a well-covered Wellstone press conference pointed out inaccuracies and Boschwitz voting patterns contrary to the interests portrayed in the ads.)

During this period the Boschwitz campaign also aired seventy-three different *radio* ads all over the state. These messages were targeted to geographical areas. In each radio spot, Boschwitz himself spoke to "what Rudy did" for that particular area (constituent service, efforts on local projects, work on the farm bill, and so on). Their polling did not pick up significant impacts on Boschwitz's standing from these ads (Mason 1991b).

Boschwitz Communications: The Final Three Weeks

On October 14 Boschwitz and Wellstone faced off in a televised debate. It was the first real exposure of the challenger to a truly mass audience in the state. It was also the day before the news stories broke about the "morals" allegations against the Republican gubernatorial candidate. Boschwitz's campaign manager said: "Everything started slipping the day after the first debate." That debate was not really a prime communication effort for the incumbent. Boschwitz spent much of the evening on the defensive, with Wellstone aggressively asserting the inside-Washington theme. That point also began the final phase of the Boschwitz communications effort.

Since they were not facing a widely known, formidable DFL challenger, the Boschwitz camp's original strategy was to "lay low politically, concentrate on promoting his senatorial activities" in Washington, ride the advantages of incumbency, and run a healthy but not excessive number of ads (first and second waves) that would bolster the senator's image. Boschwitz would then retain large resources to begin a "One Month Campaign" beginning in October that would steamroller the opposition candidate (Mason 1991a, 95). Campaign staff had also planned a three-week caravan around the state to "touch voters" and get some local news coverage. Campaign manager Tom Mason observed: "People [activists and consultants] say you don't get a very big pop [in the news media] from caravanning. But I say, those days are over. You get your big pops from *paid* media, and on the campaign trail you primarily go out and touch voters" (Mason 1991b).

In the final phase of the campaign, the staff explored negative ad approaches to define Wellstone. But focus groups in mid-October responded to the negative test ads with a feeling that the "attacks were bullying against an underdog opponent" (Mason 1991a, 95). (This is interesting in light of the continuing effort of Wellstone to portray himself as David against Goliath [Smith 1990b, 1B].) Interestingly, in one of those focus groups:

> One group of suburban voters had been particularly bewildered by our assertion that Wellstone may have bragged to students that he was more of a socialist than a Democrat. . . . We decided to test the concept. . . .
>
> It brought an immediate response, but not the one we had hoped for.

"Rudy's a socialist too," one person protested. "Haven't you seen him at the State Fair, shaking hands and meeting people? He's as friendly as anyone."

I watched, astonished, behind the one-way mirror as several heads nodded their agreement. Nobody corrected her. Focus groups can shake your confidence in representative democracy. (Mason 1991a, 95)

Despite the bad reaction of focus groups to negative ads, as October passed the midpoint, as Senator Boschwitz remained stuck in Washington with the budget mess, and following the first debate, the senator's campaigners felt they needed to more forcefully define Wellstone. During early to mid-October there "had been lively debates within the campaign as to whether we should really come after Wellstone or whether that would just give him added publicity" (Mason 1991b). But in six days following the stories on the Republican gubernatorial candidate and the TV debate, Boschwitz's "lead over Wellstone fell from 20 to only 7 points in the tracking polls" (Mason 1991a, 94). They decided to go with a tough negative ad, though one with a bit of humor.

The first ad of the final wave was actually a local remake of a classic by Robert Goodman for a race in Kentucky in the 1970s. The ad showed a farmer (actually an actor) standing in a stall with a group of cows, with the farmer saying, "He wants to go to Washington and spend all that money on new programs; and he wants me to believe he won't raise my taxes?! You know, maybe Prof. Wellstone ought to have my job, because in my job we deal with that kind of thing all the time." At that point the farmer takes his pitchfork and pitches a bunch of manure into a truck.[4] Depicting Wellstone as the worst of big-spending liberals, the ad initiated the theme of the final period. But Minnesota's premier political reporter on TV recalled that in the climate of Minnesota politics in 1990, "people reacted badly" to this ad—it just seemed like another nasty attack (Kessler 1991).

In the final two weeks, five television ads continued focusing on a central Republican theme, the "big-spending liberal" charge. The first two of these ads began running the last week in October. One ad showed an adding machine toting up numbers while a voice-over (not Boschwitz's) talked of how Wellstone would increase spending by hundreds of billions of dollars and "your tax dollars will pay for it." It ended with: "If you think taxes are high now, you haven't met Paul Wellstone." The second ad used a dollar bill as the central image, with an old picture of Wellstone with a full coif of frizzy hair to visually suggest a wild-eyed radical background. The narrator (not Boschwitz) says: "Wellstone wants us to send our money to the bureaucrats in Washington. Hundreds of billions of dollars in new taxes to pay for his programs . . ."

The third and fourth ads using the big-spender theme ran in the final week and were more harshly negative. The Boschwitz campaign felt it had to "hit back hard" and really define Wellstone, who had too pleasant an image by this time. The Wellstone image and defusing effort had been working—and now Boschwitz had the tough task of redefining him.

These two ads became very controversial. Both ads used the same format: a hand covering a picture, while the narrator (not Boschwitz) speaks of an unnamed candidate with appalling proposals—until the end when the hand is taken away, revealing Wellstone's face.

In one ad, called "Seniors," the hand and voice-over was female (often used for gentler messages). But the vocal tone was accusatory and harsh, especially for the punch line. The script was:

> Who is this guy? Who wants the federal bureaucracy to take over the American medical system? Who would take Medicare money from the seniors who need it so much and use it to fund his socialized health care plan? Who would eliminate Medicare coverage while doubling our personal income taxes? He's Paul Wellstone. *Not too smart* for a *college professor!*

The seniors factor was central because: "More than any other group, seniors abandoned Rudy in the days following the revelations about [the Republican gubernatorial candidate]" (Mason 1991a, 96).

The Boschwitz campaign began its effort to placate these alienated voters with 400,000 letters mailed to seniors statewide. That and the ad had the intended impact: by Friday before the election, "Rudy had regained his lead [by 3 points]. Led by seniors, who had completely reversed themselves . . ." (Mason 1991a, 97). But the excess and nature of the claims led to a negative reaction among many.

On the Saturday before the election, one of two strong "ad watches" in the *St. Paul Pioneer Press* stated: "This may be the most misleading political ad to air in the state this year. Portions of it are simply made up, and all of it is distorted." It also pointed out that Wellstone did not want to "eliminate Medicare," and "views Medicare as a sacred trust" (Orwall 1990, B3).

This was the first year the news media assumed the ad watch responsibility; in the last week of this election, some of the ad watches seemed to have real impact. Further, the CBS affiliate in the Twin Cities, WCCO-TV, did a series of ad watches. WCCO's political reporter pointed out:

> Because Boschwitz was not readily accessible [partly from being in Washington, partly by design], we did turn to the ads *as the* spoken word of the candidate. And that's something that was new. We covered his ads as if they were speeches by him. . . . We held him to his word. We looked at every word in the ads, because that was what the people were hearing. . . . (Kessler 1991)

The Medicare claim also brought the still highly respected Walter Mondale out of his relative inactivity regarding the campaign. In a press conference with Wellstone, Mondale denounced the claim as "beyond any conceivable standards of honesty and permissible exaggeration" (Smith 1990d, 1B)—which was a major news story.

The second of the hand-over-picture ads used a man's hand and voice-over (in less harsh tones) to say, "this Wellstone guy is a new face, but do you really know who he is and what he's likely to do?" The big-spender point is again made, but with claims like "uncontrolled spending that would double the national debt" and proposed programs that would "double the taxes of everyone making over $20,000." Again, the reaction from more neutral sources was one of excessive claims, out of legitimate bounds. Another ad watch in the *Pioneer Press* said: "Nearly every major claim in this ad is inaccurate, misleading or distorted" (Orwall 1990, B3).

The final ad sought to tackle the growing anti-incumbent sentiment. It only showed Boschwitz speaking. The idea was for him to look senatorial and suggest that Boschwitz had been trying to get the Senate to act sensibly, but: "They just don't want to make the hard votes. . . . People are mad at us and they are right." He ended with a simple plea for votes. An underlying message was to awaken people "from their trance" of a positive image of Wellstone: "In effect, we were saying, 'snap out of it; [Boschwitz] is a guy you like and respect. And don't vote one way [for Wellstone] just because you don't like the political environment we've all been thrust into.'" (Mason 1991b) As the *Star Tribune* reported: "Give a hand to Boschwitz for candor under pressure, even if he does leave one a bit confused about whether he is a 'they' or an 'us'" (Smith 1990c, 1B). The confusion was, of course, intentional.

A final nonmedia message must be noted. The Boschwitz campaign decided to send a letter to the Jewish community which was intended to shore up support among Jews while raising questions about how strong a member of the Jewish community and how strong a supporter of Israel Wellstone was. Although both candidates were Jewish, it pointed out that Wellstone's wife was a non-Jew and alleged that he had "raised his children as non-Jews." Interestingly, top staffers said they thought they had the letter "killed" or at least softened at one point, and that Boschwitz didn't see how anyone could interpret the letter as religious ill will—until the storm broke (Mason 1991b, Novak 1991). The media got ahold of it on the final weekend and the reaction was a virtual firestorm of controversy. This gave added impetus to voters to link Boschwitz with the mud of campaign '90.

"Earned Media" and News Coverage of the Campaign

Challengers usually have a harder time getting airtime and print space in the news. This campaign followed that pattern for most of the election, as this

TABLE 3.1.   Minnesota Senate Campaign 1990 in Minneapolis *Star Tribune*

Story Orientation	Preprimary	Postprimary	Last 3 Weeks	Totals
Boschwitz	(+) 22	(+) 15	(+) 6	(+) 37
	(−) 18	(−) 27	(−) 22	(−) 45
	Neutral: 23	Neutral: 15	Neutral: 11	Neutral: 38
Wellstone	(+) 16	(+) 20	(+) 13	(+) 36
	(−) 10	(−) 11	(−) 8	(−) 21
	Neutral: 10	Neutral: 11	Neutral: 7	Neutral: 21
Total Number of Stories	Preprimary	Postprimary	Last 3 Weeks	Totals
Boschwitz	63	62	42	125
Wellstone	41	49	38	90
Nichols	19	—	—	19

Note: (+) = overall, reflected positively on candidate; (−) = overall, reflected negatively on candidate.

author has discussed elsewhere (Alger 1991, 190–92). The very negative coverage of Congress and the President during the fall budget fiasco may have partially overcome the usual positive coverage individual members of Congress get from the home state media, however.

WCCO-TV did a simple analysis of coverage of Boschwitz and Wellstone in the two major papers (*Star Tribune* and *Pioneer Press*) up to primary election day (aired September 12). They checked the databases of the two papers and simply counted name mentions (including some trivial mentions); the incumbent received more than twice the number of mentions than the challenger by September 11.

A simple content analysis of coverage in the state's leading paper, the Minneapolis *Star Tribune,* was conducted for this study. All stories, editorials, columns, and cartoons involving the candidates that appeared in the paper from January 1 through election day were recorded and analyzed.[5] (Purely trivial mentions were eliminated.) The findings were slightly surprising for the general election period (table 3.1). The pattern through the primary was the usual one: the incumbent received the lion's share of coverage, most of which was positive. In contrast, more of the stories in which Wellstone appeared were ones shared with other candidates. Further, the whole series of these preprimary stories conveyed a dominant impression of Boschwitz's invincibility, especially due to his huge advantage in funds. The gap in coverage narrowed in the general election, however, and in the last three weeks it nearly evened out. In contrast to the norm of general election coverage, there were more negative than positive stories and editorial material on Boschwitz. In the final three weeks Boschwitz had twenty-two negative to only six positive stories. This drop was partly a function of the striking developments at the end of the campaign but was also a product of the Wellstone communications, to which we turn next.

The Challenger's Construction of Campaign Communications

For the challenger's campaign, several basic elements of reality conditioned the approaches to construction of campaign messages. Wellstone's name recognition was low, and he had little money compared with Boschwitz's vast war chest. Additionally, Boschwitz had a benign image, but it was not deeply held, and key Wellstone advisors "felt early on that people had not really had a chance to truly look at Boschwitz, they have not really seen the substance of Boschwitz and how he had voted on issues that mattered to them" such as children's welfare, the environment, and budget and tax policy favoring the wealthy. They also felt there was a trend toward populism in reaction to the developments and policy patterns in the 1980s (Forciea 1991b). The increasingly anti-Washington feeling was another factor.

There were five general aspects of the communication strategy, the first of which concerned the need for the ads to be different from standard political fare and to create interest and have "talk-value" for the news media and for the public. They had to become "coffee shop talk" and to be unusual and intriguing enough so public and media would be actively watching for the next ad (Forciea 1991b).

The ad team for the campaign—a group of top commercial ad people from the Twin Cities led by Bill Hillsman, plus strategist Pat Forciea—understood the nature of television as a "reach medium" and that the context in which ads appear on air is critical to their memorability. First, as Hillsman points out, channel X "doesn't just run political commercials all at once in a station break. You're in competition with every other commercial on the air, such as the Pepsi ad that cost $475,000 to shoot." Thus, to have significant impact, particularly on limited funds, something different and interesting needs to be done to grab and hold viewers' attention—especially with the pervasive availability of remote control. To do that "you can speak to people's self-interest," but in general, "entertainment value" is a key to holding that attention (Hillsman 1991). Research by Charles Atkin validates Hillsman's practitioner's knowledge. Atkin found: "Attentiveness is mainly a function of the entertainment quality of the messages and the partisan dispositions of the receivers. Those who feel that a candidate's ads are entertaining pay more attention, particularly uncommitted voters" (Atkin 1980, 19; also see Kern 1989).

The central instrument used for that purpose was humor. Besides getting attention, the humor served another important purpose: humorous ads could be "more effective [than straight attack ads] because they decreased the possibility of backlash against the user." (Kern 1989, 93). The Wellstone campaign made a conscious decision to use humor—because negative politics is risky (witness the bad reaction to Boschwitz's cow manure ad). This is particularly the case when the candidate using it is unknown. Yet the feeling was that such "humor took the edge off our attacks" (Forciea 1991). Indeed, a reporter for the *Star Tribune* found that some of the ads "were strongly negative, but there was no *feeling* of malice in them; the lighter tone of them took the edge off the negative content" (Smith 1991).

Bill Hillsman's understanding of TV included another point that contradicted conventional wisdom about memorability. There was much talk of the need for a central theme for the campaign—including a crystallization in the form of a slogan. Hillsman and colleagues saw the need for an "umbrella campaign," something that would give particular ads consistency and a common core, but they did not see a traditional slogan as necessary. They knew the ads needed a certain and relatively consistent "look," as commercial ad people phrase it, and "tone" in the ads. That is, the visuals, the sound, the type of action, and the structure of how all that came together in the ad had to have a similar look (somewhat like style) and a similar tone so as to establish that basic look and image in the minds of viewers. This idea is in accordance with studies finding a low concentration level in the average TV viewer (Kubey and Csikszentmihali 1990) and that people do not tend to remember much in the way of specifics of such TV communications but that a relatively simple residual impression is left (Graber 1988, Lodge et al. 1989). (For discussion of theory and empirical research variously related to this, see Alger 1995, chap. 4; Geiger and Reeves 1991; and Hochberg 1986.)

The Hillsman team said the visual nature of television, the sound, and the basic look of an ad are what have impact and are remembered. In particular, "it is the visuals that are remembered" (Hillsman 1991)—the "live" visuals and sound, including facial expressions, demeanor, and the general dramatic intensity of video are memorable, especially when used in connection with good narrative. (See Alger 1995, chaps. 3 and 4.)

Hillsman also saw TV as a profoundly personal medium—and if the character of the ads fits the character of the candidate, they have a deeper and more lasting impact. As Dorothy Davidson Nesbit, in her discussion of "videostyle" in senate campaigns, said: "Videostyle is the presentation of self through televised advertising" (Nesbit 1988, 20). Wellstone was a populist and was naturally quite down to earth. Correspondingly, the ads "couldn't be too slick, we couldn't shoot him in 35 millimeter [film], it wasn't supposed to look glossy." But Wellstone was a very energetic, dynamic—even frenetic—individual, so the ads showed a great deal of dynamism.

Additionally, as Jamieson and Campbell have shown: "The language of the television screen is the language of close-ups. . . . These typical close-up shots reflect the personal and social contact that is characteristic of television. . . . Distance is related to intimacy. Television simulates intimate relationships. . . . The reliance on close-ups creates new rules for our sense of interpersonal space" (Jamieson and Campbell 1983, 45). Wellstone was very intense, however. Early on advisors told him his speaking style was "too hot" for TV and he had to tone down his delivery. In some early ads by another adman, Wellstone was "too much in people's faces. He's too intense so we always shot him in what we call a medium shot, but never in extreme close-up. [And] if there was something he was really *into* we wanted it pretty far back" (Hillsman 1991). WCCO-TV's Pat Kessler noted the same thing: "What the [Hillsman] ads did was to cool him down a bit—and yet, in the process, they didn't take away that very human emotion and passion that he had" (Kessler 1991).

One other media principle was to "seduce" viewers' attention by "not revealing what this is about until the latest possible point. This presents a mystery to the viewer" and intrigues that viewer into watching. The Wellstone ad called "Dust" provided the best illustration of this technique: It starts out with a "tight shot" of just a hand drawing a $ sign in dust on a window, and then a skull and crossbones, so "the viewer is almost forced to figure it out." But then, "the camera pulls back and the viewer sees it is Wellstone and it's the windows of his [campaign] bus that he is drawing on" (Hillsman 1991). Meanwhile, a message about the influence of money and the incumbent's bad environmental record is sonorously but firmly verbalized in voice-over. In such an ad "the viewer [is] well 'into' the ad before the 'thinking function' [is] engaged" (Kern 1989, 30). Further, "the technique helps overcome the resistance people have to political ads" (Hillsman 1991). The simple but striking visual of the hand drawing in the dust also illustrates a basic theoretical point about people's attention. As cognitive psychologist Henry Gleitman has written: "We focus on the figure [in our view], not the [back]ground; we are more likely to notice shapes that are moving, rather than those that are stationary. Such examples indicate that perception is selective. . . . Our ability to take in and interpret the myriad stimulations around us is finite, and so our perceptual system is forced to choose among them. . . . [and] the major means of physically selecting the stimulus input are the movements of the eyes" (Gleitman 1986, 191–192).

In addition to gearing strategy to making memorable ads, the second basic aspect of the communications strategy was to coordinate activities to attract news coverage with the ad campaign. For example, the day the "Kids" ad on support for children's welfare issues was introduced, Wellstone was giving speeches and doing news events on that theme.

The third aspect of the strategy was to use symbols to capsulize main themes and to crystalize an appropriate image in memorable form. An old school bus that had been converted into an RV, with a platform on the back, was painted the green-and-white campaign colors and became the leading symbol of this populist, low-budget campaign: "The bus became a celebrity." It also broke down a lot—which just seemed to endear it all the more to average folks; it was something they could relate to—and it symbolized the difference from the first-class-only Boschwitz operation. The bus was used as a feature in the grass roots campaign, and it was used "every chance possible in the ads," so it helped tie the two realms together (Senese 1991). Another principal symbol was Wellstone's "David Versus Goliath" theme. Wellstone insightfully contravened the standard advice in the TV debate and insisted on having the podiums of the five foot, five inch Wellstone and the over six foot Boschwitz placed close together. He was right: this visually illustrated and symbolized that David vs. Goliath theme. (During the last days of the campaign, the get-out-the-vote callers gleefully borrowed from that and said he "could best represent 'the little guy'—because he *is* one.")

The fourth aspect of communications strategy involved a focus on issues and the incumbent's record. As the *St. Paul Pioneer Press* editorialized (1990a, 2G), Wellstone "is fiercely insistent on running a campaign of issues and substance, not paid-for political images." This commitment to discussion of the issues was principally carried out in a series of fairly detailed position papers and in the detailed, frank answers to issue questions asked in his meetings with newspaper editorial boards.

In truth, however, the issue commitment was only minimally manifested in the ads, which focused on raising the name recognition level and on building a positive image and those "bonds of trust" for Wellstone, while raising doubts about Boschwitz's image and breaking his bonds of trust with the public. The prime issue theme was turning Boschwitz's huge campaign war chest against him. The idea was to make it so that every time people saw the Boschwitz ads they would think of how much money he was spending and, ultimately, how he was trying to "buy the election" (Hillsman 1990, 1991). This strategy was crucial, because by the time the Wellstone ads could get on the air, Boschwitz had already made heavy TV buys. An example is illustrative. Wellstone had been counseled to take advantage of events that symbolized or illustrated a main theme of the campaign. Because such an event is a "news peg" on which reporters and editors can hang a story, the idea is to do something to present the campaign theme in that connection. In the tortuous national budget discussions in the fall, President Bush had flip-flopped on whether he would accept a tax increase; after indicating he would, and with a proposal to increase taxes on the wealthy offered by Democrats, Boschwitz and sixteen other Republican senators went to the White House to tell Bush not to raise taxes on the wealthy—

"or at all." Wellstone referred to "the Gang of 17" (good sound bite) and noted that most of those senators, including Boschwitz, were millionaires.

As a principal reporter said, "Money [became] the central issue in the campaign, in two senses: 1) Boschwitz represented the rich and was successfully portrayed as their defender, and 2) he had all that money in his campaign, which was successfully portrayed as coming substantially from special interests." He was portrayed as representing the kind of "politics as usual that people were fed up with" (Smith 1991, Smith and McGrath 1991).

The Wellstone Ads

"Fast-Paced Paul," a thirty-second spot, was the first ad in the Hillsman series for Wellstone. It was aired in August before the September 11 primary and rerun in the general election. The money theme is present in the opening line, which also shows how the substantive themes, along with the underdog image, are woven into the fabric of the verbal and situational humor.

The opening "scene" is simply a semi-close-up of Wellstone as he says, in a rather pleasant way, "Hi, I'm Paul Wellstone and I'm running for the U.S. Senate. Unlike my opponent, I don't have 6 million dollars, so I'm going to have to talk fast." The ad then performs the classic first-stage function of introducing the poorly known candidate and of providing a little biography—the "ID spot, the first act of the classic advertising strategy" (Diamond and Bates 1984, 302). The next scenes are Wellstone literally introducing the viewer to his family, his "house where I've lived for 21 years" [the Norman Rockwell–style home], and his son's farm. Wellstone is then seen, in increasingly rapid succession, in a "nature" scene talking about pollution cleanup, in front of a hospital talking of "leading the fight for national health care," in front of a school noting his work in and concerns for education, and so on, and, while the film speeds up, finally climbing into the campaign bus which, with the film speeded up, takes off almost like a Corvette.

The ad is done in a breezy, lighthearted way and, with the increasing speed of the action and Wellstone's natural gift before the camera, it even provides a hint of madcap comedy. The daring nature of the ad is illustrated by the hesitation of the candidate and certain advisers about airing it. The candidate and some other prime staff people thought it "wasn't senatorial enough" (they thought it looked something "like a Harpo Marx movie"); in fact, the chief strategist unilaterally decided to air it while the candidate was out of town, because of the latter's doubts. Interestingly, the ad was actually intended to lampoon the standard introductory bio ad: "The feeling in doing it was actually to make fun of political commercials because that's what everybody does" (Hillsman 1991).

Dorothy Davidson Nesbit suggests a "courtship" metaphor for candidates to win voters' hearts and minds. Thus: "Initial attraction is sparked by candidates' introductions to the electorate" (Nesbit 1988, 19). "Fast-Paced Paul" gave Wellstone a memorable introduction to the public, with the key themes interwoven with a humorous appeal to affect, which served well for that "initial attraction."

Years ago noted adman Tony Schwartz said: "Commercials that attempt to *tell* the listener something are inherently not as effective as those that attach to something that is already in [the voter]. We are not concerned with getting things *across* to people as much as *out* of people" (Schwartz 1974, 96). As Kern says: "In an age of changing values and feelings about institutions, the key is the use of visual or audible cues which evoke a more personal experience with which the viewer can identify" (Kern 1989, 29). "Fast-Paced Paul" effectively did that; some of the later ads did it even better.

"Faces," the second Hillsman ad, again used the money issue. The thirty-second ad opens with a picture of Boschwitz while the voice-over (Wellstone's own, as in most of the ads) says, "You'll be seeing this face on TV a lot. It belongs to Sen. Rudy Boschwitz who's got 6 million dollars to spend on commercials [*sic*]." Then a picture of Wellstone is shown, with the voice of Wellstone saying, "This is a face you *won't* be seeing as much on TV. It's *my* face. I'm Paul Wellstone, and *unlike* Mr. Boschwitz, I didn't take money from out-of-state special interests. . . ." Then the visual is a picture of Boschwitz again, with Wellstone's voice-over concluding, "So when you get tired of seeing *this* face, just imagine it was the face of someone [while Boschwitz's face is visually transformed into Wellstone's face] who is better prepared and in a better position to represent *your* interests." Then, unexpectedly, Wellstone adds, as an afterthought, "Not to mention, better looking!" Again the touch of humor is added that softens the negative comments. (The candidate didn't like the tag line at first, thinking it out of place and egotistical—until he realized it wasn't to be taken seriously since he was, in truth, obviously not another Robert Redford.) Following the basic strategy, this ad explicitly sought to get people to think of Boschwitz's millions every time they saw one of his ads on TV.

"Looking for Rudy" was a two minute ad using a narrative story as its vehicle. It was later voted by *Campaign* magazine's readers as the "best ad in political history." The outline of the idea was borrowed from the film "Roger and Me," in which the character played by Michael Moore keeps looking for the head of General Motors. In this case, the idea was to open by having average Joe and Jane note the need for debates, and then to have Wellstone going to Boschwitz's campaign headquarters, his Senate office, and elsewhere looking for Rudy to have debates. The "live television" encounters with Boschwitz staffers, who proved to be perfect foils at a couple of junctures, and

Wellstone's talent "on his feet" and in front of the camera make this spot striking. Beside specifically suggesting Boschwitz was avoiding debates, the underlying idea was to give the feeling of the "regular guy against the system" (Hillsman 1991). It was also a way to break his bonds of trust with the public by suggesting he was hiding from cross examination and would not engage in debate on the issues with his challenger—a genuine sin in civic-minded Minnesota.

The footage was all shot "on the fly" with a handheld camera and was intended to "look like a news crew, like 60 Minutes-style journalism" (Hillsman 1991). The idea of having a TV news look to an ad was not new, but the "60 Minutes" feel gave the ad special impact. The spot didn't get aired until October because of refinements and lack of funds.

After the video was shot but before the ad ran, Boschwitz announced an agreement, in principle, to debates with Wellstone. Correspondingly, their campaign felt the ad, when it finally ran, was unfair in suggesting he was avoiding debates. But Boschwitz's advice to others to avoid debates and the fact that the debate negotiations were strung out for a good while presented credibility problems. And, after a televised debate had been set for Minneapolis for October 14, Boschwitz said he was too busy in Washington to come out to Minnesota for the debate, or couldn't tell until the last minute (though the TV station set to air the debate and the League of Women Voters found no official meetings or events scheduled that day). This cancellation reinforced the "Looking for Rudy" message, and Wellstone furthered the narrative in his comment to the media: "Now I'll have to go to Washington to find him." The 2 minute ad was aired only two or three times in the Twin Cities due to cost, but the Wellstone campaign maximized its impact by previewing it for reporters and getting news coverage of the spot, and it was taken to TV stations in "outstate" areas, most of which aired segments as news stories, especially since it had become something of a sensation in the campaign. As Jamieson and Kaid, et al. have shown, this also served to add legitimacy to the ad (Jamieson 1992; Kaid, et al. 1993).

"Kids" was the other award-winning Hillsman ad. This thirty-second spot tackled the Boschwitz record on children's welfare in an attention-grabbing and memorable way. The visuals were a series of cute small children sitting at a table and trying to write oversized checks to "Rudy" for large sums. Few come out coherently; one kid toward the end writes a check to "Ruddy" for a "zillion." The voice-over (Wellstone) again weaves in the money theme and links it to special interest politics: "If kids had money, maybe Senator Boschwitz would listen to them. If kids had money, maybe Senator Boschwitz would vote in their interest. If kids had money, maybe he wouldn't have one of the worst records in the Senate on children's issues. . . ." The sound of a cash register punctuates the narrative. The principal reporter covering the senate campaign for the *Pioneer Press* concluded: "'Kids' is just a devastating negative ad—but it is also so god damn funny. When that kid holds up that check to 'Ruddy' for a 'zillion' it really has impact and is memorable. It is a crucial visual image" (Orwall 1991). The ad also served to counter the Boschwitz image effort aimed at suburban women. "Kids," like "Dust," was a strong effort to break the bonds of trust with the public as well as dovetailing an issue with the character of Boschwitz by raising doubts about the empathy and caring shown in his record.

"Face to Face" was the thirty-second ad that Wellstone himself wanted to do: "I just want to look into the camera and talk to the people straight from my heart about how I know they are fed up with politics as usual and how I want to change things." The ad starts with a medium shot of Wellstone and then slowly closes in to a semi-close-up. The specific inspiration for the ad is noted in his opening line: "I speak in our schools, and the kids tell me politics is 'fake,' 'corrupt,' 'phony.'" He talks of how politics doesn't have to be that way and can be about the improvement of people's lives. The ending is: "In this decade of the '90s, we must do much better for ourselves and our children. This is *your* government—and together, we can take it *back.*"

Hillsman did not like this ad at the time and still does not. He thought it was "a waste of money," was too conventional, and that the scarce dollars were needed to do ads with greater impact, especially ones that would "knock down Boschwitz's approval level" (Hillsman 1991). But there was a good deal of feedback during the campaign that people were very struck by the straight-talking sincerity of the spot—particularly in the unusually mud- and scandal-filled 1990 campaign in Minnesota. And its very difference from the other clever, entertaining ads made it unexpected ("What will he do next?") and gave it impact. It seemed like a direct view of the real person and the passionate concern of Wellstone.

"Newspaper with Bus" was a thirty-second ad aired the first week in November. It was the last in the regular ad series and was in the spirit of the first: fast-moving and humorous with use of the candidate as central comic figure and the (now famous) bus as the setting and, literally, the vehicle for the punch line. The substantive point of the ad was to trumpet the good endorsements of his candidacy by the two major newspapers in the Twin Cities—which included deprecation of Boschwitz's legislative record. The ad opens with a visual of a tied-up stack of each paper landing on a walk with a thud (a sound all can relate to), and then in voice-over and print on screen, a key endorsement passage is recited. Then comes the visual and verbal punch line and comic touch. The voice-over (not Wellstone) says: "Requests for reprints of the preceding endorsements will be enthusiastically answered by one of our many volunteers. . . . ." Meanwhile, the visual shows the back of the campaign bus with Wellstone on the speaking platform, a newspaper delivery bag slung over his shoulder; as the bus starts to move down the street, Wellstone reaches into the bag, pulls out a paper, and throws it on a house's lawn. While this is happening, the film is speeded up, as in "Fast-Paced Paul," which ads to the comic effect of the candidate himself being the "enthusiastic volunteer." (As he starts, he breaks out in a smile and looks right into the camera, as if he's letting the audience in on the joke.)

"Bunch of Boschwitz" was the final Wellstone campaign ad, hastily put together the Sunday before election day in response to the "Jewish letter" and the harshly negative Boschwitz ads of the last week. The ad was not clever or cute. It was hard-hitting and drew on political cartoons, newspaper articles, and column headings, and it quoted the *Pioneer Press* ad watch noted earlier, all to denounce the message in the Jewish letter and the negative tactics of the last week. It was the ultimate message to raise questions about Boschwitz's character and to break his bonds of trust with the public.

Constructing Communications, Construction of Meaning with Press and Public

Reflections by principal reporters covering the campaign provide some insight into the Wellstone campaign's construction of meaning through its campaign communications. Dennis McGrath of the *Star Tribune* found: "I just don't think most of the other more standard ads really stuck in people's minds. These did. The Hillsman ads were so effective because they were so simple and devastating. They really caught peoples' attention" (Smith and McGrath 1991). Political reporter Pat Kessler of WCCO-TV pointed out: "Those ads boosted his name ID tremendously; and they made people have good feelings about him." Also: "It was like guerilla warfare through TV ads. . . . But the Boschwitz people didn't get it" (Kessler 1991). The *Pioneer Press*'s Bruce Orwall saw the humor in the Wellstone ads as "reflective of the style of humor you see in the David Letterman show or Saturday Night Live, which people have become used to in recent years—sort of hip, a little sarcastic and not so respectful of authority" (Orwall 1991).

The Wellstone campaign, as the campaign of an underdog, sought to construct a message and image of its candidate and of the opponent that would help create the desired meaning of that electoral choice in the public mind. Hillsman and the staff drew on the political climate and, as a candidate who did more grass roots campaigning than any other candidate, Wellstone drew on the public's expressions of concern about issues, trends in who benefited from public policy, and the desire for new leadership out of the pattern of "politics as usual." The Wellstone ads in particular also constructed meaning for people by creating a vivid image of the person who was the candidate. Crucially, as we noted earlier, adman Tony Schwartz says: "Commercials that attempt to tell the listener something are inherently not as effective as those that attach to something that is already in [the voter]." The ads jointly constructed meaning with voters as they sought to form their judgments about the candidates.

Regarding the personal aspect, the *Star Tribune*'s Dane Smith wrote shortly before the election: "Wellstone's ads . . . appear to have done an effective job of conveying the impression that Wellstone is a warm, funny, sincere man with a stable family" (Smith 1990c, 5B). A further element of the meaning constructed by the Wellstone ads served to "defuse" his two potential vulnerabilities as a left-winger and as an out-of-control spender and to build resistance to messages of threat from Boschwitz regarding throwing old people off Medicare or the like. As the *Pioneer Press*'s Bruce Orwall said: "The ads set up Wellstone as this cuddly figure. . . . Paul's ads made him so beloved. And then Boschwitz comes on with these attacks. Nobody's going to believe Wellstone's going to shut down old people, . . . People were offended at this—now Boschwitz was attacking the teddy bear [of Wellstone] in the ads" (Orwall 1991).

The Wellstone campaign also tried to construct a message and image that would be carried through the news media and affect the meaning of the election choices that the media communicated to the public. The process of interaction and negotiation of the campaign with news media is long and elaborate—and the Wellstone campaign staff increasingly learned what would "get good press" as they went through the negotiation process.[6] The underdog found it hard to get much news attention in the earlier going, but the news media were also aware of the climate of opinion, especially the disgust with politics as usual and with big-money politics, and the media's desire for a good story with striking visuals and characters was also a part of the process.

It was a part the Wellstone campaign played to. In fact, one key finding of this research is that the Wellstone ads thereby "primed" the news coverage. As Iyengar and Kinder have discussed: "By priming certain aspects of national life and ignoring others television news sets the terms by which political judgments are rendered" (Iyengar and Kinder 1987, 4). When we listen to the principal reporters discuss what dominated the discussion in the election, *including the news coverage,* it suggests that an ad series like that of the Wellstone campaign can actually prime campaign *news coverage* of the candidate to a significant extent. The *Star Tribune*'s Dane Smith said money was the central issue of the campaign and it was the ads that were effective in communicating that, a conclusion echoed by the *Star Tribune*'s Dennis McGrath. Indeed, Smith noted the vigorous efforts by the Wellstone campaign to generate news coverage, especially on the money theme, "But frankly, those free media efforts did not have so much impact. The money theme was much more effectively gotten across through the paid media efforts" (Smith 1991).

The director of the Minnesota Poll noted that through the summer Boschwitz had a very benign image, and he even seemed "above politics." But he and reporter Bruce Orwall found: "By the last month of the campaign, Boschwitz was no longer a plaid shirt guy; he was now the rich guy who liked to raise money, who looked like a venal guy who was a big bucks hound. I attribute this almost entirely to Paul Wellstone's ads being able to cast that image" (Orwall 1991). The Boschwitz campaign was overconfident and failed to use its communications to try to define the opponent, who, by conventional campaign and news standards, was vulnerable to such definition. Meanwhile, the Wellstone campaign creatively used mass communications to develop a positive image of him, to defuse his chief weaknesses, and to sharply define the incumbent. In 1990, we saw the first stage of profound public concerns about politics as usual and a readiness to try something new and different, which was registered more generally in 1992 and 1994. The Wellstone campaign grasped this, drew on it, and in conjunction with that public concern, successfully led the construction of the meaning of this electoral choice. As WCCO-TV's Pat Kessler concluded: "From the very beginning, the rap on Wellstone was that he was too liberal . . . ; he can't get elected. Then the ads came on . . . and TV transformed him. . . . Because he was portrayed in a certain way in the ads, he was a *nice man*. That may have been the key to the election. By the end of the campaign, a number of people had real doubts about Boschwitz and were ready to vote against him. And, because they felt comfortable enough with Wellstone, because they felt he was a nice guy and committed and full of passion, they were willing to vote for him" (Kessler 1991).

NOTES

I want to thank Tom Mason (Boschwitz campaign manager), Jay Novak (Boschwitz press secretary), Pat Fociea (Wellstone strategist), Bill Hillsman (Wellstone ad team leader), Jeff Blodgett, Dick Senese, Mark Anderson (Wellstone campaign), Dane Smith and Dennis McGrath (Minneapolis *Star Tribune*), Bruce Orwall (*St. Paul Pioneer Press*), and Pat Kessler (WCCO-TV) for giving generously of their time; thanks to Tim Nokken for research help.

1. Wellstone subsequently cochaired the Dukakis campaign in Minnesota. Interestingly, the Jesse Jackson connection was never prominently pushed by the Boschwitz campaign, and it was only in the last two weeks of the campaign that the leftist, out-of-the-mainstream line was used substantially. The Boschwitz campaign was overconfident (on September 12, Boschwitz said he would "win by 20%"), and Wellstone had challenged use of the Jackson line by saying he "would match my support of Jesse Jackson with Boschwitz's support of Jesse Helms any day."

2. The picture showed the senator at an international conference on environmental issues. This ad gave Wellstone an opening for a press conference with an environmental

group leader to contest the claim, saying he had a weak record on environmental policy and had not played a significant role at that conference.

3. The cartoon showed Boschwitz dragging a big bag of money labeled "Big Bucks Campaigning" and carried the lines, "Washington hasn't changed Rudy Boschwitz . . . He's *always* been that way."

4. This version of the ad is not as effective as the original, which did the humor more adroitly and wryly. The farmer's vocal quality in the original ad sounds more like a laconic lament with a tinge of humorous reflection, whereas the Boschwitz farmer's vocal quality sounds like a nasty accusation.

5. The story or other news item was the unit of analysis; on each a judgment was made whether it was, on balance, positive, negative, or neutral regarding the candidate(s) involved.

6. WCCO's Kessler noted that Wellstone's campaign "frequently put him in a standard press conference room [using standard speech to get across his points]. This did not tend to get covered." But in a later press conference, Wellstone "went through Boschwitz's FEC report, page after page, noting campaign contributions and throwing each page over his shoulder. That got on TV." In mock disgust, Kessler called it "that cheap stunt!" But he also said: "If there is a more effective way to communicate it through symbols on TV, that's OK" (Kessler 1991).

CHAPTER 4

The Psychology of Mass-Mediated Publics

W. Lance Bennett and John D. Klockner

Bennett and Klockner argue that the voicing or silencing of public opinion in the news is constructed through a process based on an ecology of interests. Shared norms among journalists, elites, and publics enable these diverse players to judge which voices should be included and excluded from news accounts in this ecological process. In particular, voices in the news reflect the application of elite indexing and "what's personal" norms by journalists. Analysis of a broad spectrum of issues in the news shows that public opinion is either excluded from or discredited in mass media news about foreign policy and macroeconomic trends, while numerous grass roots voices are included without qualification in news reports of social, moral, and pocketbook economic issues. These patterns of voiced and "silenced" opinion may hold the key to the psychology of citizen-government relations in different policy areas, explaining, for example, the relatively high levels of activism and popular challenge to governmental authority on matters such as abortion and prayer in school and the greater tendencies toward acquiescence in the spheres of foreign and monetary policy. The result of these mass-mediated political realities is a "dual democracy" with strong mobilization of opinion, citizen action, and elite responsiveness in some areas and a much weaker civic culture in others.

It should come as no surprise that different kinds of voices are heard in news accounts of different kinds of issues. Public officials and experts are likely to dominate stories about foreign policy and macroeconomic matters, while news scripts about social policy, morality, and pocketbook economics are more likely to include the viewpoints of grass roots groups and people in the streets. As the data reported in this chapter will indicate, this pattern even applies to the use of public opinion polls, which are more likely to be cited in the coverage of social and moral issues than in stories about foreign affairs or monetary policy. Moreover, when polls are included in the latter areas, they are frequently qualified as the opinions of the uninformed, whereas polls on subjects such as abortion or the environment are usually reported at face value as legitimate opinion. These broad patterns of reporting social voices in the news have been replicated in research on varying forms of opinion expression, ranging from polls (Bennett 1989, 1990) to protest movements (Gitlin 1980, Entman and Rojecki 1993).

This chapter explores the possibility that these patterns of public opinion in the news constitute an important part of the "social reference" context within which individuals develop their senses of personal power and efficacy, along with their political priorities and inclinations toward political action. The theoretical premise is that individual thought and action are affected by perceptions of one's relation to public opinion in the larger society (e.g., Noelle-Neumann 1984, Herbst 1993). The media, in turn, are the dominant purveyors of public images and, more importantly, images of publics (Edelman 1988). If different images of publics are attached systematically to different spheres of politics, important consequences may follow for the formation of individual consciousness and political action.

The Media and the Divided Democracy

Which brings us to the idea that the media portray what might be described as a split power system or a "divided democracy." On one side of the split news screen, average individuals see people like themselves speaking and acting confidently and often effectively in pursuit of policy goals in areas such as civil rights, social morality, and environmental protection. On the other side of the split screen, however, ordinary citizens see few people like themselves defining problems or pursuing solutions in areas such as banking and credit policy, trade, corporate taxation, military and defense spending, or the conduct of foreign alliances.

There is a good commonsense explanation for this dichotomy. Topics such as abortion, prayer in school, and the environment are considered "personal" issues about which people are understandably concerned, active and informed. As such, citizens ought to have a more privileged voice in the media marketplace of ideas about issues that are "up close and personal." Conversely, why should the news emphasize the voices of uninformed and apathetic publics in high-risk areas such as public finance and or military spending that are better handled by experts and "trustee officials"? At a minimum, this rationale sets up a self-fulfilling information system in which citizens without the information or interest needed to participate in particular areas are denied these essentials in public communication.

Self-fulfilling or not, there is much to reinforce common sense on this subject. Yet there are several anomalies and puzzles that warrant deeper analysis. First, consider the question of whether people really know more about the legitimacy of fetal claims to "rights" than they knew about the legitimacy of Nicaraguan claims to sovereignty at the time of the U.S.-backed war that all but aborted the Sandinista revolution. Although public opposition to U.S. Nicaraguan policies held firm for the duration of the Contra war (despite an active "public education" campaign by the Reagan administration), the few opinion polls cited in news stories (even in the influential and generally antiadministration *New York Times*) were discounted on grounds of low public information (see Bennett 1989). Meanwhile, as Nicaragua debate was confined largely to elite opinion, stories about abortion on the same news pages gave frequent voice to grass roots opinion from protest groups and cited numerous opinion polls at face value.

The plot thickens when we see that many seemingly "personal" issues such as affirmative action in the workplace and inflation in living costs often cross the line and behave more like impersonal, officially dominated political topics. Moving across the public voice line in the other direction are what seem to be more distant issues such as sanctions against South Africa and strategic arms reduction initiatives (see poll data later in this chapter). Moreover, it is not uncommon for a single issue to change its vocal composition in the news over time as did Vietnam after 1968 (Gitlin 1980, Hallin 1986). Such anomalies lead us to suggest that "what's personal," politically speaking, may be as much a product as a producer of the array of voices and viewpoints heard in mass media news and commentary.

The idea that the private political world is in part constructed by distant media images is given further support by comparative analyses of other nations where media systems are more aggressive in setting the political agenda, where citizens are more likely to take an interest in foreign policy and economic affairs, and, perhaps most important, where journalists often display greater diversity in constructing the scripts for news stories than they do in the United States (Patterson 1992). Such comparisons are complicated by the fact that private political experience is also mediated by other factors such as stronger labor movements that stimulate economic debate and vulnerable international positions that may motivate greater personal interest in world events. However, there is little doubt that the media not only affect what people think about (Iyengar and Kinder 1987), but influence patterns of reasoning and influence as well (Iyengar 1992). It also seems reasonable to think that images of public opinion may affect individual levels of political interest, efficacy, and action.

Common Sense and Journalism Norms

Despite the possibility that "what's personal" may be as much an effect as a cause of the construction of publics in the news, common sense continues to favor the intuitive assumption that the marginalization of popular voices in particular media representations is an appropriate response to public apathy and ignorance. Not surprisingly, journalists also have adopted commonsense assumptions about "what's personal" as guidelines in news construction—a practice that reinforces the vicious circle. Whether they are journalists, scholars, or members of "informed" publics, those who subscribe to this conventional wisdom should at least consider the proposition that their own common knowledge is constructed, in part, by taking these media constructions at face value.

Whatever its sociological basis may be, it is clear that publishers and news executives often use the "what's personal" norm in bottom-line calculations about "what sells," which, in turn, helps them in deciding what news stories to tell and how to tell them (Bagdikian 1992). Add to this the widespread belief among journalists (also backed up by marketing research) that stories about foreign affairs and economic technicalities are lost on the general news audience, and it is easy to see why reporting in these areas is often written from the viewpoint, and for the edification, of the elite stratum of the media audience.

One senses, for example, that the *New York Times* is written for a rarefied stratum of elites and intellectuals, inviting the populist charge that it is, variously, an elite, effete, or liberal publication. One suspects that those who level such charges are unlikely to write any more intelligent public policy scripts in their ideal versions of the news, but that is another story. The point here is that such elite news organizations cue the daily news agendas of the hundreds and thousands of lesser print and broadcast news organizations. A normative system of this order requires not just broad, commonsense agreement on norms, but daily exemplars from leading news organizations about how to apply those norms. And when an information system of this magnitude produces symbolic patterns as striking as the representations of publics that emerge in our data set, those representations just might have psychological effects worth thinking about.

When viewed as a professional journalistic gloss on common sense, the exclusion and inclusion of voices in the news is not a conspiracy between profit-conscious media executives and power-hungry rulers. The process is more of an ecology of interests, and an ecology of often uneasy interests at that. The frictions and strategic calculations on the part of news organizations and political organizations can inject surprising episodes of investigative journalism and some detailed explorations of public policy. However, as shown by Ettema et al. (1991), these glimpses of independent journalism are often idiosyncratic and lacking in overriding and broadly integrative political points. This conclusion was also reached by Iyengar (1992) using a very different set of data and analytical methods.

Reflecting this odd mixture of business, entertainment, advertising, audience-drawing, and public information interests, the journalism product is not guided primarily—or, perhaps, even much of the time—by a norm of educating the public. The assumption that people are generally uneducable in a mass communication context (or, more basically, that they tune out and turn off "highbrow" media in favor of more shallow and sensational alternatives) is the founding assumption that keeps this constructed world reproducing itself. Indeed, all normative orders rest on founding assumptions that are as unprovable as they are convenient. It is on such assumptions that the perpetuation of and belief in other norms depends. Thus, most journalists and news watchers would agree that it makes little sense to introduce the views of uneducable publics into representations of politics that are believed to be beyond them.

It is conceivable that journalists could take up the defense of the public interest on behalf of such hapless publics. Yet such advocacy journalism is clearly not within the mainstream normative order of contemporary American press-politics. To the contrary, at the hint of such an idea, the public is suddenly transformed by both politicians and news executives into a noble body whose very sovereignty depends on independence of thought and neutrality of information. Armed with such contradictions, journalists seldom become very specific about the nature of the public interest. Indeed, political reporting is seldom even clear about what constitutes an abuse of power in the absence of official pronouncements from government authorities who express often calculated measures of concern about such abuses. Thus, Richard Nixon's Watergate transgressions were pegged journalistically at the levels of seriousness assigned them by an impeachment-minded Congress. By comparison, Ronald Reagan's Iran-contra abuses (and earlier clandestine harbor-mining activities) were pegged as lesser offenses by more appeasement-minded congressional players.

Such variations in news coverage fall within the ecology of interests (and related norms) that join journalists and political actors in the production of familiar patterns of news content. These patterns arguably reflect the primacy of economic considerations on the part of the media and the primacy of considerations about political power on the part of elites. Since media profits depend on audiences, and political power is contingent upon public acceptance, both sides represent their activities in the most public-minded ways imaginable (Edelman 1964, 1988). Indeed, an important feature of this information order is that these separate-yet-inseparable ecological interests (media profits and elite conservation of power in key affairs of state) find their respective legitimacy through more broadly shared social norms. We further suspect that patterns of political voices in the news seem more "natural," and therefore more acceptable, when viewed as the expression of public interests in a pluralistic democracy, rather than as a hegemonic product of overlapping corporate and state interests. The bedrock of commonsense, after all, is that people are more naturally concerned about issues such as abortion than about how to respond to the North Korean nuclear capability. Far from dismissing the "naturalness" of these public responses, we seek an understanding of how they are produced in and by communication processes.

Opening and Closing the Opinion Gates: Norms about Power

In this ecological process the "what's personal" norm is probably just one of several considerations used by journalists, elites, and publics in judging the appropriateness of voices included in and excluded from news accounts. On political matters, another deceptively simple norm explains even more about how journalists open and close the news gates to political viewpoints. The American democracy rendered as journalistic norm goes something like this: since the public elects officials to govern, the decisive debates among those officials should drive the content and composition of voices in news coverage. In other words, the social composition and content of political news is implicitly indexed to the range and intensity of ideological conflict among elites responsible for making policy decisions on a given issue. If elite debate is unwise or fails to represent political currents in society, so this commonsense logic goes, then it is the responsibility of the people to elect better or different rulers. The logic is immaculate: the people elect rulers, rulers debate issues, and journalists report those debates to the people. The problem with this reasoning is that it paints a simple, one-way picture of causality. In areas such as foreign policy and economic affairs, elites have evolved norms of greater consensus and secrecy surrounding their debates (also for good commonsense reasons). The result is that indexing news coverage to official debates in areas driven by elite norms of consensus and secrecy is likely to drive popular voices farther to the margins of the media, which, in turn, reinforces elite supremacy and public apathy and allows many key decisions of state to proceed in the absence of much critical public scrutiny.

The indexing norm explains why many foreign policy stories in the news adopt the ideological tone of the administrations pushing these policies while marginalizing critical voices from below (see, for example, Herman 1985, Entman and Page 1994, Dorman and Livingston 1994). The indexing hypothesis also accounts for those occasional triumphs of adversarial and investigative journalism in which publics are brought into the political fray (e.g., Vietnam, Watergate, Iran-Contra) and, not surprisingly, become interested participant-observers in stories that affect and include them more centrally. Such moments of adversarial journalism occur when elite consensus breaks down. Hallin (1986), for example, has documented the shift in media coverage of Vietnam as war policies moved from a protected sphere of elite consensus to an increasingly embattled sphere of legitimate controversy in Congress and between Congress and the administration.

There are limits to what indexing explains, however. Since the assumptions underlying indexing involve power and democratic representation within institutional decision processes, cases in which power and decisions move outside of Washington institutions call up other news construction strategies. For example, the election "horse race" script is not based on indexing (Zaller with Hunt 1994). And indexing does not fully account for the presence of so many foreign voices in coverage of Reagan's bombing of Libya (Althaus et al. 1994)—a case in which the path of power moved from Washington to the capitals of NATO allies.

Yet indexing does account for a large range of political content cues in the news. For example, content analyses of *New York Times* coverage of Reagan administration Nicaragua war policy (Bennett 1989, 1990) show that even the antiadministration views expressed on the *Times* editorial pages (both official editorials and invited commentaries) rose and fell with the levels of opposition expressed in congressional committee and floor votes on Reagan funding requests for the war. Extending this finding to the majority of foreign policy crises since World War II, Zaller, Chiu, and Hunt (1994) found a strong correlation between congressional hawkishness and more generalized media hawkishness on the crises in question.

Why the Symbolic Construction of Publics Matters

Thus, the proposal here is that voices in the news reflect the application of elite indexing and "what's personal" norms by journalists. The resulting construction of public opinion on the news pages seems generally plausible or even "natural" because the underlying journalistic norms have some broad intuitive appeal as social common sense. Yet the normative construction of publics in the news may set in motion patterns of ideological debate, public apathy, and arousal that structure the distribution of power and participation on various concerns of state and society. This process of constructing publics is ecological rather than conspiratorial, and thus accounts for dynamics that move issues in and out of public attention and that move publics in and out of issue debates. Thus, when partisan and institutional splits cued journalists to play up Vietnam, Watergate, and Iran-Contra stories, increases in public interest followed, which further fueled a journalistic opening of the news gates on these issues in keeping with the "what's personal" norm.

Both the "what's personal" norm and the public opinion it may generate are held in check by indexing. For example, Iran-Contra reportage steered a safe course around the inclusion of voices and evidence that pointed to involvement by President Reagan or (then) Vice President Bush. In a later round of self-criticism, several journalists (e.g., Armstrong 1990) raised the possibility that the relatively narrow opening of the news gate on Iran-Contra stemmed, in part, from congressional disinterest in pursuing the matter aggressively to its roots in the Oval Office or in the Constitution. Some journalists also pointed to the popularity of Ollie North as a problem for the political tone of the story. It was apparently too tempting to play North as a folk hero rather than as a villain due to the strength of his personal following. Thus, both indexing and "what's personal" norms may have led journalists to pull their punches on Iran-Contra, while different configurations of these norms opened the news to a broader range of voices and issues on Watergate and Vietnam. By contrast, the media free-for-all debate on abortion is typical for issues where elite divisions are pronounced, personal interest among news consumers is high, and there is little indication that elites are seeking to establish consensus (or that continuing dissensus has much effect on the stability or status of the state).

The cumulative effect of these gatekeeping norms is to build up general patterns of public inclusion in and exclusion from debates and ideological exchanges in the marketplace of ideas. The next section explores some of the characteristics of these patterns of public opinion construction. In the concluding section of the chapter, we suggest several models of mass psychology that may be helpful in understanding the impact of these images of publics on the formation of individual political consciousness.

A Tale of Two Democracies

Let's return to the cases of Nicaragua and abortion, two of the leading issues of the 1980s. Both issues were high on the agendas of the Reagan administration, both received considerable attention from elites in national institutions, both were targeted for action by interest groups and protest organizations, and, not surprisingly, both issues received massive media attention. For example, a headline search of a Lexis-Nexis database of six national newspapers (not including the *New York Times*)[1] revealed 4,251 articles on abortion during the period 1980–1989. The same six-newspaper database turned up 3,355 stories on Nicaragua over the same period. Suffice it to say that Nicaragua and abortion were among the most covered and talked about issues of the 1980s.

The important question is: Who was doing the talking in these news stories? A hand-coded study of *New York Times* index entries looked at whether policy opinions were expressed in an article, who expressed those opinions, and the direction of the opinion. (See Bennett 1989 for a description of the coding instructions). Two coders were trained for these tasks and achieved inter-coder reliability levels of .9 or higher on each task. Abortion stories and op-ed pieces were coded for 1981–86, while Nicaragua articles and op-ed pieces were coded for 1983–86, a period corresponding to the years of open policy debate between Congress and the White House prior to the out-

TABLE 4.1. **Breakdown of Opinions in Articles and Editorials on Nicaragua and Abortion Reported in the** *New York Times*

	Total Number of Stories and Editorials	Total Number of Opinions	Number of Opinions in News Stories
Abortion[a]	1,015	923	794
Nicaragua[b]	2,148	1,177	889

[a]1981–86
[b]1983–86

break of the Iran-Contra scandal. The search resulted in the breakdown of stories, editorials, and opinions shown in table 4.1.

The higher ratio of opinions to news in the case of abortion (.91) compared to Nicaragua (.55) suggests that much Nicaragua coverage was devoted to descriptive articles about the war and conditions inside the country. This sharp contrast in the opinion-to-coverage ratios suggests that abortion is, in the most obvious respect, a story about public opinion—and not just any public: the publics constructed for the two stories are dramatically different slices of society.

As the data in table 4.2 show, government officials were given the lion's share of opinion on Nicaragua, 51.3 percent, compared to only 32.4 percent of the voice slots in news and editorial opinion on abortion. Even more interesting is the dominance of "social voices" in the abortion case, with representatives of interest groups, participants in demonstrations, and interviews with people in the street accounting for 38.3 percent of all opinion, compared to a small (11.8 percent) proportion of "social voices" admitted into the newsprint debate on Nicaragua. Citations of public opinion polls followed the same pattern, with polls constituting only 2.5 percent of all opinion on Nicaragua while representing 8.6 percent of opinion on abortion. (Note here that the methods for drawing the samples in the studies reported in tables 4.1 and 4.2 were different than in table 4.3. In particular, the first study included all articles and editorials with a mention of Nicaragua or abortion in the text. The second study was restricted just to news articles that mentioned the issue in the headline. The time frames of the two studies differed as well.) Further diminishing the weight of the little public opinion that was cited on Nicaragua, news accounts generally qualified the polls as the products of uninformed citizens (see Bennett 1989). Polls on abortion were reported at face value without commentary on the qualification of the public to hold opinions on the issue. These patterns of opinion, along with editorial page breakdowns and opinions from other (primarily foreign) sources, are shown in table 4.2. It is worth noting that the opinions of foreign voices (primarily Sandinista officials and Contra

TABLE 4.2. Breakdown of Opinions on Nicaragua and Abortion Reported in the *New York Times*

Issue	Total Opinions		Government Officials		Polls		Social Voices		Other (Foreign)		Op-Ed Pieces		*NYT* Official Editorials	
	(N)	(%)	(N)	(%)	(N)	(%)	(N)	(%)	(N)	(%)	(N)	(%)	(N)	(%)
Abortion[a]	923	100	299	32.4	79	8.6	354	38.3	62	6.7	69	7.5	60	6.5
Nicaragua[b]	1,177	100	604	51.3	30	2.5	139	11.8	116	9.9	206	17.3	84	7.1

[a] 1981–86
[b] 1983–86

TABLE 4.3.   Opinion Polls in News Coverage of Domestic and Foreign Issues:
New York Times, 1980–90

(a) Domestic issues			
Headline	Total	Polls	Percentage
Gun control	70	3	4.3
Abortion	1,388	120	8.7
Drug testing	138	8	5.8
Tax reform	115	4	3.5
Inflation	874	4	0.5
Unemployment	259	5	1.9
Pollution	311	9	2.9
Acid rain	305	6	2.0
School prayer	61	12	19.7
Busing	166	5	3.0
School integration/desegregation	62	4	6.5
Homelessness	67	2	3.0
Minimum wage	148	4	2.7
Affirmative action	82	3	3.7
Domestic issues total	4,046	189	4.7

(b) Foreign issues			
Headline	Total	Polls	Percentage
Persian Gulf	238	0	0.0
Grenada	337	7	2.1
El Salvador	478	2	0.4
Guatemala	383	1	0.3
Honduras	328	1	0.3
Nicaragua	1,488	9	0.6
Trade deficit	255	2	0.8
South Africa divestment	173	0	0.0
Libya	697	3	0.4
Terrorism	397	4	1.0
Afghanistan	321	0	0.0
Arms control	287	4	1.4
Panama	665	8	1.2
Foreign issues total	6,047	41	0.7

spokespersons) were featured nearly as prominently as representatives of the American general public in the Nicaragua policy debate. (Note that foreign officials were counted as policy or opinion voices only when they specifically addressed Reagan administration policy. Otherwise, their actions were coded in the "descriptive" category.)

As these data show, government officials set the tone of debate on Nicaragua, while polls, along with a broad spectrum of social voices, set the tone of the media debate on abortion. Further reinforcing the elite tone of the former issue, a full 24 percent of the opinions on Nicaragua were contained on the editorial pages, compared with only 14 percent of the total viewpoints on abortion.

The Public Opinion Index and the Divided Democracy

Important clues explaining these patterns are provided by the duration and the extent of elite divisions in each case. To put it simply, government officials were more evenly divided on abortion, and those divisions remained strong over the whole period under study. The percentage of pro choice voices among government officials cited in the news averaged 45 percent over the six-year period, providing a fairly consistent balance to the average of 55 percent of the officials who went on the record opposing abortion. This persistent elite split opened the news gate to a large number of social voices (38.3 percent of the opinion total) who were reported by journalists as holding remarkably similar ratios of pro and con opinion as the elites (42 percent pro choice, 58 percent antiabortion among social voices). In the Nicaragua case, by contrast, official opinion was much more heavily skewed in favor of the proadministration line, with elite opponents of government policy (primarily registered through and around congressional debates) averaging only 33 percent, leaving a vocal White House with the lion's share (67 percent) of the "pro-Contra" opinion among officials in the news record. Not only was the opposition weak, but it eventually collapsed altogether under pressure from the administration to re-establish consensus in foreign policy, compounded by a White House intimidation campaign aimed at vulnerable House Democrats up for reelection in 1986. As a result, congressional opposition collapsed (ironically, just before the outbreak of the Iran-Contra scandal), and Reagan secured passage of his full $100 million military aid request for the war against Nicaragua. With the disappearance of congressional opposition, virtually all other social opposition (what little there was) disappeared from the news as well. One suspects that the small volume of "social voices" in Nicaragua coverage reflected the media indexing of a relatively fragile congressional opposition, compounded by press sensitivity to traditional pressures for bipartisan consensus in foreign policy.

In many ways, the most surprising finding of this study is that indexing also applies to editorial opinion in the media—at least "media of record" such as The *New York Times*. To wit: the opposition voices on the *Times*'s own editorial page disappeared after a consensus was hammered out in the institutional power circles. A study of *Times* editorial (and invited op-ed) opinion shows that levels of the paper's own opposition rose and fell with the rising and falling opposition in Congress. Even though the eventual collapse of the House opposition appeared to result from White House intimidation through media campaigns in vulnerable members' home districts, the *Times* also folded its tents on the issue. The implication of this pattern seems to be that opinion (including editorial opinion in this case) is so tightly indexed to elite divisions that when elite divisions disappear, so does "responsible" editorial opinion in foreign affairs—even if the reassertion of elite consensus was due to anything but enlightened judgment on the part of the national leadership. (See Bennett 1989 and 1990 for more detailed analyses of these data.)

As this "tale of two issues" illustrates, norms pertaining to conflict and consensus among the officers of government seem to explain much about the construction of opinion both in news stories and on the editorial pages of the nation's leading newspaper. While it is impossible to conduct such painstaking case studies for dozens of issues in the entire U.S. media, it is possible to get a rough sense of whether this pattern generalizes to other media and other issues in the foreign and domestic policy spheres. The patterns of opinion polls reported in news coverage of different kinds of issues offer a rough test of the generalizability of our thesis. Just as opinion polls were reported much more often in abortion stories than in Nicaragua coverage, we would expect opinion polls to show up more often in stories about most domestic issues than in stories about most foreign issues. Again, the reason is not the domestic-foreign split per se, but the likelihood of elite consensus and conflict in the respective areas, bolstered by the "what's personal" norm that assumes greater public interest in domestic issues. While it is not possible to report a full "voice in the news" analysis for each of the domestic and foreign policy issues chosen for the following study of the 1980–90 time period, we can show patterns of opinion polls reported in the news about some of the most prominent issues of that decade.

Research Design

The studies reported in this section were all based on samples of domestic and foreign issues that appeared on the front pages of leading national newspapers, as lead stories in newsmagazines, and on network nightly news broadcasts (per the Vanderbilt Television News Index) during the 1980s. The sample included a balance of issues that were cited in Gallup polls as the "most important issue facing the country," along with issues that were not cited as "most important" despite receiving prominent news coverage. The total number of issues on the domestic side was fourteen, and the number on the foreign side was thirteen, due to the original existence of two issues on South Africa (corporate divestment and government sanctions) that became confounded in media coverage and had to be collapsed. Since all of our comparisons are based on poll averages within stories, these differences did not contaminate the basic domestic-foreign comparisons or the significance tests reported herein.

The issue samples (shown in tables 4.3 through 4.5) were searched in the Lexis-Nexis database in three separate studies of different media domains: (a)

TABLE 4.4. Opinion Polls in News Coverage of Domestic and Foreign Issues: Other National Papers, 1980–90[a]

(a) Domestic issues			
Headline	Total	Polls	Percentage
Gun control	361	32	8.9
Abortion	4,251	384	9.0
Drug testing	552	19	3.4
Tax reform	572	32	5.6
Inflation	2,050	31	1.5
Unemployment	594	5	0.8
Pollution	1,581	21	1.3
Acid rain	439	2	0.5
School prayer	107	11	10.3
Busing	375	9	2.4
School integration/desegregation	166	3	1.8
Homelessness	174	5	2.9
Minimum wage	299	8	2.7
Affirmative action	304	7	2.6
Domestic issues total	11,825	584	4.9

(b) Foreign issues			
Headline	Total	Polls	Percentage
Persian Gulf	779	14	1.8
Grenada	440	6	1.4
El Salvador	1,634	10	0.6
Guatemala	566	0	0.0
Honduras	771	1	0.1
Nicaragua	3,355	20	0.6
Trade deficit	725	4	0.6
South Africa divestment	482	2	0.4
Libya	1,716	7	0.4
Terrorism	1,375	10	0.7
Afghanistan	925	0	0.0
Arms control	737	26	3.5
Panama	2,233	19	0.9
Foreign issues total	15,738	199	0.8

[a]Includes data from the *Boston Globe, Chicago Tribune, Christian Science Monitor, Denver Post, Los Angeles Times, Providence Journal, San Francisco Chronicle, Tulsa Star, Sacramento Bee,* and *Washington Post.* While the search period is 1980 to 1990, the various papers entered the Lexis-Nexis database at different times. For example, the *Christian Science Monitor* runs from 1980, but records from the *Los Angeles Times* begin in 1988. Thus, the numbers of citations do not include all articles for each paper on each issue for the entire search period.

TABLE 4.5. Opinion Polls in News Coverage of Domestic and Foreign Issues: *Time* **and** *U.S. News and World Report,* **1980–90**[a]

(a) Domestic issues			
Headline	Total	Polls	Percentage
Gun control	27	2	7.4
Abortion	150	22	14.7
Drug testing	5	1	20.0
Tax reform	69	10	14.5
Inflation	175	5	2.9
Unemployment	46	6	13.0
Pollution	37	5	13.5
Acid rain	13	0	0.0
School prayer	12	0	0.0
Busing	25	1	4.0
School integration/desegregation	8	1	12.5
Homelessness	25	0	0.0
Minimum wage	13	0	0.0
Affirmative action	23	0	0.0
Domestic issues total	628	53	8.4

(b) Foreign issues			
Headline	Total	Polls	Percentage
Persian Gulf	22	2	9.1
Grenada	72	0	0.0
El Salvador	132	2	1.5
Guatemala	10	1	10.0
Honduras	17	1	5.9
Nicaragua	135	3	2.2
Trade deficit	16	0	0.0
South Africa divestment	5	0	0.0
Libya	66	1	1.5
Terrorism	138	3	2.2
Afghanistan	74	0	0.0
Arms control	78	2	2.6
Panama	63	1	1.6
Foreign issues total	828	16	1.9

[a]Search periods correspond to the length of inclusion in the Nexis-Lexis database, 1981–90.

New York Times headlines containing the issue or a cognate term; (b) a national ten-newspaper comparison sample, also using headline searches (see the note on table 4.4 for description of this sample); (c) a subject search of the news magazines *Time* and *U.S. News and World Report.* Articles naming the various domestic and foreign policy issues in the headline (or newsmagazine subject) were then searched for the use of the words *poll* and *survey.* In an improvement on the earlier studies reported in tables 4.1 and 4.2, we then called up the context (a ten-word span on either side) of the reference to a poll or a survey and coded for whether or not the reference was, in fact, to an opinion or survey on the issue in question.[2]

Eliminating extraneous mentions of polls (e.g., polling places in elections in Nicaragua, or opinion polls in South Africa) ended up increasing the size of the public opinion gap between domestic and foreign issues. For example, uncorrected polls appeared in 2.5 percent of *New York Times* Nicaragua coverage in the 1983–1986 period reported in Table 4.2, while the corrected coding for the entire 1980–1990 period in Table 4.3B shows a stunning result of just .7 percent. Part of this difference may be due to higher levels of public policy controversy in the 1983–1986 period than during the rest of the decade, but part of it also reflects the greater reference to non-U.S. public opinion polls in foreign policy coverage. Note, for example, that the corrected and uncorrected percentages of polls reported in abortion coverage are the same in the two samples.

The Findings

The overwhelming pattern in all three of our media samples is that polls appear significantly more often in domestic news reports than in foreign issue coverage. However, there are some interesting ratio differences as we move from the *New York Times* (the most skewed, at a 6.7-to-1 ratio), to the national paper sample (close to *NYT* at a 6.1-to-1 ratio), to the newsmagazines (a bit closer at 4.4 to 1).

The *New York Times* poll coverage reported in table 4.3 clearly introduces the public more prominently into domestic than foreign issues, with polls appearing in 4.7 percent of domestic, and 0.7 percent of foreign studies. In addition, we see that within the 4.7 percent of domestic headline stories containing polls, some issues such as school prayer and abortion feature public opinion more prominently than do others, particularly those on the economic end of the spectrum. This is precisely what we would expect from the indexing and "what's personal" norms. The coverage featuring public opinion most prominently was school prayer, abortion, school integration, drug testing, and gun control, in that order, while items at the bottom end of the spectrum were all economic policy issues. The standard deviation around the poll averages for domestic issues (.044) is more than twice that for the poll distribution on the foreign issues (.0188). The difference between these group averages based on a t-test (2-tailed, unequal variance) is $p < .005$.

The means of 4.7 domestic and 0.7 foreign were weighted averages based on the number of stories. There is, however, no theoretical reason to be concerned about outliers such as abortion and school prayer. To the contrary, these issues should be outliers according to the theory. However, unweighted averages were also taken to address criticisms that a few issues were driving up the effects. In an unweighted average of straight poll percentages, the domestic issue average was 4.4 percent and the foreign average was 0.6 percent, with a *t*-test significance of $p < .005$. These patterns were remarkably similar in the sample of other national papers reported in the following paragraph, suggesting that the *New York Times* does, indeed, cue mainstream press coverage patterns.

Notice, for example, that the domestic and foreign means in the sample of other papers reported in table 4.4 are virtually identical to the *Times*, at 4.9 and 0.8 respectively. Moreover, the patterns of variance in both groups are almost exactly the same as well, with a standard deviation around the domestic issue mean of .044 and a standard deviation around the foreign issue mean of .016. The significance of the *t*-test is $p < .01$. As with the *Times* study, the theory predicts both the number and the kind of outliers on the domestic list, but a more conservative unweighted mean comparison still shows the domestic-foreign split to be highly significant, with means of 3.2 percent and 0.9 percent, respectively, and a *t*-value significant at $p < .004$. These patterns are also similar for the newsmagazines, although the levels of foreign policy polls and polls in general are somewhat higher.

As shown in table 4.5, the overall levels of poll reporting are higher in newsmagazines, and the gap between domestic and foreign issue coverage is not as great. However, the reporting of polls occurred in 8.4 percent of domestic stories and 1.9 percent of foreign stories, leaving a considerable public opinion "cue gap" between the two areas. Not only is this gap substantial, but it is in the same direction as those found in the aforementioned samples.

What may be more interesting than the size of the difference is the newsmagazine tendency toward an "all or none" approach to polls, suggesting that magazines use their polling operations more intensively on some issues than on others. This difference in poll patterns emerged in both domestic and foreign issue coverage, as reflected in larger standard deviations around the means (.071 and .034, respectively). The basic pattern of greater poll cuing in domestic versus foreign issue coverage remained significant at a *t*-test level of $p < .05$ for both weighted and unweighted means.

While the patterns of poll reporting in all three media samples are similar in direction and difference, the higher volumes of polls used in newsmagazines may be worth exploring further. For starters, newsmagazines seem to build more perspective or thematic context in their reporting than do other news outlets, which should make their reporting more accessible in the terms outlined by Iyengar (1992). Indeed, this pattern may help explain the finding by Neuman, Just, and Crigler (1992) that people get much more information out of newsmagazine coverage than from newspaper reporting on the same issues. These and other possible consequences of opinion poll cuing in the news lead to the theory building and hypotheses for future research contained in the remainder of this chapter.

Images of Publics and the Public Self-Image

At the very least, it is clear that grass roots voices are privileged in news accounts of domestic moral issues while elite voices are privileged in coverage of foreign policy matters. As noted at the outset, there are good commonsense explanations to account for this, including the traditional claims of elites to greater latitude in foreign policy for reasons of national security, public apathy, elite expertise, and the importance of bipartisan consensus. However, these legitimating explanations also constitute what amounts to an ideology of elite power in the most important matters of state.

When viewed as an ideology of power rather than simply as a rationale or a causal explanation, this general wisdom about who should have a say in public debates becomes potentially important as a psychological context in which various political issues and conflicts may be judged by the public itself. In particular, diminished and discredited grass roots voices in news about foreign policy may constitute psychological grounds for continued public ignorance and apathy in those areas. A psychology of commonsense may be set in motion, reproducing the very conditions of apathy and ignorance that justify differential levels of power and access to public discourse between elites and the general public.

There are several psychological models that help define the dynamics of this vicious circle. Each model represents a different component of the psychological process, from (1) a greater reluctance of people to express opinions about foreign policy, to (2) the assumption that elites ought to have more say in these matters, to (3) the greater willingness of the people to abdicate political action in foreign policy to elites, while reserving for themselves action prerogatives in the domestic (particularly moral) arena.

1. The "spiral of silence" (Noelle-Neumann 1984) explains the process through which people suppress their own opinions (or fail to form them in the first place) when surrounding social opinion is similarly silenced or dominated by a vocal point of view. In the case of foreign policy, mass opinion is relatively silent in news coverage of most issues while policy options are dominated by elite voices that generally strive toward consensus. As a result, it is hardly surprising that most people confess ignorance and lack of interest in foreign policy areas when interviewed by pollsters.

As table 4.6 shows, people are dramatically less likely to form opinions at all on foreign policy questions. The "no opinion" response is over 20 percent on four of the six Gallup poll foreign policy issues included in this study for the

TABLE 4.6. Gallup Polls in the *New York Times*, 1980–86

Headline	Number of Articles	Number of Polls	Percent No Opinion
Abortion	657	44	3.8
School prayer	58	7	5.7
Death penalty	171	15	8.3
Gun control	48	2	5.3
Affirmative action	90	2	6.5
Busing	150	6	6.0
Domestic total	1,174	76	5.9
South Africa (sanctions)	1,285	23	13.0
Nicaragua[a]	1,000	16	24.0
Lebanon[a]	1,514	15	15.0
Central America[a]	198	16	24.5
El Salvador[a]	376	11	31.0
Middle East[a]	151	1	25.0
Foreign total	4,524	82	22.1

[a]Handling by Reagan administration

1980–86 period. By contrast, all the issues on the domestic side show "no opinion" rates under 10 percent. (The issues were chosen for diversity of subject matter. Poll results were gathered after the issue lists were composed.) The first step toward abdicating an area of political power is to stop forming opinions about it at all. This seems to be the pattern in a startling number of foreign policy cases.

2. "Superstitious learning" (Skinner 1953) next explains how people make sense out of the state of dual democracy in which they find themselves. Searching for clues in complex and often incomplete behavioral environments leads people (and in Skinner's experiments, pigeons) to invest their most salient behavioral routines with superstitious meaning. Thus, the random moves made by a pigeon prior to the appearance of a pellet of grain in the reward tray become internalized as a necessary "dance" that must be performed in order to receive food. Similarly, life in a foreign policy communications environment that is all but devoid of credible grass roots voices may lead easily to the attribution of diminished right to express a viewpoint on the part of ordinary individuals. The superstitious conclusion easily drawn from this perception is that the vocal elites who occupy the public limelight actually have something more meaningful and reasoned to say about foreign policy initiatives. Given the modern legacy of third world debt, failure of development, low-intensity warfare, and dubious U.S. entanglements, attributions of greater

elite insight are at the very least questionable. Indeed, as Page and Shapiro's (1992) impressive analysis of public opinion on a range of complex policy issues shows, there are reasons to credit publics with greater rationality than that for which they are often given credit. But rationality is not at the base of a mass political psychology that legitimizes the exclusion of these publics from particular policy debates.

The important question here is not who is right and who is wrong about any policy question, but who abdicates public debate prerogatives and consequent political power to whom. Superstitious learning about relative levels of elite expertise and popular ignorance may help sustain elite power and legitimacy in some of the most important matters of state. By contrast, a parallel superstitious learning process may lead people to look in just the opposite way at the unchallenged reporting of high volumes of grass roots voices in areas such as abortion and school prayer. The sensible (if superstitious) conclusion about public debate on these moral issues is that ordinary people know what they are talking about, and insofar as elite political fortunes hang in the electoral balance, rulers had better listen. Thus, our public life is driven by intense debates about moral issues (that happen to be) of little consequence for the conduct of business or international politics, while the key affairs of state pass through the public side of the political system relatively unscathed by controversy or by credible popular challenges to elite power and decision prerogatives.

3. A social imitation model of learning (Bandura and Walters 1963) links opinion formation and attributions of legitimate political privilege to action imperatives. A social imitation model suggests that when people see others like themselves marginalized in a sphere of political action, the most obvious individual response is to seek out a marginalized political participation niche as well. In other words, people who see others like themselves expressing few credible opinions and taking even fewer effective political actions are likely to "learn" that foreign and economic policy are areas that do not warrant much, if any, participation from the "little people." By contrast, individuals who see people like themselves expressing strong views on abortion or prayer in school (and taking political actions inside the news frame) are provided clear models from which they can imitate similar styles of political thought and action.

Two Political Worlds

The psychological dynamics of public opinion in the news may create (at least) two political worlds. In the first, individuals are reluctant to form and express opinions, turning over the political floor to elites who, in effect, think and act for them. In the other political world, people form and express opinions more freely, act in a variety of ways, and often seek to discipline elites both as candidates and officeholders. The first world resembles an oligarchy run by the captains of industry, finance, and state. The second is more like the textbook democracy that we read about in high school civics. A cynical interpretation would say that the mass communications system helps create democracy in those areas that matter least, while draining interest and popular involvement away from the most consequential areas of state power. A less cynical interpretation merely points out that the same citizens seem capable of quite different levels of political thinking and action depending on the political subject matter. In either case, media portrayals of this split reality may support the impression in the minds of news audiences that this dual democracy is appropriate and even "natural."

NOTES

The authors would like to thank Thomas Tsai for invaluable help with data gathering and graphic display. Coding on the early Nicaragua and abortion case studies was done by Steve DeTray and Laura Matson. Coding of the later poll in the news studies was done by Naomi Stacy and John Klockner. Earlier versions of this paper benefited from the comments of Susan Herbst. These ideas were also vetted in presentations at the 1990 annual meetings of the International Society of Political Psychology in Washington, D.C., and at a joint political science-communication lecture at Northwestern University. The helpful comments of those in attendance are gratefully acknowledged.

1. The papers in the Lexis-Nexis "education" database used for this search were: *Chicago Tribune* (November 1988–December 1990); *Christian Science Monitor* (January 1980–December 1990); *Los Angeles Times* (January 1985–December 1990); *Greensboro News & Record* (April 1988–December 1990); *Newsday* (May 1988–December 1995); *Tulsa World* (February 1988–December 1990).

2. The coder assigned to this task was trained in an earlier study and achieved 90 percent or better reliability with a second coder, based on a set of blind examples provided by the authors. This level of reliability was maintained in this study as well.

CHAPTER 5

Media Discourse as a Framing Resource

William A. Gamson

People use media discourse as one among several resources in making sense of political issues. Sometimes they combine media discourse with experiential knowledge and popular wisdom to bridge public discourse and personal experience; at other times, they use it in isolation from other resources or largely ignore it. The particular ways in which they use it to build and maintain a frame for understanding depends heavily on the issue involved, although individuals may also vary on the same issue. This chapter explores this process of using media discourse by examining the conversations of 188 ordinary working people on the issues of affirmative action, nuclear power, troubled industry, and Arab-Israeli conflict.

One might imagine that with thousands of studies of people's voting preferences and attitudes on every conceivable issue, we would thoroughly understand how people think and talk about politics. Indeed, we do understand a lot about the end product—the content of the opinions they express. But on how they get there, on what the issues mean to people and how they reach their conclusions, we are still groping.

Surveys of political attitudes frequently ask people about issues on which there is a rich public discourse, presented selectively in mass media accounts and commentary. Most students of public opinion assume that this media discourse is somehow reflected in the attitudes people express but would be hard-pressed to specify exactly how it is used in thinking and talking about various issues. Media discourse is clearly not the only resource that most people use to construct meaning on political issues. Faced with a cacophony of media clatter, popular wisdom, and knowledge from their own lived experience, whether and how they make sense of it all remains a substantial mystery.

Imagine a group of ordinary working people carrying on a conversation in which they are trying to figure out how they think about complex issues such as affirmative action, nuclear power, troubled industry, and Arab-Israeli conflict. Each issue is a forest through which they must find their way. These are not virgin forests, however. The various frames in media discourse provide maps indicating useful points of entry, provide signposts at various crossroads, high-light the significant landmarks, and warn of the perils of other paths. However, many people do not stick to the pathways provided, frequently wandering off and making paths of their own.

From the standpoint of the wanderers, media discourse is a cultural re-source to use in understanding and talking about an issue, but it is only one of several available. Nor is it necessarily the most important one on some issues, compared, for example, with their own experience and that of significant others in their lives. Frequently, they find their way through the forest with a com-bination of resources, including those they carry with them.

Peer Group Observations

My colleagues and I conducted thirty-seven peer group conversations among 188 participants in the greater Boston area in 1986–87. The following profile is based on information they provided in a questionnaire filled out in advance of the discussion. They were heterogeneous in race and gender but less so on age. Slightly more than half were white (54 percent) and female (56 percent). More than three-fourths were between the ages of twenty-nine and forty-nine, with a median age of thirty-three and only one percent over sixty-five. In religion, they were a mix of Catholics, Protestants, and nonreligious, with only one Jewish participant. Irish was the most frequently cited ethnicity among the whites, but they comprised only 15 percent of the total sample.

Almost 90 percent were currently employed in the paid labor market, with only 4 percent unemployed and 3 percent full-time homemakers. About 30 percent were in service jobs of one sort or another, with another 24 percent clerical and office workers; only 12 percent worked in manufacturing jobs. Cooks and kitchen workers, bus drivers, medical and lab technicians, nurses, firefighters, and auto service workers were some of the specific job categories that included five or more people.

We deliberately tried to exclude from the sample people who were current students or college graduates. Groups were formed by recruiting a contact person who then would invite three to five friends. Although the contact person was not a college graduate or currently enrolled student, we could not fully control whom she or he invited. Hence, some 6 percent of the total sample were college graduates, but 58 percent had no education beyond high school or trade school. About one-third had some post–high school technical training or col-lege short of a baccalaureate.

Certain contextual issues would remain even if we had a perfect random sample of all Boston-area working people. We asked them to discuss four issues: affirmative action, nuclear power, troubled industry, and Arab-Israeli conflict. Boston has its own special history and set of geographical factors that influence Bostonians' understanding of these issues. Residents of cities that did not experience the bitter racial clashes over school busing in the 1970s would not necessarily discuss the affirmative action issue in the same way. The Seabrook and Pilgrim nuclear reactors are close to Boston and received much local publicity over a number of years, creating a special context for the discussion of nuclear power. The unemployment rate in the Boston area was only 4 percent at the time of these conversations on troubled industry.

The timing of these conversations played a role on all issues. They occured soon after Chernobyl and at a moment when affirmative action was under challenge by the Reagan administration; before the *intifada* but not long after the Achille Lauro hijacking and the bombing of Libya. These contextual characteristics of time and location influenced the extent to which results can be generalized, independently of the representativeness of the sample.

We recruited contact people at multiple sites and ended up with participants from thirty-five different neighborhoods or separately incorporated communities in the Boston metropolitan area. We chose public sites where a recruitment table for the project was not out of place and it was possible to carry on a conversation and establish some rapport with potential recruits. This parameter led us to focus on neighborhood and community events of various sorts—festivals, picnics, fairs, and flea markets, for example. We also posted notices of research with a phone number to contact us at various neighborhoods and work sites. We avoided recruiting at any event or site associated with a political cause or tendency because we were eager to avoid any kind of political atypicality.

To minimize a sample biased toward those with a special interest in discussing issues in the news, we paid people enough to make the monetary incentive attractive. The desire to earn a little money, we reasoned, was a better motive for participating than the more atypical motive of special interest in politics. Judging from a combination of self-reported interest on the questionnaire and the discussions themselves, there is no evidence that our participants were unusually high in political interest, but there is good reason to suspect that we lost the apolitical end of the spectrum. Only 2 percent of our sample claimed that they followed the news "hardly at all." For some people, the risk of embarrassment or humiliation inherent in talking about politics for a gallery of university researchers was not worth the modest payment involved. The most important bias in our sample, then, is the underrepresentation of an apolitical stratum of people who simply don't attend to politics at all.[1]

The Context

The peer group conversations used here are a variant of the more generic technique of *focus groups*. The technique's greatest advantage is that it allows us to observe the process of people constructing and negotiating shared meaning, using their natural vocabulary. We were concerned with the threatening nature of the task for working people who do not normally carry on a sustained conversation about public issues. By going to participants instead of having them come to us, we hoped to put the interaction with the facilitator on a more equal footing. Most of the groups were run in people's homes where our facilitator and observer were present as guests, even though participants were being paid and did not control the topic of conversation. By holding discussions on the participants' own turf among people they knew and felt comfortable with, we hoped to minimize some of the constraints in the situation and to make them less fearful that they would expose themselves as political incompetents.

To encourage conversation rather than a facilitator-centered group interview, the facilitator was instructed to break off eye contact with the speaker as early as politeness allowed and to look to others rather than responding herself when someone finished comment. If a discussion got off the track, the facilitator would move it back on by going to the next question on the list. But we encouraged a conservative approach to what was considered "off the track" since, in negotiating meaning on any given issue, participants typically brought in other related issues. Decisions on what is or is not relevant are intimately tied to how an issue is framed, and the facilitator tried to avoid imposing or suggesting any particular frame.

The facilitators were instructed to follow a standard script, especially in describing each issue under discussion. They aimed for a discussion of approximately twenty minutes on each issue, using a series of follow-up questions to the open-ended one with which each discussion began. Once most people had responded to a question and no one else sought the floor, the facilitator would move to the next question on the list. These follow-up questions also served as a reminder of the issue in the event that a discussion had rambled.

One follow-up question asked about whether people were personally affected by the issue, a second asked about whether large groups stood to gain or lose, and a "cartoon" question showed them a series of four or five cartoons on each issue. Each cartoon represented a different way of framing the issue in public discourse. Finally, they were asked for their judgment of what should be done about the issue.[2]

Conversational Resources

When people state an opinion in a conversation, they usually explain to others the basis for their conclusion. Sprinkled through their conversations are numerous examples of claims about the world that frame the issue in a particular way and serve to justify this framing.[3] I focus on three types of conversational resources: *media discourse, experiential knowledge,* and *popular wisdom.*

Media Discourse

Every group on every issue in our study showed some awareness that there was a public discourse around them, even if they made minimal use of it and frequently apologized for not having better command of it. In fact, most groups drew on it in some fashion, even if they failed to integrate it with other resources. On some issues—and in some groups on most issues—it was the main or even exclusive resource they used in constructing meaning. Other resources appeared only sporadically on matters that were tangential to their framing of the issue.

The public discourse that people draw on is much broader than the "news" and takes many forms. In discussing affirmative action, for example, several groups in our study quoted the advertising slogan of the United Negro College Fund: "A mind is a terrible thing to waste." A variety of movies and television programs were brought in more than once, including *Silkwood* and *The China Syndrome,* in discussions of nuclear power.

Nor did participants confine the media discourse on which they drew to the immediate issue under discussion. Frequently they attempted to understand one issue by comparing it to other related issues. On nuclear power, more than one-third of the groups discussed the explosion of the space shuttle *Challenger,* which had occurred earlier in the same year. About one-fourth of them introduced the conflict in Northern Ireland in discussing Arab-Israeli conflict.

Often it is difficult to know for certain whether a remark draws on media discourse because people do not identity the source of their knowledge. Those in our study who followed media discourse on the troubled steel industry, for example, would have known the story of U.S. Steel. Buttressed by low-interest government loans, the company chose not to reinvest in modernizing its plant facilities to produce steel competitively; instead, it embarked on a policy of diversification, acquiring the Marathon Oil Company in the process. Eventually, it even dropped *steel* from the company name, becoming the USX Corporation.

It would appear, in the conversation that follows, that Bob was aware of this part of the public discourse and was drawing on it as a resource. The group was responding to the initial, open-ended question on troubled industry:

Participants:
Madelyn, a worker in a candy factory, in her fifties
Bob, an assistant manager at a car wash, in his thirties
Daniel, a printer, in his twenties

Madelyn: These people have a hard time to find another job. Some of them are older people, and then they have to relocate, and not even live in the community they were brought up in.

Bob: That's true.

Madelyn: And then business suffers, too, you know, because the thing shuts down, these people have to move it, they don't have the money to spend.

Bob: Like in the steel industry, in the Midwest. The steel industry is just about gone in the United States. Although, probably, we have the most knowledge about it and the best people to do it. There's no money in it for the businessmen, so they don't put it out.

Madelyn: Yeah, and in Maine there's a paper mill that's in big trouble. They were on strike because they don't want them to have seniority. They're trying to make slaves out of them, you know. So, if the company won't back down, he says they won't give them what they want. So you know what they're going to do? They're going to shut down, and they're going out to Minneapolis or somewhere like that. And they tell them, like, "you come if you want," and there's about 1,200 people working there, and that's all there is, is that paper mill.

Daniel: You want to buy a house up in Maine—

Madelyn: You can get them cheap.

Daniel: You can. A house—

Madelyn:—$18,000—

Daniel: Yeah, $18,000, but then, there's no work up there. But there's work in certain mills, but the guys are on strike and who wants to be a scab and cross the picket line, especially since that guy's been putting his blood, sweat, and whatever into it and you're going to go across the line and they're going to start trouble, and they're going to threaten your families and stuff.

Madelyn: They follow them home, see where they live. And they threaten to burn their house down—

Daniel: The government—President Reagan should do something. He's out for himself. He's not for the poor people. That's my feeling about him. You know, they should get somebody else in office.

Madelyn: Like Nancy.

(laughter)

Bob did not flag his source of knowledge by saying, "I saw *a program on television* about the steel industry or I *read an article* that the steel industry is just about gone in the United States." However, the content implied awareness of the U.S. Steel story or others like it. Fortunately, most uses of media discourse in our groups were not as subtle and inferential as this one and instead were quite explicit. More than 95 percent of the usages that we coded fell into one of the following categories:

1. Spotlighted facts. The advantage of media frames for journalists is that they serve as guidelines in helping select what information to spotlight and what to ignore. Facts take on their meaning from being framed in some fashion. Many facts are spotlighted by certain frames and ignored or discounted by others. People bring in a variety of these informational elements from media discourse to support the frames that spotlighted them. Their information may or may not be veridical, and sometimes it is challenged and corrected by others, but accuracy is not the issue. As used here, the words *fact* and *knowledge* always include implicit quotation marks that beg the question of their truth and treat them all as factual claims.

To illustrate how spotlighted facts support particular frames, take the explosion of a nuclear plant in Chernobyl in the Soviet Union, an accident that occurred only a few months before our study's conversations took place. Chernobyl entered the conversation in some form in 86 percent of the groups. Not everyone got the name exactly right, but we included here such variations as Chernova, Grenoble, or just "Russia." The context made it clear enough what they were talking about.

The mere mention did not indicate what about Chernobyl was relevant, but it became clear as the conversation continued. The most frequent point was that Chernobyl illustrated the dangers of nuclear accidents: people can get killed immediately or experience delayed injury through radiation effects. (No frame in media discourse challenges this fact, but it is certainly not emphasized by supporters of nuclear power.) Instead, they spotlighted another fact: Soviet nuclear reactors were designed less safely than U.S. reactors. By implication, the U.S. nuclear industry had this potentially dangerous technology under control.

About 17 percent of the groups explicitly introduced this fact, as in the examples below.

Participants:
Ida, a bookkeeper, in her late sixties
Ruth, an office supervisor, in her fifties

Ida: You see, our plants are built better than that one as it is. There's something—(pause) they're supposed to have here.
Ruth: I was just wondering how long it had been in operation before they had this accident? (pause) It certainly wasn't a new plant.
Ida: No, it wasn't. But it didn't have the safety features that our plants already have.

Participant: Joe, a firefighter, in his fifties

Joe: Look at Chernobyl. They're comparing it to the nuclear power plants in the United States. They can't do that! Chernobyl happened with stuff that the United States did in the nuclear power forty years ago. That plant's antiquated. Know what I mean?

Drawing on this spotlighted fact in the conversation always occurred in the service of a pronuclear frame that discounted the significance of the Chernobyl accident for the future of nuclear power in the United States. Ida was a minority of one on nuclear power in her group, and no else helped her to construct her preferred frame. No one, for example, supplied her with the term "containment structure" when she searched for details on why U.S. plants are safer. The alternative package that the others were developing did not spotlight the fact that the Chernobyl plant had a different and inferior containment structure. Hence, it was not a relevant resource for their purposes, and the conversation quickly moved on to other aspects of the issue.

2. Public figures. Conversations in our groups frequently brought in public figures who were seen as significant actors on the issue. In 1986, Ronald Reagan made the most appearances, entering the conversation on every issue, although infrequently on certain ones. On troubled industry, he sometimes entered as a symbol of union busting, and reference was made to the breaking of the air traffic controllers' union. On affirmative action, Reagan came up in many black groups as the ringleader of the effort to take away "all the things that we have fought for" (as one woman put it).

Many other public figures made their appearance more selectively on a given issue. Lee Iacocca made frequent appearances in discussions of troubled industry, and, perhaps more surprisingly, Libyan leader Muammar Gadhafi appeared in almost one-third of the discussions of Arab-Israeli conflict. As with Chernobyl, different uses can be made of the public figures invoked. Iacocca was typically presented in a hero's robe as the savior of the moribund Chrysler corporation. But occasionally a group used the enormous compensation Iacocca received to draw a different lesson from the Chrysler story. Similarly, Gadhafi was typically cast as a crazy fanatic and villain, but again oppositional readings occasionally occurred. "I like Gadhafi because he's flashy," said a woman in one group.

The use of public figures in a conversation was counted as a resource only if it was used to develop and support a shared framing of the issue. Celebrity gossip that did not make a relevant point did not count. The remark about Gadhafi's personal style, for example, was not used to support any particular frame and would not qualify as an example of using media discourse.

3. Catchphrases. People signal the use of media discourse by using particular catchphrases that are a prominent part of it. On affirmative action, for example, about one-third of our groups use the phrase "reverse discrimina-

tion." To allow us to infer the use of this resource, they must have used the actual language of public discourse and not merely a paraphrase that expressed the idea. It was not enough, for example, that they claimed that whites were being discriminated against if they did not use the phrase "reverse discrimination."

Other phrases came up much less frequently, including "A mind is a terrible thing to waste" and "Last hired, first fired" on affirmative action. On troubled industry, people occasionally spoke of the "foreign trade deficit" and "buy American"; on nuclear power, "no nukes" and "split wood, not atoms" were invoked a few times. However, no catchphrase from the public discourse on Arab-Israeli conflict appeared in more than one group.

Experiential Knowledge

People in our study frequently made their points in these conversations by telling a story. Sometimes these stories were about someone they read about or heard on a radio talk show, but the majority of them were anecdotes about themselves or someone they knew personally. These stories had a point to make, and if a speaker was uncertain about whether the point was clear, the story made the lesson explicit.

While every story had its unique features, the stories also formed generic types, related to the framing of an issue. Comments about the "hard time" involved when people got laid off their jobs might have stimulated either a supporting *hardship* story or a discounting *readjustment* story. A hardship story typically emphasized the impact on people's self-esteem and the devastating effect on their families as well as the economic difficulties involved; a readjustment story typically emphasized the importance of personal motivation in overcoming life's inevitable adversities. Such generic stories recurred on every issue and contributed to framing it in particular ways; the choice of one rather than another was crucial to the construction of a shared meaning on the issue.

These personal anecdotes were one of the primary mechanisms in using experiential knowledge as a conversational resource. Such knowledge has a privileged place; it says, "I know because I saw it myself, firsthand." One does not contradict or deny other people's experience, although it may be discounted as an exception or countered with one's own experiential knowledge to support an alternative framing. More typically, people will add their own stories of the same genre, further buttressing a collective frame.

Experiential knowledge may be direct or vicarious in varying degrees. Sometimes the story is not about oneself but about one's spouse, partner, or child. At the other extreme, people tell stories about friends of friends or someone they once knew at work. It is difficult to know exactly where to draw the line at which experiential knowledge is so vicarious that it hardly seems personal at all.

Empathy allows people to transcend their own personal experience and to imagine how they would feel in another person's situation. For example, Madelyn was able to experience vicariously what it must be like for older workers with families to leave "the community they were brought up in" and move to "Minneapolis or somewhere like that." But being able to make this empathic leap is not the same as using one's own experience as a conversational resource. It does not claim the privilege of something witnessed or experienced directly. Hence, we coded as experiential knowledge only those claims that were based on one's own experiences and those of immediate family or household members.

Popular Wisdom

People in our study brought to bear many popular beliefs that transcended the specific issue in question. Frequently, they flagged their references to this resource by using such phrases as "That's the way life is," "In my experience . . . " "It's human nature," "As everyone knows," and the like. When they told a story, they often began or ended it by a general rule of thumb that related the experience to some popular maxim that it illustrated. Or, conversely, a statement of some proverb stimulated the introduction of experiential knowledge to make the same point concretely.

Popular wisdom as a resource depends on shared knowledge of what "everyone" knows. While everyone's experiential knowledge is in some respects unique, popular wisdom depends on the common elements. Hence, the greater the degree of homogeneity of life experience among a group of people, the greater the popular wisdom available to them as a resource. Popular wisdom frequently is part of a particular subculture, rather than part of a broader national culture. In our study groups, the popular wisdom expressed was often oppositional.

The two major devices by which popular wisdom entered these conversations are (1) rules of thumb, including proverbs, maxims, and biblical sayings, and (2) analogies to everyday life situations. In the following example, Tom implied a rule of thumb and Luke made it explicit in discussing the initial, open-ended question on nuclear power:

Participants:
Tom, a salesclerk in a stereo store, in his early twenties
Luke, a salesclerk in a department store, in his early twenties

Tom: I don't feel that the federal government can really guarantee the safety of nuclear power. I know they have got pretty strict regulations.

There's no guarantee. At any time a leak could erupt and cause a very, very disastrous situation.

Luke: Any time a human being is in control of it, anything can happen.

There were many paraphrases of this same generalization in other groups—for example, "You can't avoid human error," or "It's human nature to cut corners." Competing maxims are used to frame the nuclear power issue in a different way. "Everything in life has risks" or "You can get killed crossing a street," for example, use popular wisdom to debunk the special dangers of nuclear power.

Popular wisdom is also introduced through analogies between the issue and familiar situations from everyday experience. In the following example, a discussion of Arab-Israeli conflict, Evelyn offered a rule of thumb about how to handle intractable fights, and Thomas likened the Arab-Israeli conflict to a family feud.

Participants:
Evelyn, a nurse, in her thirties
Lucas, a worker in a shelter for the homeless, in his twenties
Thomas, a tailor, in his thirties

Evelyn: I think that when you have two sides fighting, if you can't stop the fight, after numerous attempts, walk away and leave them. The United States does not have to live over there in Palestine or Israel; they've got the United States. Come home; let 'em fight it out until it's over. Because you wouldn't go leave your home to go and witness some fight with somebody a thousand miles away. Why? It makes no sense to me.

Lucas: They have to have, both of them have to, ah, acknowledge each other's right to exist somewhere.

Thomas: You know, the war between these two—it, it's a lot deeper than just—it's not money or, power or—it's just a, ah, like a family feud. (laughs)

Lucas: Yeah, a family feud.

Comparing Resources: Personal versus Cultural

Any single resource has its limits. By using a combination of different types of resources to construct a shared frame, a group gives it a solid foundation.

Let me concede at the outset that none of these resources is purely personal or cultural. Even our personal experience is filtered through a culturally created lens. "Big Brother is you, watching" in Miller's (1990) clever phrase. We walk around with hyperreal images from movies and television and use them to code our own experiences. Media discourse is not something "out there" but, rather, something inside our heads.

At the other extreme, people bring their own experiences and personal associations to their readings of cultural texts. Media images have no fixed meaning; they involve a negotiation with a heterogeneous audience that may provide them with meanings quite different from the preferred reading. Gadhafi's sartorial style may signal craziness to the photojournalist or editor who spotlights it, but it signals panache and flashiness to some viewers. Media images, then, are not purely cultural but are infused with personal meanings as well.

Nevertheless, the mix of cultural and personal varies dramatically among the three types of resources. Our experiences may have cultural elements, but they are overwhelming our own private resources, not fully shared by others. People distinguish between knowing something from having experienced it and knowing something secondhand or more abstractly, and they generally give a privileged place to their own experiential knowledge. Experiential knowledge is valued precisely because it is so direct and relatively unmediated. While there is plenty of selectivity in the memory of experiences, it is our own selectivity, not someone else's.

Media discourse, at the other extreme, is a useful resource precisely because it is public. In spite of personal elements, it is possible to talk about the accident at Chernobyl on the basis of assumed common images and factual knowledge. If everyone may not know the particular element of media discourse referred to, it is nonetheless public knowledge, available to anyone who wants to know. Unlike personal experience, you can look it up. Media discourse, then, is predominantly a cultural resource.

Popular wisdom is in the middle, an amalgam of personal and cultural. On the one hand, it embodies the lessons of personal experience. One's experiences take on meaning by being linked to these rules of thumb. They help transform the unique experience of different individuals into a bit of popular wisdom that invokes others' similar experiences. By bridging the personal and cultural, popular wisdom helps make experiential knowledge relevant to framing the issue under discussion.

Popular wisdom is also part of the media discourse on these issues. Analogies to everyday life and popular maxims are often invoked to make abstract frames more immediate and concrete. Popular wisdom is not only a conversational resource but a resource for sponsors of different media frames and for journalists as they interpret events. By linking media discourse to popular wisdom, it is thus brought closer to experiential knowledge.

Iyengar and Kinder (1987) offer experimental evidence of the special impact of integrating the personal and cultural. First, they reviewed a large number of studies that showed that Americans sharply distinguished the quality of their personal lives and their judgments about public issues. For example, crime victims did not regard crime as a more serious problem for society as a whole than did those personally untouched by crime; people's assessments of economic conditions were largely unrelated to the economic setbacks and gains in their own lives; and the war in Vietnam was not rated as a more important problem among those who had close relatives serving there than among Americans without such personal connections to the war.

Iyengar and Kinder then designed a series of experiments to test more subtle connections between media coverage and personal effects. One experiment concentrated on three issues—civil rights, unemployment, and social security. Their procedures involved showing edited television news broadcasts to their subjects, varying the amount of coverage of these issues systematically. (Stories on a variety of other issues were included as well.) In different conditions, subjects saw either no coverage, intermediate coverage, or extensive coverage by varying the total number of stories on each of the three issues.

Their subjects varied on whether they were in a category that was personally affected. Blacks were contrasted with whites on civil rights, those out of work with those currently working on the unemployment issue, and the elderly with the young on Social Security. All subjects were asked at the end to name the most important problems that the country faced.

Iyengar and Kinder found that on two of the three issues—civil rights and Social Security—members of the personally affected group were especially influenced by the amount of television coverage they watched. On the unemployment issue, they found no differences between the employed and unemployed. Only this last result is consistent with the earlier studies showing the lack of relationship between people's personal lives and their views on public issues.

Iyengar and Kinder interpreted their results in ways that suggest the integration of personal and cultural resources. "We suspect," they wrote, "that the key feature distinguishing civil rights and social security is that they are experienced psychologically both as personal predicaments and as *group* predicaments." Although they do not use the term, collective identity processes come into play that do not operate on unemployment. It is not merely that "I" am affected but that "we" are affected, and they are especially sensitive and responsive to media coverage that suggests that "our" problem is an important problem for the country.

In sum, by failing to use all three resources in constructing a frame, a group is unable to bridge the personal and cultural and to anchor their understanding in both. By failing to link their understanding of an issue with popular wisdom and experiential knowledge, their issue understanding is ad hoc and isolated from their more general understanding of the world. Hence, there is a special robustness to frames that are held together by a full combination of resources.

Resource Strategies

Groups in our study were not asked to reach a consensus and hence were under no external pressure to come up with a shared meaning. However, the demands of conversation included their own built-in pressure. When there was disagreement, participants frequently searched for points on which they could all agree. More important, it was difficult to carry on a conversation if they could not even agree on what the issue was about and what was at stake. Hence, there was a group dynamic that pushed participants toward a common framing, even when they disagreed about solutions.

Nevertheless, not all groups succeeded in constructing a shared frame on every issue. I treat them as having such a shared frame if either of the following conditions is met: (1) At least two participants contributed to the elaboration and construction of the frame and no one challenged or attacked it directly, or (2) Someone was explicitly critical and offered an alternative but no one else contributed to its construction and the group defined the person as offering a minority view[4]

Overall, more than 80 percent of the issue discussions resulted in a shared frame, but each issue presented its own separate challenge. As figure 5.1 shows, groups were overwhelmingly likely to come up with a shared frame on troubled industry, affirmative action, and nuclear power but less likely on Arab-Israeli conflict, where only about two-thirds of the groups (68 percent) did so.

When they did develop shared frames, their resource strategy varied from issue to issue. Since popular wisdom was almost always used at some point, the critical variable was the extent to which they integrated both experiential knowledge and media discourse in developing their frame. In particular, I distinguished three resource strategies:

1. Cultural. These discussions rely on media discourse and popular wisdom in framing the issue but do not integrate experiential knowledge in support of it.
2. Personal. These discussions rely on experiential knowledge and popular wisdom in framing the issue but do not integrate media discourse in support of it.
3. Integrated. These discussions rely on a full combination of resources, bringing together media discourse and experiential knowledge.

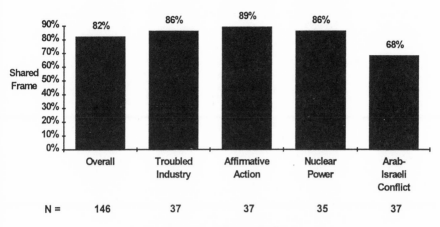

Fig. 5.1. Shared frames by issue

Resource strategy, as figure 5.2 shows, is heavily issue dependent. While some groups made slightly more use of media discourse than others, such differences were overwhelmed by issue differences. Integrated resource strategies were quite likely on affirmative action and troubled industry but much less so on nuclear power and Arab-Israeli conflict, where less than a third of the groups used the full array.

With respect to resource strategies, nuclear power and Arab-Israeli conflict were very similar issues. The conversations overwhelmingly began with media discourse; in contrast, less than half the groups began with this resource on troubled industry and less than one-third on affirmative action. A substantial minority also drew in some relevant personal experience on nuclear power and Arab-Israeli conflict as well, but the predominant strategy was cultural.

I initially thought that the issues of nuclear power and Arab-Israeli conflict were so far removed from people's daily lives that it surprised me to find such a substantial minority introducing experiential knowledge in support of their shared frame. The following example illustrates the variety of experiences that people bring to bear on such issues as the enforcement of safety regulations and the realism of evacuation plans. This is the same group from which Tom and Luke were quoted earlier to illustrate the use of popular wisdom on nuclear power; now they are discussing the initial, open-ended question on nuclear power:

Participants:
Luke, a salesclerk in a department store, in his early twenties
Pat, a salesclerk in a department store, in his early twenties

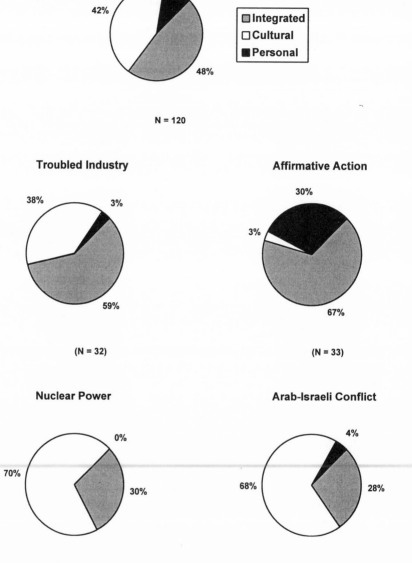

Fig. 5.2. Resource strategy by issue

Tom, a salesclerk in a stereo store, in his early twenties
Rich, a photographer's apprentice, in his early twenties

Luke: One time this guy told me about—I was on the Hudson on this
   boat and we passed by this nuclear power plant. And he said,
   "Yeah, well they were—there was this thing about how they're
   not running it safely and—
Pat: —That's the one the Mafia were running?
(laughter)
Pat: True. There was one.
Rich: Our power plants? Uranium smuggled in from Colombia.
Luke: No. They were supposed to be showing these safety films.
   They were say—well, something like the government said, "You
   have to show safety films to all the workers." And it turned out that
   they got the safety films and put 'em, like, in a drawer, and they
   ordered porno flicks—and they sat around and watched porno
   movies instead of watching what they were supposed to. So, that is
   what scares me.
Rich: From my window at school, I could see the Yankee—no, what
   was it? What was the one in Vermont? Vernon, the Vernon power
   plant.
Pat: You could see that?
Rich: Yeah.
Pat: You could see the lights of the plant?
Rich: You can see the lights—about eighteen miles down the river.
   And they were *busted* every three or four months for venting off
   the steam, which is really illegal. You're supposed to cool it with
   the water tanks and everything. But it cost a lot of money and they
   didn't care. I mean, they're run so lax.
Tom: There's a place in Charlestown—I used to work on these boats
   and there's a dock out there with a sign that says, "Radiation
   Hazard—No Swimming." Turns out the nuclear submarines used
   to dock there and pump out the coolant water, into the water in
   Charlestown.
Luke: They did a thing at our school. The power plant in Vermont
   that he was talking about. We used to have every Wednesday and
   Saturday, they had this safety whistle that would like—drills.
   They'd just test the whistle.
Rich: Yeah. How do you know what to do, though?
Luke: Well, see the thing was—the plan was that buses from North-
   ampton or Amherst—like the public transportation buses were
   supposed to drive up there and get all the people and bring 'em

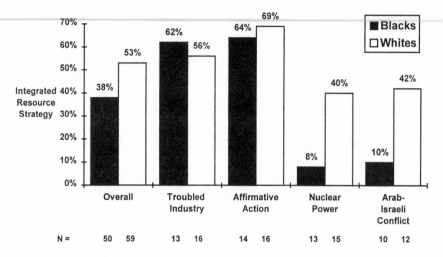

Fig. 5.3. Resource strategy by race

down. There's two things, two problems: first of all, if there was actually a meltdown or something, there's no way you can get—we're so close, and we're downriver—there's no way you can get away in time. And also, do you think that a bus driver in Northampton who's farther south is actually gonna drive up towards the nuclear power plant to get people?

(laughter)

Integrated resource strategies were quite common on affirmative action and troubled industry, but the two issues showed an important difference. Affirmative action was the only issue on which personal strategies were more common than cultural strategies and the first resource utilized was more likely to be experiential knowledge than media discourse. Personal strategies outnumbered cultural by ten to one on affirmative action, but on the other three issues combined, cultural strategies outnumbered personal ones by fifty to two ($p < .001$).

In many respects, black and white groups followed similar resource strategies. They were almost identical in the resource they used first, and the pattern of their resource strategies was the same over the four issues. For whites and blacks alike, affirmative action was the highest in integrated strategies, followed closely by troubled industry, with nuclear power and Arab-Israeli conflict well back. But as figure 5.3 shows, there were some overall differences.

Whites used an integrated resource strategy in 53 percent of their issue conversations with a shared frame, compared to 38 percent in the black groups (p = n.s.). A look at the individual issues reveals that it is primarily the media discourse issues of nuclear power and Arab-Israeli conflict that account for the difference. White groups were more likely to draw on experiential knowledge as well in constructing a frame on these issues, but this was rare in black groups. On affirmative action and troubled industry, there was little or no difference.

Media Effects on Public Opinion

I do not argue that working people are well served by media discourse in their efforts to make sense of the world. The limitations that many media critics point out are reflected in media discourse on the four issues examined here. Media dependence, however, is only partial and is heavily influenced by the issue under discussion. Among our groups, on certain issues—nuclear power and Arab-Israeli conflict, for example—media discourse was typically their first resort. Even on these issues, though, they found more than one frame available, leaving them at least a partial choice as well as the necessity of using other resources to complete the task. They controlled their own media dependence, in part, through their willingness and ability to draw on popular wisdom and experiential knowledge to supplement what they were offered.

If media dependence is only partial when media discourse serves as the starting point, it is even less so where experiential knowledge is the primary resource for finding a path through the forest. Lack of dependence, however, does not imply lack of use or influence. Even on affirmative action, where an overwhelming majority of the groups in our study introduced experiential knowledge, most drew on media discourse and popular wisdom as well in constructing a shared frame.

Graber (1988), although she approached the issue of media effects in a different way, simultaneously examined both news content and audience response and reached similar conclusions. Carrying on the tradition begun by Lane (1962), she did a long series of intensive, open-ended interviews with twenty-one participants over a year. At the same time, she analyzed the content of their major sources of news, including the most widely read daily newspaper plus national and local television news.

On media effects, Graber suggests a "modulator model" in which media impact depends on the relationship of the audience to the issue. On many issues, people "round out and evaluate news in light of past learning and determine how well it squares with the reality that they have experienced directly or vicariously" (Graber 1988, 93). All of her panelists, despite inattention, substantial forgetting, and limited learning, had developed a knowledge base about issues currently in the news. "What they knew," she concludes, "and the deductions and inferences that sprang from that knowledge, evidently was not limited to what the media supplied."

These results suggest a reframing in the long standing debate on the magnitude and nature of mass media effects on public opinion. The effects discussed here are effects in use. Instead of treating media content as a stimulus that leads to some change in attitudes or cognition, it is treated as an important tool or resource that people have available, in varying degrees, to help them make sense of issues in the news. When they use elements from media discourse to make a conversational point on an issue, we are directly observing a media effect.

I do not mean to imply that the media element—for example, a spotlighted fact or a particular depiction of a public figure—"caused" the person to think about the issue in a predetermined way. The causal relationship is complicated and bidirectional, as the tool metaphor implies. One chooses a tool, but some tools are cheap and available everywhere while others can be found only in side streets and out-of-the-way places. One chooses a tool partly for convenience and ease of access but also for its suitability to the job at hand—in this case, to make a particular point in conversation.

The results here suggest that the causal process differs quite a bit from issue to issue and from group to group on the same issue. Media influence depends on which of the three discourse strategies a group is using: cultural, personal, or integrated. It is impossible to say from examining effects in use whether the way people privately think or feel about an issue has been changed by their media exposure, but the results suggest some conditional hypotheses:

1. Cultural strategies. People who use cultural strategies to understand an issue will be subject to substantial media effects and will be heavily influenced by the relative prominence of media frames. Their attitudes and beliefs will be relatively unstable and subject to change as media discourse changes.

2. Personal strategies. People who use personal strategies to understand an issue will be relatively immune to media effects, ignoring or discounting the relative prominence of frames, including even those that support their experiential knowledge and popular wisdom.

3. Integrated strategies. People who use integrated strategies will be selectively influenced by the relative prominence of media frames, responding to the degree that these frames are consistent with their popular wisdom and experiential knowledge. They will be constrained by omissions from media discourse but relatively immune to differences in the relative prominence of visible frames.

Conclusion

Resource strategies among working people are heavily issue specific. They use a combination of experiential knowledge, popular wisdom, and media discourse in framing issues, but the particular mix varies. For some issues, media discourse and popular wisdom are the primary resources, and they generally do not integrate experiential knowledge in the framing process. For other issues, they generally begin with experiential knowledge and popular wisdom. Sometimes they also bring in media discourse in support of the same frame, but sometimes they ignore this resource. Nuclear power and Arab-Israeli conflict exemplify the former kind of issue and affirmative action ex-emplifies the latter; troubled industry falls somewhere in between, but it is very rare for people to ignore media discourse in framing it.

There are theoretical reasons for expecting that frames based on the integration of all three types of resources will be more robust. Such frames enable people to bridge the personal and cultural and to link issue frames to broader cultural themes. If this is true, then we should expect the framings of affirmative action and troubled industry to be especially robust, since the majority of our study groups followed an integrated strategy in constructing them. Nuclear power and Arab-Israeli conflict, where the majority of groups used media discourse and popular wisdom but not experiential knowledge, should be more subject to fluctuations in the prominence of different frames in media discourse.

Are college-educated professionals different in their resource strategies? Probably they are more likely to attend to the media spectacle and to rely on it more heavily as a primary resource. Perhaps they are also less likely to draw on popular wisdom and experiential knowledge and, therefore, to use integrated resource strategies in the framing process. If so, this suggests the intriguing hypothesis that they are more likely than working people to be affected by shifts in the dominant media frames on an issue. But that is a topic for another study.

NOTES

1. This stratum is generally estimated at anywhere from one-fifth to one-third of the population. See Neuman 1986 for a good discussion of the "three publics," including a politically involved group of 10 to 15 percent and a very large "middle mass" who are marginally attentive to politics but accept the duty to vote and the norm that it is important to keep informed to some degree about current events.

2. For more precise methodological details, see Gamson 1992.

3. The concept of frame seems both indispensible and elusive. It plays the same role in analyzing discourse that the concept of schema does in cognitive psychology—a

central organizing principle that holds together and gives coherence and meaning to a diverse array of symbols.

4. Groups often used different shared frames at different points in the discussion, employing some quite briefly while elaborating others at length and at many points. I counted as their shared frame the one used most exclusively in the total conversation in analyzing the resources used to construct it.

CHAPTER 6

Cognitive and Affective Dimensions of Political Conceptualization

Marion R. Just, Ann N. Crigler, and W. Russell Neuman

In this chapter, Just, Crigler, and Neuman examine how individuals construct political meaning by framing political issues along two integrally related dimensions. The first dimension, the frame, is primarily cognitive in nature and contains information about the structure and general parameters of the object under consideration. The second dimension, the tone, is primarily affective and represents the emotions associated with the object. Analyses of in-depth interviews on the topics of the Strategic Defense Initiative, apartheid in South Africa, drug abuse, and AIDS reveal that individuals use a small number of frames, such as "human impact" or "economics" to discuss these topics. The frames are particularly useful to individuals as they can be associated with a wide range of emotional tones. The cognitive aspect of frames in conjunction with the tone of frames is critical to understanding individuals' diverse constructions of political meaning.

A reasonable understanding of the key political issues facing a polity is a prerequisite of meaningful political participation. Modern behavioral research has debated the question of what kind of an understanding on the part of the mass public might be considered reasonable. This chapter focuses on one aspect of the controversy: how people construct meaning about the important issues facing the polity.

Previous research in political science and psychology has focused on levels of ideology and sophistication in individual thinking about politics. Survey research tended to show that people have relatively unsophisticated belief systems as measured on a liberal-to-conservative ideological continuum (Converse 1964). The belief-systems approach has dominated research on the political understanding of Americans. It has also been criticized on theoretical grounds for denying alternative organizations or structures of attitudes and beliefs (Lane 1962; Neuman 1986; Graber 1988; Rosenberg, Ward, and Chilton 1988).

Political cognition research has also contributed to the debate about political conceptualization. Two approaches are prominent: developmental analysis based on Piagetian psychology and schema theory or the related concepts of scripts, frames, and themes. Rosenberg, drawing on Piagetian theory, suggests that the lack of observed voter sophistication can be explained by the different structures of thinking being employed by the respondents and the researcher. He argues that individuals exhibit styles of political thinking that correspond to different stages of cognitive development and that people at the earlier stages simply do not have the cognitive skills necessary to think in Converse's ideological terms. Rather, Rosenberg and his colleagues find that political thinking, indeed thinking about a broad range of topics, reflects the cognitive operations available to the individual, such as differentiation, identity, or causality (Rosenberg, Ward, and Chilton 1988, 34).

The schema theorists take a different approach. They argue that Converse's emphases on the liberal-conservative continuum precludes examination of other possible schema that individuals use to organize, manage, and store political information. Various researchers have used different definitions of schema, but the term generally describes "the set of cognitions relevant to some concept. The cognitions may be few or many, highly structured or ramshackle" (Kuklinski, Luskin, and Bolland 1991, 1342). Most research employing schema emphasizes the multiplicity or organization of cognitions around a particular concept. While many researchers recognize that cognitions may be charged with affect, a major criticism of schema theory is that it neglects emotion (Kuklinski, Luskin, and Bolland 1991), especially as compared with the older concept of attitude. In fact, Conover and Feldman distinguish the two approaches primarily in terms of their emphasis on affect or cognition: "The central meaning of the attitude concept—the meaning common to all competing definitions—is fundamentally *affective* in nature . . . At its core a schema is fundamentally a *cognitive* structure" (1991, 1366). While there is still a great deal of controversy about the differentiation of schema and attitudes, both the critics and defenders agree that the contribution of schema is to the understanding of how mental contructs influence information processing (Kuklinski, Luskin, and Bolland 1991; Lodge and McGraw 1991; Conover and Feldman 1991; Miller 1991).

More recently the concept of schema or frames has been employed to encompass both the way in which information is presented in media and the way individuals process that information (Lodge and McGraw 1991; Entman 1993). Frames usually refer, however, to structures smaller than schema, that select or highlight particular bits of information in constructing an argument or in evaluating an object. In content analysis, frames are used to show how the authors have called attention to particular aspects of problems, such as the "Cold War" frame of international news (Gamson 1992), or the "personalizing" frame of domestic policy-making (Bennett 1993). Entman argues, however, that the salience of the frame represents an interaction between the audience and the text and "even a single unillustrated appearance of a notion in an obscure part of the text can be highly salient, if it comports with the existing schemata in a receiver's belief systems" (1993, 53). Kahneman and Tversky's pathbreaking work (1984) showed how framing a problem in positive or negative terms could influence the policy choices people make. In spite of the important lesson about the affective tone of communication illustrated by their experiments, the emotional dimension of schema or frames has received little attention in the study of political conceptualization.

This study takes as its premise that people do not separate cognition and affect in their natural speech—nor do journalists. Even the objects selected for attention in a discussion carry with them an affective component. For example, in news about the scourge of crack cocaine, the frame is very different if the object of the story is the addict herself or her helpless infant. News about Star Wars/SDI that focuses on missile "throw weight" is very different from one that looks at the problem of protecting families from nuclear disaster.

Attention to political discourse reveals that understanding does not occur in a vacuum of emotions or affective evaluations of situations, persons, issues, or ideas. The rational cognitive aspects of political understanding are intertwined with an emotional or affective component and tied to particular objects. Psychologists, philosophers and other social scientists have long engaged in debate over the dominance of cognition over affect. (See, for example, Aristotle, Plato, Aquinas, Arnold, Lazarus, Ortony et al., on the primacy of cognition; Darwin, Freud, Wundt, Singer, Tomkins, Izard, Plutchik, and Zajonc on the centrality of affect.) While important work has been undertaken recently to compare the cognitive and affective dimensions of political conceptualization (Conover and Feldman 1986), the jury is still out on the issue of which comes first.

We take a different approach by assuming that cognition and affect are two integrally related dimensions that are difficult to separate in an individual's thinking and talking. The first dimension, the frame, is primarily cognitive in nature and contains information about the structure and general parameters of the object under consideration. The second dimension, the tone, is primarily affective and represents the emotions associated with the object. We emphasize that the object highlighted for discussion is an important element in political discourse, especially because many objects are culturally defined with common frames and tones (Entman 1993).

This study demonstrates that when individuals talk about political issues they frame the discussion around particular objects or aspects of a problem and infuse that discussion with one or several emotions. We find that frames are highly versatile. People commonly use only a small number of frames, such as "human impact" or "us-them" to discuss a variety of political issues. What makes these recurring frames so useful is that they come draped in such a wide range of emotions. We illustrate the use of five of these frames in interviews on the topics as Star Wars/SDI, the problem of apartheid in South Africa, drug abuse, and AIDS.

Methodology

In order to examine the frames and affective dimensions of public understanding about politics, a series of in-depth interviews were conducted. Four political issues—the strategic defense initiative (SDI), apartheid in South Africa, drug abuse, and the deadly disease AIDS—were discussed during the one- to two-hour loosely structured conversations. A stratified sample of twenty-eight adults participated in the study; seventeen women and eleven men ranging in age from eighteen to seventy-five (see appendix A). The interviewees were recruited from a list of mall shoppers who had previously participated in an experiment on political learning from the news media. Therefore, a considerable amount of personal, political, and conceptual information was already available on each person, so the interviews would focus on the individual's conceptualizations of the issues. The interviewers, however, were not aware of the interviewees' previous answers.

The interviews were loosely centered around six general questions and emphasized the individuals' cognitive and affective responses to the issues (see appendix B). The goal of the interviews was to elicit information from people "in their own voices" rather than to emphasize the replicability of a highly structured interview (Mishler 1986). This methodological approach was used to provide an opportunity for the natural expression of individuals' political conceptualization and the integration of the cognitive frames and affective dimensions. The approach avoids the compartmentalizing of cognition and affect that inevitably arises in other more structured research techniques, such as surveys or experiments.

The interviews were tape-recorded and transcribed to aid in the analysis. As the richness of this method lies in the detailed natural language of the interviewees available for analysis, frames and affective dimensions were drawn from the readings of the interviews. The frames were not formalistically defined by a predetermined list of key words, and the analysis did not follow the word-count style of traditional content analysis or the linguistic approach of discourse analysis. Two teams of readers read each interview aloud and discussed the cognitive frames, affective dimensions, and policy preferences in each interview. Both teams repeated this process for all the interviews, after which the teams met to compare results. While no formal measure of intercoder reliability was calculated, a high degree of convergence was evident in the findings of the reading teams.

Political Conceptualization: Frames, Affect, and Objects

Analysis of the interviews reveals that people appear to use only a small number of identifiable frames to structure their understanding of the four political issues. The analysts identified a half dozen predominant frames used to discuss these diverse political issues in the twenty-eight interviews. The frames include human impact, economics, control, us-them, and equality. Several of these frames appeared in almost every interview. Many interviewees used several of the frames in their discussions of particular issues, sometimes in the same passage.

A close reading of the transcripts revealed that these cognitive frames were indeed suffused with affect. As people talked about issues, their language reflected their evaluative judgments and emotions about the political objects and issues they discussed. While the number of frames used in discourse was limited, the tonal range of the affect was wide. The political opinions expressed by the interviewees grew out of the confluence of the frame, tone, and objects selected for discourse.

While some individuals were less emotive than others, the union of cognition and affect was apparent in all the interviews. An examination of the most prevalent frames illustrates how affect is so closely bound to the cognitive structure of political understanding.

The Human Impact Frame

The interviewees who drew upon a human impact frame discussed the selected political issues in terms of the effects they have on people. About half of the interviewees tended to look at the human side of events and tended to use emotionally laden terms to evaluate the positive or negative impact of policies, events, people, and problems. Illustrating the affective dimensions, they used language of (dis)interest, caring, worry, and compassion for themselves and others. For most of these interviewees, the human impact frame tended to be used across all four issues. We expected that there might be a gender difference in the use of this frame, but we found that the same proportion of women and men interviewed related the issues to their impact on people.

Interviewees applied the human impact frame and its associated affective dimensions to different objects: the self, groups to which the interviewee belongs, and groups to which he or she does not belong. (The naming of groups is related to the us-them frame discussed subsequently.) Expressions of concern for one's self and the effects of an issue on the individual were seen in most of the interviews, if only in passing.

Analysis of the human impact frame illustrates that if only the cognitive structure or frame is examined, researchers miss the variety of political views expressed about different political objects and would fundamentally misunderstand individuals' conceptualizations of the issues. For example, a middleaged woman emphasizing the human impact frame in discussing AIDS expressed little interest in the topic, but potential fear, when responding to the question of how important AIDS was to her.

> Not very. It would be, if my lifestyle were different, you know, if I, if I (pause) I'll tell you, if I were single, but I have a steady boyfriend. If I were single, I would be terrified.

A male postal clerk in his mid-fifties also expressed a lack of concern, but combined that emotion with empathy, compassion, fear and sorrow for those with AIDS.

> And, I can look at it [AIDS] and say, well, almost draw a fence around myself and I, um, isolate myself from these other problems that are going on like cocaine and AIDS, because I'm not going to be able to be promiscuous with anybody. I might like to, I'd like to, but I'm not going to be able to because for one thing, I'd be afraid to . . . I don't equate myself with ten thousand people having AIDS, because I believe it's so far away from me and it will never touch in my life, but it's going to eventually, somebody, something. I feel bad, feel I gotta, and if they are homosexuals, and they've got AIDS, or if heterosexual, I'm not going to criticize lifestyles; it's too bad, I feel it's a shame if they have it. I don't believe it's a punishment, because they're homosexual . . . they're poor victims.

Fear and worry were also associated with the human impact frame for issues that affected groups with whom the interviewees identified, in this case, one woman's daughter. The woman stated that

> you never heard of drug abuse when I was growing up . . . But as the years came by, especially since my daughter was born, I worried about it, because I know that schools were having problems with drug abuse and I was really worried about how she would react to it. . . . I still have that fear that she just might be pushed into it . . .

It is possible to use the human impact frame and yet care very little about the group. The same male postal clerk who felt empathy for AIDS victims acknowledged the problems for blacks in South Africa but felt little empathy or compassion for them and wanted to focus attention on the poor in this country instead.

> South Africa is supposed to be a bad place for blacks to be there . . . I don't know what they live like. I know what Americans (live) like. Some

live very well, and some live in real abstract [*sic*] poverty. And I'd like to see us take care of poor people in this country. The old people in this country, the sick people in this country. Then, when we've cleaned up our own act, let's go out and spread our doctrine someplace else.

In each of these examples, the cognitive frame of human impact is present, but the affective dimension ranged from fear to compassion to lack of interest. The objects of affective attention and the evaluations of those objects also varied even with a single frame, so that an individual might exhibit a lack of interest regarding the self, but fear regarding the human impact on children. These dimensions can have substantial effects on individuals' political opinions and policy preferences. AIDS, for example, was seen by many people as having an enormous impact on human beings, but individuals who did not favor government action accepted AIDS as divine retribution for the sins of loose living, while those who favored a stronger AIDS policy were distressed and frightened, seeing AIDS as a disease that was killing friends and innocent children. Still other interviewees eschewed the human impact frame even in a health issue such as AIDS, and instead framed the problem in economic terms.

The Economic Frame

Approximately half of our respondents used an economic frame at some point in talking about these four political issues. Both men and women talked about the issues in economic terms, making judgments by citing costs of policies, by suggesting a profit motive, or by linking the issue to the national or world economy. Whether individuals attached positive or negative affects to this cognitive frame, different policy evaluations and preferences resulted. The economic frame was expressed most frequently in terms of social costs: SDI, for example, was often seen in terms of the program's cost to the taxpayer. One retired woman discussed with positive anticipation the economics of SDI and was even willing to pay for it.

I don't know much about the technology, but it's expensive . . . But, to me, even if it's expensive, I just as soon pay taxes for it, if it would help, if it was something that would help us.

For other interviewees, the costs of SDI were expressed negatively. SDI was seen as a waste of money because it was not likely to work, was not expected to be implemented much less deployed, and was possibly a big business "racket." A retired man expressed a great deal of suspicion and skepticism about expenditures on "Star Wars," as SDI became commonly known.

[Star wars is] no way near completed and if they do complete it, it couldn't possibly do what we're seeing over here that they're doing. And if I sound a little bit (pause) you know, I'm very suspicious of (pause) oh Eisenhower always said you gotta watch out for the military, it's one big racket, you get these big contractors making billions of dollars and like I said . . . you got drug abuse, you got AIDS and here we are throwing 2 trillion dollars over to the defense which is kind of . . . I think it's a big waste of money, because every time you make a bomb, what do you get out of it? What use do you get out of it? It's not like making a pair of shoes or a coat or something.

When the object was the situation in South Africa, the framing of issues in terms of cost and wastefulness was associated with emotions of anger and disgust. In the following example, a male engineer in his fifties displays his anger about the supremacist government of South Africa.

It's absolutely atrocious. I think the supremacists in South Africa ought to be done away with as completely as possible . . . Blow the ship out of the water. Whatever it takes and I don't think we ought to waste money on throwing them in jail. I think it's a waste of resources.

On the other side, a twenty-six year-old female accountant used an economic frame to explain apartheid but expressed acceptance of white rule.

[If] South African whites pulled out of South Africa, it would be a poor, squalid country in no time. If you ask me, the black Africans, they cannot, they don't have the knowledge or they don't have the wealth to make South Africa into a predominant black country. And, I think the white South Africans are keeping the South African economy in a pretty high standard.

By framing issues in economic terms, there is often an implied division of the world into those who have and those who have not. This is closely related to the us-them frame.

The Us-Them Frame

An us-them frame is used by many of the interviewees. As noted earlier, the us-them frame is inherent in the naming of groups in the human impact frame and is implied in both the control and economic frames. The us-them frame applies a polarized structure to politics (McClosky 1967). The affective dimensions and the groups identified as "us" and "them" vary substantially.[1] For example, the woman who accepted white rule in South Africa as an economic good also used an us-them frame to structure her political understanding of the world. She has divided the world into white and black. Later in her discussion of apartheid in South Africa, she brought up racial relations in the United States in a very polarized way and affectively laden with feelings of mistrust, rejection, and distress.

> But, I think most Americans, including myself, I don't look down on the blacks. I don't feel superior to them, but I don't want to mingle with them. I don't mind if I work with them, but I don't want any of my kids to marry one of them. And, I don't particularly want to socialize with them. And, this country here, they want to push immediately, immediate equality in South Africa. And it can't be done.

More than one-third of the interviewees saw SDI as the United States versus the Soviet Union. The emotions felt toward the Russians were, however, diverse. For instance, a retired man described the Russians' fear and his own mistrust and dislike of them in discussing SDI.

> As far as Star Wars, it sounds good. The fear that comes from, well Russia is the one who has the great fear, and it's understandable. They fear that it could be employed as an offensive weapon, see. I think, perhaps, that comes from because of their own nature, you see, myself, I don't have a very high opinion of communistic government. I think with every move they make is done to gain something, to gain an advantage, or put somebody at a disadvantage and so, I think perhaps, they suspect us of the same thing.

Another retired, sixty-six year-old man felt that the Russians are like him and want peace, but he was not completely sure; in fact, he was "in definite doubt."

> I really believe that Russia really and truly wants peace as much as I do. And, the average Russian person doesn't want to kill the average American person. . . . And, I can't see why this country can't learn to coexist . . . that's how I feel, right, I could be a hundred percent wrong. That's because I'm in definite doubt. . . . I mean, I don't think they want to kill me.

The us-them frame was also used to describe AIDS. Some, but not all, of the interviewees saw AIDS as a disease associated with homosexuality. The "us" and "them" refer, respectively, to those without AIDS, who tend to be heterosexual, and to those with the disease. The emotions felt for the "them" vary substantially. A retired man saw homosexuality as "against the law of God" but felt sorry for the "many innocent people"—that is, children and those who have had blood transfusions—who suffer.

> If I could help the innocents and put the rest of them out on an island, I would do it. That's my feeling about it. I don't have that much sympathy for (pause) so, I don't think I'm much help to you on that, because I'm fed up with hearing about that.

A young woman accountant had just the opposite feelings for those with AIDS, even though she also viewed homosexuality as a sin.

> I think it's horrendous the way AIDS victims are treated, however they got it has to be separated from the fact that they're sick people now (pause) and they shouldn't be treated like lepers.

As is evident in these quotations, the affective tones of the frames and the objects of the emotions have substantial impacts on people's political judgments and policy preferences. In particular, emotions of anger and its objects were highly political, as were emotions of compassion and its objects.

The Control Frame

The control frame was evident in an individual's reference to a sense of power or powerlessness with regard to an issue. In fact, the control frame might more appropriately be called the lack of control frame, as descriptions of helplessness and inefficacy predominated. The control frame was evident in approximately half of the interviews and was used far more frequently by women than men.[2] The control frame was manifested in three ways: a lack of personal control, a belief in fate or the inevitable progression of time and events, or the existence of other powerful forces, such as God, governments, and Ronald Reagan.[3]

Many of the interviewees who expressed a lack of personal control associated this aspect with a lack of emotional interest in the topic. A middle-aged female secretary, who used many frames including the control frame when talking about SDI, said that SDI was not at all important to her.

> I mean, the whole thing bores me to tears . . . So, I just (pause) I don't even listen to them [politicians], because there's nothing I can do to make any change.

Two other women also reported a lack of control but associated that frame with dislike of and frustration with their own situations. An eighteen-year-old woman said, "I mean, I don't like it, but there's not too much I can do to change it though." The other woman, a thirty year-old teacher, connected her own frustrated powerlessness to her status as one of the "little people" whose fates are controlled by a relatively distant powerful elite.

> Somebody higher has the control over this [SDI]. We don't have control. We can vote for things, but um, vote for the nuclear arms to stop. I signed a petition yesterday for, ah, to stop nuclear waste dumps, and that's about all we can do as the little people.

Another woman's lack of personal control was accompanied by anger, contempt, and hatred of powerful others who are in control. In this case, her affective evaluation was directed toward Ronald Reagan as the sponsor of SDI. The sixty-five year-old woman remarked in connection with the issue of Star Wars:

> The president really should have been impeached, but he got away with it. I'm sure if I had my way, I'm not even afraid to go to Washington and look him right in the eye and say: "Mister, you're a big liar and you're a big thief and you're treacherous to your own country, because you knew all the time about Iran. You knew a lot of things, but you got away with it, because no one put the finger on you because you are the president and they're afraid of getting you impeached and disgraced."

Ronald Reagan is not the only controlling force to become the object of negative emotions. In discussions of South Africa, interviewees expressed shock, outrage, and sadness for the situation in South Africa, even though they felt there was little they could do. A fifty-one-year-old secretary who saw the South African government as a "gigantic foot just stepping on them [blacks] and keeping them down" expanded her disgust to include the United States as well:

> I'm appalled. I'm appalled to see human beings (pause) like something like that goes on in our day and age. I'm appalled at our country doing business with South Africa right up until a couple of years ago when so much pressure was put on them not to (pause) I just wish that something could be done about it.

A sixty-five-year-old man also expressed sadness and an implied inability to do anything in South Africa, but with a very different twist. The object of his feelings was not the evils of apartheid or the American government, but the changes being pressed by blacks. In addition, he wondered if American blacks were instigating the changes. This is another example of multiple frames being used, in this case, control and us-them.

> I'm wondering if some of our people in this country, black people didn't go over there and do some (pause) a lot of this stuff, telling them how to become more on their own . . . But, from what I do and what I see, it seems it's kind of more-or-less sad that they've done too much.

In sum, then, the control frame is most often an expression of powerlessness on the part of the individual who sees fate, inevitability, and others as having more influence over the course of events than he or she does.

Conclusion

The investigation of frames shows how individuals apply these limited number of frames across diverse issues. The economic frame, for example, was employed to communicate about the cost of SDI, the economic incentives of colonialization in South Africa, the profits from drug sales, and the enormous social cost of health care for AIDS victims.

While coders converged in their identification of frames used in the discourses, the assessment was not simply based on the presence of particular words but rather on the explicit and implicit meaning of phrases and larger word groupings. So, for example, key words such as *cost, expense, profit,* and *dollars* are commonly employed in the economic frame, and a key word in the control frame is *control,* but it is more typically characterized by phrases such as "there's nothing I can do" or "that's about all we can do as the little people." Sometimes the frame is embedded in larger chunks of discourse, for example, a lack of control and the existence of powerful others as expressed in the following remarks by a thirty-year-old female teacher:

> We don't get to vote on a lot of big issues. It makes me angry that people say, the United States this and the United States that, and it isn't the United States people, it's just the little president up there, House and Cabinet, making these decisions.

Or in discussing the human impact of AIDS, a twenty-one-year-old female interviewee told the following story about her friend David:

> My friend saw him a month before he died. And he said, "How are you feeling, David? How are things going? He said, "Great. Everything's going great." You know, he's one of those . . . if he had said well, they gave me like three weeks to two months to live, you'd be like . . . Oh my

God. You know what I mean? And people would feel bad for him. He didn't want that. He wanted people to treat him how they usually did so he didn't say anything. And then when he died, it was kind of a surprise to everyone. But I feel worse for his mother, because David died and two weeks later, his father died of a brain tumor. So that poor mother had to sit there and watch her husband and her son die slowly. You know, this one dies and two weeks later this one dies. I don't know how that woman survived it. I think that's terrible.

As the previous examples illustrate, frames are most commonly expressed with affective tones. People sometimes say, as in the preceding two quotations, "I feel angry" or "I feel terrible"; but in addition, affect is expressed implicitly, often in the selection of words and phrases describing particular objects, such as "big business" or "the little people." Metaphors such as "a gigantic foot, just stepping on them" or "you become a slave to it [drugs]" powerfully convey the emotional dimension of cognitive frames. The inseparability of cognition and affect was in fact recognized by some of the subjects. A forty-six-year-old female receptionist explained it this way:

I think [people] separate the emotional facts from the intellectual facts. You know, people use their emotions like when an AIDS kid comes into a school, well then you don't want your kid to have any contact with it because you're not quite sure. Even though intellectually, you may accept the facts that you can't get it by casual contact and so forth. I suppose if it came right down to protecting your family, that little doubt would creep in.

We did not find a consistent correlation between using a particular frame and having a particular liberal or conservative view of politics. Liberals, for example, often focused negatively on President Reagan while conservatives concentrated on the Russian threat. In the case of South Africa, liberals' arguments were directed against white supremacists while at least one conservative expressed negative sentiments against American blacks who had "gone over" to incite South African black resistance. Even a single individual could be torn between seeing AIDS as an issue involving people with "loose morals" and "innocent victims." Very different policy preferences related to these disparate objects, as indicated by the remark of the homophobic man quoted earlier: "If I could help the innocents and put the rest of them out on an island, I would do it."

The integration of the frame, affective tone, and object characterizes natural political discourse and conveys the political element. Cognition alone, as employed in the schema or developmental psychology approach to political understanding, cannot capture the essentially political quality of discourse about public issues. As a compassionate retired male interviewee in his mid-sixties explained:

> You worry about drugs, you worry about AIDS, you worry about SDI because of the money that's spent and it's not being spent on the people that need it. You worry about all these things because it's human beings behind it that's being affected by it.

The remarks illustrate the use of both economic and human impact frames, but they also demonstrate the inseparability of cognitive and emotional tones of frames as well as the critical selection of objects of discourse. We propose that not only the analysis of popular conceptualization of political questions, but the study of news would be enriched by a concept of framing that specifically and prominently acknowledges the emotional tone of the frame, especially as it is culturally ascribed. In fact, the objects and emotional tone of the frame, which we have described here in popular discourse, may be the key to the power of the frame in media texts and visuals.

APPENDIX A

Twenty-eight adults participated in in-depth interviews for this study. The interviews were assigned identification numbers, and participants' gender, age, and occupation were noted as follows.

Interview ID Number	Gender	Age	Occupation
1029	Male	75	Retired
1036	Female	18	
1047	Male	36	Jeweler
1052	Male	57	Postal Clerk
1126	Female	67	Retired Teacher
1138	Male	31	
1220	Female	61	Retired
1260	Male	56	Self-employed Engineer
1263	Female	35	Full-time Homemaker
2004	Female	18	Bookkeeper
2014	Female	63	Retired
2020	Female	18	Student

2109	Female	51	Secretary
2121	Male	27	Student
2124	Male		
2153	Female	28	Laundry Worker
2201	Female	48	
2202	Male	66	Retired
2223	Male	71	Retired
2230	Male	65	
3031	Female	21	Cashier
3049	Female	30	Teacher
3051	Female	65	
3101	Female	62	Retired
3103	Female	26	Accountant
3119	Male	72	Retired
3252	Female	48	Registered Nurse
3254	Female	46	Receptionist

APPENDIX B

Interview Questions

There are lots of current events. It would certainly be difficult to follow each one in detail. We're just interested in what you think.

1. If you had to explain the general idea of _____ to someone who doesn't know about it, how would you explain it?

    Anything else?

    Are there any images or pictures that come into your mind when you think about that issue?

2. How do you feel about _____ ?

    What did you think about when you told me how you feel?

How did you come to have that opinion?

3. How did you find out about (or how do you know about) _____ ?

(Interviewer probes here for specific sources people use.)

4. How do the media treat this issue?

Why do you think the media cover this issue?

5. How important to you personally is this issue?

How important to the country is this issue?

6. Is this issue like any other that you can think of? How so?

(Interviewer repeats questions 1 through 6 for each of the four issues.)

7. Finally, I would like you to rank the issues in order of their importance to you personally and then to the country.

NOTES

1. See Liebes and Crigler 1990 for further discussion of the range and scope of the us-them frame in the United States and Israel.

2. Three-quarters of the interviewees who used the control frame were women.

3. These three manifestations are quite similar to factors identified in the locus of control literature in social psychology. See, for example, Rotter 1966.

CHAPTER 7

Constructing Public Opinion: The Uses of Fictional and Nonfictional Television in Conversations about the Environment

Michael X. Delli Carpini and Bruce A. Williams

Delli Carpini and Williams use a constructionist perspective to analyze the use of media in the formation of public opinion. This perspective is readily apparent in their conception of public opinion as a dynamic exchange among views based on personal experience, fellow citizens, and the media. Drawing on focus group data, the authors show how citizens socially construct their views on toxic waste and the environment in interaction with other people and with fictional and nonfictional media, particularly television. Television is treated as more than a conduit of information or a source of persuasive messages. Rather, focus group participants considered TV a forum for public debate and a participant in the conversation, even talking back to the screen whether it was on or not. In addition, focus group participants noted their dependence on the media and exhibited some autonomy in recognizing and, in a few cases, resisting television's ideological slants.

Few things are more revealing of the state of a democracy than the way in which citizens receive and use political information. Indeed, John Dewey argues that societies can exist only through communication, since people "live in a community by virtue of the things they have in common; and communication is the way in which they come to possess things in common" (Dewey [1916] 1974, 4). Given its national scope, centralized nature, and near universal availability and popularity, television is a critical institution in the development and maintenance of a common political language. This process is a complex one, however, in part because politics *necessarily* involves issues that are contested (Gallie 1955–56, Connolly 1983), and in part because the information drawn from any particular source (such as television) will be interpreted through attitudes, opinions, and information drawn from other sources (Liebes and Katz 1990; Gamson 1992; Neuman, Just, and Crigler 1992).

The meaning of any concept or issue varies over time and among different people. Certain concepts, however, generate a greater variety of meaning by their very nature. These essentially contested concepts "involve endless disputes about their proper uses on the part of their users" (Gallie 1955–56, 23). Gallie considers "democracy" such a concept and Connolly (1983) includes concepts such as "politics," "political interest," "power," "responsibility," and "freedom." In the end, most of the fundamental concepts of political and social thought are likely to be essentially contestable. In turn, specific opinions about political institutions, officeholders, policies, and so forth rest upon the meaning ascribed to these more fundamental concepts and so are themselves open to negotiation.

Emphasizing the inherently ambiguous nature of politics leads to a different conceptualization of public opinion than is implied in much of mainstream research.[1] Opinions are viewed as shifting constructs that are constructed rather than retrieved (Bennett 1980, Zaller and Feldman 1992). In addition, opinions are understood as social, imbedded in a dynamic process of interaction and debate (Connolly 1983; Williams and Matheny, 1995). That is, politics is about *public* issues that are discussed *in public*. It is through social discourse, or "conversations," that opinions are continuously created and recreated. The need to consider seriously the position of others is what distinguishes private life from public life and private opinion from public opinion (Barber 1984).

Our notion that public opinion emerges from discourse is both normative and heuristic. We agree with political theorists such as Hannah Arendt and Jurgen Habermas that a defining characteristic of democracy *should be* that political decisions are reached through public dialogues in which participants draw equally from a common pool of information. However, we also argue that opinions *are* formed through interactions that occasionally approximate, and that often mimic, even mock, such public dialogue.

Envisioning public opinion as a conversation is especially useful in understanding the political relevance of television. As the central source of information in the United States, television provides both the topics and the substance upon which most political conversations are based. In addition, however, our conversational metaphor points to a more active role for television in the shaping of public opinion. Put simply, we argue that the interaction between television and a viewer is similar to a conversation. Of course in an important respect this conversation is one-sided: viewers are seldom seen or heard.[2] And yet the viewer is engaged in a conversation in many important respects. The most obvious example would be when he or she "talks back" to the set or, more indirectly, when two or more viewers comment to each other about a show as it is being watched.

But even when sitting in silence, viewers are interacting with television in ways that are more analogous to conversation than to reading, to writing, or even to contemplation or deliberation. Certainly viewers interact with television in ways that are more similar to conversing than to other commonly used metaphors, such as inputting data or being inoculated. This is so because television consciously mimics the elements of immediate, personal exchange. The information transmitted is ephemeral. Messages are contained in a combination of aural and visual cues, including tone of voice, body language, and so forth. Televised conversants (whether newscasters, celebrities, or fictional characters) are often familiar to the viewer. The illusion of intimacy and dialogue is heightened by techniques such as looking directly into the camera or directly addressing the viewer through asides or stock phrases such as, "We'll be right back" or "I'll see you next time." Television, therefore, serves not only as a source of information for future conversations, but also as both a regular "conversant" in an ongoing discussion and, ultimately, as an important forum for political discourse in the United States.

Focus Groups as a Method of Social Inquiry

The conversational metaphor leads to a somewhat different set of expectations and concerns than those derived from most mainstream metaphors. Opinion formation and opinion expression are no longer seen as two fully distinct processes. Nor are the processes of interpersonal and mass-mediated communication viewed as truly distinct. Rather, opinions "exist" only within interactive, dynamic contexts. In short, public opinion does not *follow* interactions with television, friends, coworkers, and so forth, so much as it *is* that interaction.

Focus groups offer a promising way to explore this dynamic model of opinion formation in general, and of television viewing in particular.[3] The focus group is a "carefully planned discussion designed to obtain perceptions on a defined area of interest in a permissive, nonthreatening environment" (Krueger 1988, 18). While often used in conjunction with other methods such as experiments and surveys, the information generated from focus groups can stand alone as a way of providing insights into opinion formation and even allow for what Krueger calls cautious generalizations (43–44). This information can be analyzed qualitatively (as one might do with an in-depth interview) or quantitatively (by careful content analysis).

Admittedly, focus groups have certain limitations when compared to other methods of inquiry. The setting is less natural than participant observation. The researcher has less control than in an in-depth interview or an experiment. Results are less easily analyzed and generalized than in survey research. However, focus groups have some significant advantages over these other methods. They allow one to examine the role of social interaction in opinion formation and expression. They combine the probing and flexibility of in-depth interviews with the ability to talk to a larger number of people. They help guard against researcher bias and shortsightedness by guaranteeing that interaction is not exclusively with the researcher him- or herself, and by allowing enough open-endedness for unanticipated views to emerge from the discussion. And they strike a compromise between the generalizability of quantitative analysis and the depth of qualitative analysis.

Focus groups are especially appropriate for exploring the social aspects of public opinion: "The hallmark of focus groups is the explicit use of the group interaction to produce data and insights that would be less accessible without the interaction found in the group" (Morgan 1988, 12). They are also appropriate for examining the relationship between television and politics, especially in light of the conversational metaphor presented earlier. The ubiquitousness of television; the assumption that messages and audiences interact in complex ways that allow for multiple meanings to emerge from the same broadcast; an understanding that television watching is often a social activity in which viewers converse with each other and with the TV: all of this suggests the need to think in terms of *the uses* of television rather than simply its effects. It also suggests that such uses will be subtle, varied, fluid, social, and context dependent. Focus groups, more than most quantitative methods, allow for a systematic examination of television and politics that is sensitive to the complexity of this relationship.

Discussing the Environment: A Case Study in the Construction of Public Opinion

The findings presented in this chapter are based on nine focus groups conducted in 1990–91.[4] Given our desire to simulate conversations people have in more natural settings, we opted for relatively small groups.[5] In the end, one group consisted of five people, five consisted of four people, and three consisted of three people. Ages varied from eighteen to seventy-two, with a median age of thirty-nine.[6] Occupations ranged from student, to government employee, to full-time homemaker, to both blue- and white-collar worker (one participant was unemployed). Twenty-one of the thirty-four participants were women. Three of the participants were black. Overall our "sample" was slightly less affluent than the larger population from which it was recruited. Based upon responses to a brief telephone survey administered during the initial recruitment, as well as to a self-administered survey completed prior to the start of the focus groups, our participants varied in the strength and direction of their partisan affiliation, their ideological self-placement, and their views concerning issues such as the environment, prayer in schools, government aid to minorities and women, abortion, and defense spending. They also varied in their self-professed interest in politics, their likelihood of talking about politics with friends, and their television-viewing habits. In short, while

not a random sample of either the local or the national population, our participants brought a range of backgrounds, beliefs, and opinions to the discussions.

The topic of discussion in each of our nine focus groups was "environmental pollution." Three of the discussions (one from each age group) were
preceded by viewing an edited version of the made-for-television docudrama
"Incident At Dark River," which dealt with the issue of toxic waste. Another
three groups began by viewing an episode of the CBS newsmagazine *48
Hours*, also dealing with the issue of toxic waste.[7] In both cases, the broadcasts
were introduced as "a way to get us thinking about the topic." The remaining
three groups watched no television and simply began by discussing their views
on environmental pollution. The focus groups without television lasted approximately one and a half hours, while those with television averaged an
additional forty-five minutes.

The discussion protocol was loosely structured and designed to stimulate
discussion rather than to uncover particular pieces of information (see appendix). The protocol was identical regardless of whether television was present or
not, with two exceptions. First, in those groups where television was viewed,
discussants were asked what they "thought of the show," prior to turning to a
more general discussion of the environment. And second, at the end of sessions
that had begun by watching television, discussants were asked a few specific
questions about the programs. Other than this, however, the broadcasts were
not referred to by the moderator.

Overall, the focus groups were intended to provide three types of "data."
First, since at various points in the protocol we directly asked discussants about
their reactions to the show they had seen, their views of the media more
generally, their television-viewing habits, and so forth, the focus group transcripts provided information concerning people's own perceptions about their
relationship with television. Second, by asking people to engage in a public
discussion of a timely political issue, we were able to directly observe how
citizens converse and the role that television plays in that public conversation.
Third, by having people watch television and then requiring them to talk both
about the program itself and about issues touched on in the program, we were
able to approximate what we argue is the ongoing, silent conversation people
are regularly engaged in while watching television.

Given that "the richness of this method lies in the respondents' own
words," the focus group transcripts were initially "read for themes that
emerged . . . rather than coded for pre-determined categories" (Crigler et al.
1988, 8). Each transcript was read aloud and discussed by the authors in an
attempt to uncover systematic patterns (the recordings were also replayed both
to validate the transcripts and to better capture nuances in the discussion). Once
we felt that we had identified certain structures to the discussions, we repeated
the process from the beginning, this time beginning to "test" the validity of our

hypothesized pattern. This qualitative yet systematic reading of the transcripts was intended to uncover suggestive relationships.

The next step in our analysis was to systematically code the transcripts using Ethnograph, a software package developed by John V. Seidel, Jack Clark, and Rolf Kjolseth and specifically designed for analyzing qualitative data. Ethnograph allows each line of a transcript to be coded for up to twelve characteristics (for example, direct and indirect references to television, particular points of view expressed by participants, and so forth). Once coded, the transcripts can be systematically analyzed both quantitatively and qualitatively. Quantitative analysis includes examination of the frequency of certain kinds of statements (for example, the number of times unsolicited references were made to the television program viewed in the focus group). Qualitative analysis involves more interpretive readings of specific parts of the transcripts (for example, one can retrieve and examine all the statements made by a single individual about environmental activists, all the references to television made by one person, or all the interchanges between two particular discussants). In essence, Ethnograph does not replace interpretive analysis but rather eases the logistics of transcript management (i.e., "cutting and pasting," retrieving particular statements and exchanges, and the like), allowing more systematic and in-depth examination.

In presenting our preliminary findings we have several goals. First, we provide evidence for the extensive role both nonfiction and fiction television play in public discourse. Second, we show that, based on self-reports and our own observations, citizens do interact with television in ways consistent with our "conversation" metaphor. Third, we examine the fluid, often inconsistent nature of public opinion, pointing out how people socially construct rather than retrieve their views on complex issues. Fourth, we explore the role of television in this process of opinion formation, focusing on our discussants' surprising awareness of (and concern for) their dependence on the media. Finally, we provide examples of the real but limited autonomy individuals have in identifying and, where appropriate, resisting television's ideological biases.

The Ubiquitousness of Television in Political Conversation

During coding, we distinguished among three types of media references made by conversants as they discussed environmental issues: references to the specific show watched at the start of the focus group (not applicable to groups where no television was shown), references to television more generally; and references to other mass media (i.e., newspapers, magazines, radio). Included in this last category are general references to "the media." Within each category we distinguished between "direct" and "indirect" references. Direct references refer to comments in which the media were specifically mentioned (e.g., "I picked up a newspaper that had an 'Earth News' section" or "I saw this thing on TV, about how enough pollution could . . ."). When the specific reference was less clear (e.g., "If it's like they showed in Mexico City where the people can't walk down the street" or "You know, when the spotted owl was the big issue . . . they made it the owl against the lumberjacks"), the comment was coded as an indirect reference to the media. In addition, we distinguished between "prompted" and "unprompted" references. The former included any media reference made when we specifically queried about their reactions to the show or about their general views concerning how well the media cover environmental issues (see appendix). The latter included only unsolicited references to the media.

As table 7.1 reveals, media references peppered the conversations: on average, 34 percent of all statements included at least one *unprompted* media reference (row IV). The relative number of such references varied depending upon the presence or absence of television. In groups without television (table 7.2, row IV), the total percentage of unprompted media references was 27 percent, compared to 40 percent (tables 7.3 and 7.4, row IV) in groups that started by viewing a television show. Most of this difference is accounted for by continued reference to the shows after we had turned the discussion to more general issues of the environment. For example, Dan, in explaining why he trusted the opinions of certain experts, referenced a character from the docudrama "Incident At Dark River."[8]

> Yeah, especially the more respected people. Like, even in that film, you have the officials, like the Johns Hopkins guy. There, you say, "A *professor,* he must know what he's talking about."

Similarly, Ann, in trying to explain her feeling that environmental regulation can be taken too far, referred back to a segment from *48 Hours,* in which a relatively small-time polluter had been arrested.

> Well there's just so much they can do. Like that man on the show that they arrested. Why that was ridiculous. . . . He just left a can or something didn't he? I don't know, it's just silly.

We have argued elsewhere that understanding the impact of television on the construction of public opinion requires expanding the definition of politically relevant television to include both fictional and nonfictional programming (Delli Carpini and Williams 1994a). Our focus groups support this argument. When participants drew upon media in their conversations, they made few distinctions between fictional and nonfictional television. Unprompted

TABLE 7.1. References Made by All Groups

	Comments (No./Total)	Comments (%)
I. References to show		
A. Overall[a]		
Direct	240/913	26
Indirect	45/913	5
Total	295/913	31
B. Unprompted[b]		
Direct	90/713	13
Indirect	37/713	5
Total	127/713	18
II. References to TV		
A. Overall[a]		
Direct	122/1,490	8
Indirect	18/1,490	1
B. Unprompted[c]		
Direct	59/1,161	5
Indirect	14/1,161	1
III. Reference to other media		
A. Overall[a]		
Direct	126/1,490	9
Indirect	115/1,490	8
B. Unprompted[d]		
Direct	74/1,270	6
Indirect	105/1,270	8
IV. Unprompted media references[e]		
Direct	145/886	16
Indirect	159/886	18
Total	304/886	34
V. References to group members		
Direct	284/1,490	19
Indirect	57/1,490	4
Total	341/1,490	23
VI. References to Personal		
experience	135/1,490	9

Note: Although we express the frequency of comments in terms of a percentage of the total number of statements made, these figures cannot be added across categories because the denominator of each category changes with the number of possible comments.

[a]Includes all relevant references regardless of place in protocol.

[b]Excludes references to show from protocol sections III and X.

[c]Excludes references to TV from protocol sections VId (media) and XI.

[d]Excludes other media references from protocol section VId.

[e]Number and percentage of comments that contain unprompted reference to TV show, TV in general, other media, or media in general.

TABLE 7.2. References Made by Groups Without Television

	Comments (No./Total)	Comments (%)
I. References to show		
A. Overall[a]		
Direct	n.a.	n.a.
Indirect	n.a.	n.a.
B. Unprompted[b]		
Direct	n.a.	n.a.
Indirect	n.a.	n.a.
II. References to TV		
A. Overall[a]		
Direct	60/577	10
Indirect	7/577	1
B. Unprompted[c]		
Direct	16/421	4
Indirect	4/421	1
III. Reference to other media		
A. Overall[a]		
Direct	66/577	11
Indirect	52/577	9
B. Unprompted[d]		
Direct	44/504	9
Indirect	47/504	9
IV. Unprompted Media References[e]		
Direct	43/393	11
Indirect	65/393	17
Total	108/393	27
V. References to group members		
Direct	112/577	19
Indirect	20/577	3
Total	132/577	23
VI. References to personal		
experience	66/577	11

Note: Although we express the frequency of comments in terms of a percentage of the total number of statements made, these figures cannot be added across categories because the denominator of each category changes with the number of possible comments.

n.a. = not applicable

[a]Includes all relevant references regardless of place in protocol.

[b]Excludes references to show from protocol sections III and X.

[c]Excludes references to TV from protocol sections VId (media) and XI.

[d]Excludes other media references from protocol section VId.

[e]Number and percentage of comments that contain unprompted reference to TV show, TV in general, other media, or media in general.

TABLE 7.3. References Made by Groups that Watched Nonfiction Television

	Comments (No./Total)	Comments (%)
I. References to Show		
A. Overall[a]		
Direct	102/426	24
Indirect	26/426	6
Total	128/426	30
B. Unprompted[b]		
Direct	17/300	6
Indirect	21/300	7
Total	38/300	13
II. References to TV		
A. Overall[a]		
Direct	47/426	11
Indirect	10/426	2
B. Unprompted[c]		
Direct	32/327	10
Indirect	9/327	3
III. Reference to other media		
A. Overall[a]		
Direct	35/426	8
Indirect	13/426	3
B. Unprompted[d]		
Direct	13/339	4
Indirect	12/339	4
IV. Unprompted media references[e]		
Direct	35/189	19
Indirect	40/189	21
Total	75/189	40
V. References to group members		
Direct	59/426	14
Indirect	23/426	5
Total	82/426	19
VI. References to personal experience	32/426	8

Note: Although we express the frequency of comments in terms of a percentage of the total number of statements made, these figures cannot be added across categories because the denominator of each category changes with the number of possible comments.

[a]Includes all relevant references regardless of place in protocol.

[b]Excludes references to show from protocol sections III and X.

[c]Excludes references to TV from protocol sections VId (media) and XI.

[d]Excludes other media references from protocol section VId.

[e]Number and percentage of comments that contain unprompted reference to TV show, TV in general, other media, or media in general.

TABLE 7.4. References Made by Groups that Watched Fiction Television

	Comments (No./Total)	Comments (%)
I. References to Show		
A. Overall[a]		
Direct	138/487	28
Indirect	19/487	4
Total	157/487	32
B. Unprompted[b]		
Direct	73/413	18
Indirect	16/413	4
Total	89/413	22
II. References to TV		
A. Overall[a]		
Direct	15/487	3
Indirect	1/487	0
B. Unprompted[c]		
Direct	11/413	3
Indirect	0/413	0
III. Reference to other media		
A. Overall[a]		
Direct	36/487	7
Indirect	50/487	10
B. Unprompted[d]		
Direct	17/427	4
Indirect	45/427	11
IV. Unprompted media references[e]		
Direct	67/304	22
Indirect	54/304	18
Total	121/304	40
V. References to group members		
Direct	113/487	23
Indirect	14/487	3
Total	127/487	26
VI. References to personal		
experience	36/487	7

Note: Although we express the frequency of comments in terms of a percentage of the total number of statements made, these figures cannot be added across categories because the denominator of each category changes with the number of possible comments.

[a]Includes all relevant references regardless of place in protocol.

[b]Excludes references to show from protocol sections III and X.

[c]Excludes references to TV from protocol sections VId (media) and XI.

[d]Excludes other media references from protocol section VId.

[e]Number and percentage of comments that contain unprompted reference to TV show, TV in general, other media, or media in general.

references to the media were as frequent in focus groups viewing fictional as nonfictional programs, and we found little difference in the overall percentage of references to the shows themselves (32 percent in the groups viewing "Incident At Dark River" and 30 percent in those viewing *48 Hours*). Indeed, participants were more likely to make *unprompted* references to the fictional show than the nonfictional show (22 percent of all unprompted comments in the former case, compared to 13 percent in the latter).

Beyond references to these particular shows, discussants were about as likely to invoke fictional as nonfictional programs to make or refute points. For example, where possible we coded direct references to television (other than to the shows viewed during the focus groups) as to whether the programs referred to were fictional or nonfictional. There were 102 references to television that could be coded in this way. Of these, 49 were to fictional media (e.g., *The Day After, The Simpsons*) and 53 were to nonfictional media (e.g., *60 Minutes,* CNN). Groups were about as likely to reference fiction as nonfiction programs regardless of whether they had been shown "Incident At Dark River," *48 Hours,* or no television at all.

The political relevance of fictional media is also revealed by the specific public figures mentioned by our discussants. The following is an inclusive list of the people mentioned at least once in our groups: George Bush, Carl Sagan, Ralph Nader, Ted Turner, Dan Rather, Cher, Captain Planet (a cartoon character), John Ritter, Bill Moyers, Nadia Comaneci, Kitty Kelly, Nancy Reagan, Bette Midler, Ed Begley Jr., Bill Cosby, Jeremy Rifkin, Bob Barker, Phil Donahue, Oprah Winfrey, Sally Struthers, Tom Cruise, Clint Eastwood, Cindy Lauper, and Al Sharpton. At least two things seem striking to us about this list. First is the frequency with which figures from the media, especially entertainers associated with environmental issues, were referenced, often as authoritative sources. Second is the almost complete absence of government representatives: other than a *single* reference to President Bush, there were no mentions of specific elected or appointed public officials.[9]

The extent to which the mass media in general and television in particular dominated our conversations about the environment is perhaps best illustrated by comparing the aforementioned numbers to the frequency with which personal experiences were referenced. Where possible, we coded all comments that referred to personal experience as a source of information. Included here were statements based on either firsthand experience or experiences of people with whom they were familiar. Hazel's comment represents the first type of personal information, Marie's the second.

Hazel: I . . . lived in the Washington metropolitan area, and you see the dirty Potomac River out there and so many other things. . . .
Marie: My husband said plastic bags are cheaper than paper bags. . . .

How often do people draw upon personal experience in political conversations about the environment? Not very often when compared to mediated sources. Overall, only 9 percent of the comments referred to personal experience (table 7.1, row VI). This percentage varied only slightly between groups shown fictional television (7 percent), nonfictional television (8 percent) and no television (11 percent). Even when citing direct experiences, our discussants often evaluated them against information drawn from the media.

> Violet: I feel really guilty because we just had our lawn treated today and we just started it this year, but I've been reading more and more articles about how that may not be the best thing to do as far as having small children that play in the grass and I know when you read things and you see things on TV that they sort of sensationalize it, it may not always present an accurate picture, but if there's even a small chance that something could happen to one of my children, I would want to avoid it at all costs.

As the preceding quote illustrates, and as we shall discuss in more detail, people are ambiguous about their dependence on the media for information. Nonetheless, part of the media's power to shape political discourse comes from an underlying, semiconscious belief that information provided by it is more reliable than other sources, including personal experience.[10]

As final evidence of the general influence of television on political conversation, we compared how often it was addressed, relative to references to other members of the group. The latter included both direct references to others (e.g., "I agree with her") and more indirect references in which someone seemed to be taking his or her cue from the comments of another member of the group. Among the groups shown television, we found that the specific program was addressed almost as much as all the "other" group members combined. For the groups shown *48 Hours,* 13 percent of all comments contained a direct or indirect, unprompted reference to the show (table 7.3, row IB), while 19 percent of all comments contained a direct or indirect reference to other members of the group (table 7.3, row V). For the groups shown "Incident at Dark River," the numbers were 22 and 26 percent respectively (table 7.4, rows IB and V, respectively). And this comparison underestimates the frequency of overall television or media references, since it includes only unprompted references to the specific show. Clearly, television remained an important "participant" throughout the conversations.

Conversing with Television

We have argued that citizens often "discover" their political views in the give-and-take of discussions with others. Television plays a central role in this process, in that it is engaged in an ongoing political conversation: when we turn the set on, we dip into this conversation.

Some of the strongest support for our conversational metaphor comes from the discussants' own reports of their viewing habits. Literally all of them said they talked with others about what they saw on television, either while viewing or shortly thereafter, and almost all of them said they did this with great regularity. When asked to recall the last time they had watched a show and talked about it, the following comments were typical. Note how the point at which the viewer enters into television's ongoing conversation (i.e., the particular show that is watched and the specific topic it addresses) shapes the topic that is then discussed with others:

> Jane: I [talk about what's on television] all the time. So do my friends. . . . If we go out to dinner, or if there was something that really grips me. Or I might call them up and see if they read about something or watched it on TV . . . and we discuss it.
> Kara: When I watch TV with my friends, we'll get into big, big discussions about what's going on. If I watch it with my boyfriend, I'm kind of like her [points to another group member], I kind of argue with him about stuff . . .
> Paul: When my roommate and I are watching TV, he always likes to make comments about anything he's watching, and depending on my mood, I'll just take whatever's the totally opposite statement to what he says and just try and provoke an argument every once in a while, especially like on talk shows or something.

Paul goes on to recall another example that supports our argument that fictional shows can also spark political conversation.

> It seems like we were watching *LA Law* and there was some issue being discussed like the right to die or something and he said, "Well, I'd always want to do it this way" . . . and I say, "I'll remember that you want to die," or something like that. . . .

Viewers' interaction with television has a conversational quality even when one watches alone. In our focus groups, it was common to see viewers smiling, nodding, groaning, and so forth as they watched television. It was also not unusual for them to gesture at the television during discussions (even though the set was off) much as they gestured at other members of the conversation. Indeed, many viewers (as we do) talk back to the tube: only three of the thirty-four participants said they never did. Of the three, one woman said that, while she didn't, her husband did all the time. Another one of the three said: "I don't actually verbalize, but I think, boy I'd like to be . . . like on Donahue or something . . . I'd like to be there right then just to say this. . . ." More typical was Catherine's comment: "I scream at the TV, just like I scream at other people when I drive." Again, such interactions were not limited to news or talk shows. As Kara commented:

> Out loud? Yeah, sometimes. When I watch *Cops,* mostly . . . or if [a show] has a bad ending, I'll say, "she should have done this . . . I hate that damn ending."

Of course, as the following comment by Mark reveals, not everyone is tolerant of actually verbalizing the conversation we have with television.

> How do you think I lost my first wife? Sitting there and talking back to the TV. She left me for that.

The Shifting Nature of Public Opinions

One of the most consistent and telling patterns to emerge from the focus groups was the active role conversants took in attempting to make sense of the political and social world. Drawing on their own store of information and beliefs, the views of others in the group, and the views presented by television, discussants engaged in an ongoing effort to construct their opinions about environmental issues.

Key to understanding the role conversation (with both television and other citizens) plays in the formation and maintenance of public opinion is first understanding the contextual, fluid, and often inconsistent nature of opinions themselves. Freed from the forced restraints of closed-ended surveys, this aspect of public opinion becomes clear. This inconsistency in part reflects a lack of information, interest, and so forth, but more importantly also reflects the "inherent contestability" of most important public issues. An examination of all the comments made by individual discussants throughout the focus groups demonstrates that even the most thoughtful citizens express views that are contradictory. Indeed, often the most consistent views were expressed by those who were uninterested and unreflective of the issues under discussion. For example, Sarah acknowledged that she was "just not concerned about the environment at all," was "just not interested in it," and "never engage(s) in any conversation about it [the environment]." Throughout the discussion, however, she maintained a consistent (even stubborn) critique of environmental problems.

> I think they've gone too much into this pollution. I don't believe in all of it. . . . There's just a bunch of kooks around.

> Some of those people are trying to sue Ashland Oil [a local company accused of polluting the environment]. . . . They're just trying to get rich over it. Ashland is a good citizen.

> As far as recycling, it's not going to work at all unless they're paying. . . . Everybody's collecting cans because they're paying. . . . They're not going to fool with anything unless they're paying.

> I think [environmental problems] are overblown a lot so they can sell more papers. . . . I don't think most [journalists] know anymore about it than my cat.

> Some of these women [activists] that are involved in this stuff should just stay home and do something productive. . . . They're always wanting their mug on the TV.

Much more common were opinions expressed by the same person at different points in the conversation which, when placed back-to-back, appear incompatible. For example, Carol initially said "I don't think about the environment much," a point she reiterated several times throughout the discussion. But interspersed throughout these denials were comments such as the following:

> I work for a regulatory agency and we deal with hazardous materials on a daily basis. We give permits to the companies that haul the stuff in and out. The laws just do not support caring for the environment.

> I started paying attention to what was going on, you know, the garbage being dumped and other flammable and medical [waste]. I realize that it's very easy for them to unload here. . . . The law just does not support . . . Kentucky being environmentally sound.

Carol also expressed fairly strong views on the distinction between the killing of animals for sport versus for food and acknowledged having read several Greenpeace newsletters (several points of which she disagreed with). And consider the following two comments by Kara. First she says:

> I think it definitely is [possible to protect the environment in today's world]. I mean, to think there's all these big brains and all this big money for making things, surely they can come up with some way to make them in a safe manner, or to protect the public, or the land or animals . . .

Yet later in the conversation she says:

There's just a lot of other stuff you have to deal with. . . . I mean, you would just have to take over the world pretty much, it would have to be every person in the United States, every company, every—I just don't think it would be possible [to protect the environment in today's world]. . . . I hate to be Miss Negative, but I just don't think so.

A similar about-face is demonstrated in the following two comments by Mike. He first says:

I think everybody is concerned about the environment, because we all live here and I don't think anybody wants to see the earth destroyed. . . .

Yet later, in response to Tim's comment:

Tim: I don't think we're concerned at all. . . . I don't think the majority of Americans would go to a meeting, lift a finger. . . .
Mike: Yeah, I agree with that 100 percent. . . . I personally never recycled newspapers or anything until I was just about forced. . . . I think [people] are kind of apathetic towards it. . . .

On some occasions, the ambiguities inherent in difficult political issues manifest themselves within the same comment, as in the following attempt by Elaine to express (more accurately to construct) her view on whether progress is being made in dealing with environmental problems:

I'm thinking two prongs here. When you were talking about the Ohio River, just think about the pollution last year, how [you couldn't swim there]. When I was a child, you could swim there. . . . Then, on the other prong we're talking about, I just think it's great about the schools. . . . They're letting the school kids—and the school kids want to—bring these wire carts around [to recycle cans]. . . . In the early seventies the thrust of environmental education really came on board.

The Construction of Political Meaning

What *is* Carol's level of interest in environmental issues? Kara's view of the possibility of addressing the nation's problems? Mike's sense of how concerned the American public is? Elaine's level of optimism concerning the future? Our argument is that their "true" opinions do not reside in one or the other of their statements. Rather, their opinions are to be found in the full set of statements they make about a particular issue and can be understood only in the specific context in which they are made. More important, we argue that citizens play an active, if limited, role in the construction of these opinions, and they do so in part through ongoing conversations with other people and, especially, with television.

Examples of our discussants actively using their own experiences, the comments of others, and the "comments" of television abound throughout the transcripts. Many of the examples already cited in this chapter began with phrases such as "I agree with her," or "It's like on the show we saw." In addition, participants often picked up on themes, topics, and so forth introduced by other members or, in those focus groups with television, by the program they had just watched. For example, the plot of "Incident at Dark River" revolved around a local company's polluting a river with toxic waste. Similarly, one segment of *48 Hours* was devoted to toxic water pollution. In the discussions about the environment following both these shows, people were much more likely to focus specifically on industrial water pollution than were those people in groups who were without television's immediate influence (Elaine's comment is one such example). The following were also taken from groups who had viewed these shows:

> Mark: [The docudrama] really made me more aware of things that I guess in the back of my mind I knew were happening. You read occasionally about all these factories dumping in rivers and I think I've read about some things going on up on the Ohio river . . .
>
> Stephanie: One issue that's really affecting me right now . . . is the salt in the Jamestown River from that underwear company up there. You know, Lake Herrington, it's not even worth going there anymore, the banks are filled with trash. There aren't very many fish there and it's just nasty. . . .

Similarly, both programs focused attention on the human costs of pollution by emphasizing its effect on children. In the docudrama, the lead character's daughter dies after playing in a river polluted with toxic waste, while one segment of *48 Hours* centered on parents whose young son had died of leukemia, the possible result of pesticides used in the area. Comments such as the following, found in all the discussions in which television was present, were largely absent from those discussions held without first viewing TV:

> Susan: I think that [pollution] is very serious and that . . . if we don't do something our grandchildren and their children won't have a chance.
>
> Ruby: I don't have any children, but I have nieces and nephews. . . . What kind of world are they going to have? . . .

In one sense these examples simply illustrate the agenda-setting and priming effects demonstrated by mainstream research. Ruby's comment is typical: "I never really think about [environmental issues] too much unless I happen to see something on television." However, allowing people to speak for themselves, as in focus groups, also helps expand our understanding of these processes. First, our discussions suggest that the media not only shape what people *think* about, but also what they *talk* about. Second, they provide evidence that people are very much aware of this process. In some important ways, the agenda-setting function of television is not the insidious process often implied in media research.

> Tania: I think people talk about [environmentalism] more now than they did before because it's brought out so much more now. . . . But, I think now you hear so much about it that it's on your mind. Whether you're talking about it or not, you are thinking about it.
>
> Catherine: I don't think [environmental problems are] something that's a major, major concern. . . . [I]t's like . . . the war in the Persian Gulf. If you asked me about it [when it was going on], I'd say [I talk about it] every day. You know, you talk about it and so people kind of put aside other things.

Often our conversants' understanding of the degree to which they rely on the media was fairly sophisticated. Violet and Catherine, for example, noted the power of television as a visual medium to dramatize environmental issues.

> Violet: I thought [the program] was real interesting. I think lots of times . . . you know, you can have all these ideas in your head then you have this visual representation of a landfill or this visual representation of a child and here's their picture and now they've died. Or, these individuals that are actively campaigning that look like very normal people that you would not normally envision as campaigning on environmental issues. I think that's real important.
>
> Catherine: [T]hat's what the media is there for, sometimes they don't belong in people's business, but it's a good thing they're being concerned. So we can see what is going on, what needs to be done, they let us know. They're our eyes, kind of. . . . they let us see. You know, if we didn't get to see what was on TV, well, unless we went to a landfill ourselves, would we really know what it looked like? You know, in our heads, we can visualize what it looked like to have all that.

At the same time that subjects recognized their dependence on the media, they often seemed troubled and ambivalent about the potential such dependence has for selectively shaping their perception of the importance of various political issues. The public's concern over this agenda-setting process, revealed in the following quotes, is often overlooked by researchers:

> Mark: I think I'm concerned, but then on the other hand, I think I spend very little time thinking about it until I see something like this [gestures

to the blank screen] or I see the oil wells burning out of control or
something to bring it home . . . I think we need to have more hard facts
put before us. I think we need to be bombarded with more things to
make us think about it and hopefully therefore to make us act.
Hazel: I think, you know, some of the best people or the most expert
people may not have an avenue to get . . . to the public . . . if the media
doesn't involve themselves in that, then there's really no way to get the
exposure.

Some discussants moved beyond simple ambivalence to an understanding
of the reasons for the shifting nature of media coverage. Such sophisticated
understandings open up the possibility of maintaining a critical distance between the media's definition of what is important, and other hierarchies of
importance. Take this quotation from Paul, for example:

One problem with the media is that . . . if they talk about some issue then
two weeks later if it's not changed, they really don't want to do the story
again. . . . They don't want to do the same thing over and over, they think
the viewers are going to get bored and change to something else. I wonder
if the media's attention to environmental concerns is going to be fad like
and then they're going to find something else to focus on six months from
now. That can be a problem . . . when you involve the media.

The Limited Autonomy of Television Viewers

Elsewhere, after closely analyzing several programs dealing with environmental issues, including the ones we showed to our focus groups, we concluded
that these shows adopted a uniform perspective, but one that varied at different
levels of politics (Delli Carpini and Williams 1994b). When discussing "the
substance of politics" (i.e., issues that are on or becoming part of the political
agenda), such shows adopted a liberal perspective, assuming that environmental problems were worse than ever and posed a grave and immediate threat to
humans and nature, while denying the need to consider trade-offs between
protecting the environment and economic growth. However, when discussing
"the institutions and processes of politics" (i.e., the formal channels and institutions of government and the economy), the programs took a conservative
populist view. Government was painted as corrupt, incompetent, and completely inadequate to the task of dealing with the problems posed by environmental pollution, while the business sector was represented by either evasive
corporate spokespersons or disreputable owners.

Most of our discussants had the ability to critically analyze the slant of
these shows and, at a certain level, to resist or accept their messages based upon

a comparison with their own ideology. Employing our conversational meta-phor, while dependent upon the media for information and the basic structure of political discourse, people continuously integrated and critiqued the media's side of this conversation. The following comments were fairly typical:

> Mark: Well, for the purposes of the movie ["Incident at Dark River"], I guess they wanted them [presented this way] . . . but I saw it as being slanted. I think they really portrayed [the corporate executives] as not having any heart at all and, you know, being guilty. We seem to already draw the conclusion that they were guilty and they didn't care whether they were guilty or not, and if it hadn't been for the little lowly guy at the bottom there which gives us all hope that no matter how big the company, there's always somebody. . . . I thought it was biased.
>
> Richard: I think it had a pretty liberal slant, which is OK with me because I agree with it, but still you've got to admit it wasn't exactly evenhanded.

Violet, commenting on *48 Hours,* identifies the bias of the show but accepts the need for such bias in order to combat wider apathy about environmental issues.

> I think sometimes it needs to be biased in order to make people more aware of what the issues are. I think it was biased on the side of environ-mental issues, you know, that we should be more aware that these are the horrible consequences. Yes, these are consequences and yes, these are horrible, but how many times do these things happen?

Joe makes a similar point about media coverage of environmental issues more generally.

> I think some people may think they're overemphasizing environmental issues and I think that may be true, but I don't think it's bad that they do because sometimes something needs to be overemphasized in order to balance it out. That has been neglected in the past, so I think they do a good job.

Discussants also critically evaluated the reliance on sensationalism or emotionalism in both shows. Especially interesting was their ability to see the dramatic elements in *both* fiction and nonfiction. Violet criticizes one segment of *48 Hours* that dealt with a family's grief over their belief that their child had died from exposure to pesticides.

> Yeah, but then like that [show], that was really too sad. . . . I'm sure the parents were really sad and I cannot imagine losing a child, but to show

them sending balloons to heaven on a TV show like that, I think that's a bit much.

And Bob makes a similar comment about the emotional appeal of "Incident At Dark River."

I think it was definitely a bleeding-heart story. The underdog against the whole world. I mean, it brought up quite a few good issues, but I don't know if it was particularly objective.

Similarly, discussants often understood the need to distinguish the dramatic elements from the more factual bases of fictional programming. As Ruby commented, "[W]ith a movie, you find so much of it is factual and so much of it [is included] to make it interesting."

While recognizing the impracticality of only providing facts and figures on television, and the benefits of emotional appeals, our subjects were troubled and divided over the implications of television's use of such dramatic devices. This interrogation of the motives and the methods of the media was fairly subtle and not unsympathetic to the dilemmas of attracting and educating an audience.

Mark: I think a documentary usually gives us more hard cold facts [than docudramas]. . . . I mean, I found myself [after watching "Incident at Dark River"] . . . crying and I was mad, and those are the things that tend to get us fired up and ready to go out and take action right now. . . . So, I think they're both useful and, you know, we shouldn't discount either because there's something we learn from both.
Barbara: Because a documentary would be in another place, another city, you'd say, "Oh, that's in New York and New Jersey, I can't do anything about that over there." But in a fictionalized account, it's like, "Oh, I wonder what's going on in my town."
Joe: I think if it touches the emotions of a person, laughter, sadness, whatever, it's going to stick with the person longer than if you just read statistics about it. I think that's a good way to bring a message across.

And John, while recognizing the power of entertainment figures to attract audiences for worthwhile causes, is also clearly troubled by this state of affairs.

Well, they're public figures, they are recognized and I think most American people would probably in some way trust a movie star for some reason. I'm not sure why, but they're well known and they're not foreign and if you just had somebody like Ralph Nader who isn't real well known come up and start speaking on some environmental issue, no one would go to see him.

However, while these examples suggest the potential for citizens to critically evaluate and resist the media's agenda, other aspects of their use of information were much less accessible to conscious reflection. Consistent with research based on schema theory, we found several examples of the way people unconsciously used preexisting beliefs to interpret information provided by the media. For example, the most widely known environmental group was Greenpeace, which was mentioned several times in all our focus groups (the second-most frequently mentioned group, the Sierra Club, was brought up in fewer than half the groups). When asked to describe what they knew about Greenpeace, most subjects mentioned that the group was "radical," "extremist," or "violent." And in four of our groups, the following story (here told by Marcie) was recounted:

> I mean, you see them with a little rubber dinghy between the Russian trawler and the whales and that type thing which grabs your attention, but I guess they got accused of blowing up a ship once, so. . . . they also have a political activist wing.

It appears that, since the schema in which information about Greenpeace is filtered centers on images of "radical activism," the vague recollection of a ship being blown up becomes reconstructed into further evidence for this point of view: Greenpeace blew up a ship. In only one of our focus groups did someone tell the story correctly: that it had been the Greenpeace ship *Rainbow Warrior* that had been blown up.[11]

The inability of discussants to see, and so to actively use or resist, the opinions expressed by television is most apparent once one moves to what we have labeled "the foundations of politics" (i.e., the values and beliefs upon which the very ideas of politics and government are based). At this level the television programs were highly conservative, emphasizing individualism to the exclusion of any form of collective or political action (Delli Carpini and Williams 1994a). In considering such issues, discussants were largely unable to identify or critically resist the media's tendency to present individual actions as the only acceptable form of action. Possible solutions to environmental problems brought up by discussants were limited to individual activities such as recycling or shopping more wisely.

> Tom: I talk about building a geodesic dome . . . running off a windmill or solar power.
> Sandra: I do go to Winn-Dixie and take all my paper and plastic there. . . .

Jeff: I do little things, like sometimes I buy paper that's been recycled . . .

A similar ideology is revealed in their attitude toward government: it should do more, but without stepping on individual rights, and in general is too corrupt or incompetent to count on:

> Elaine: I think recycling is good, but I think the question is whether we can legally force anybody to do it. It just seems like its a private decision.
>
> Louis: What is it, 96 percent of all incumbents get elected. . . . I think it gets so corrupted that it's hard to figure out why the system doesn't work.

And collective action is either viewed with suspicion, or else is simply not thought of as a serious alternative.

> Kara: Greenpeace has knocked on my door two or three times and I will not open my door to them. . . . [They] are too militant for me and just do not agree with them.
>
> Sandra: Unfortunately I met two people who I did not particularly like who were from the Sierra Club. . . .
>
> Mike: I'm not sure if it was Greenpeace, it was one of those organizations. They invaded the Soviet Union to save some seals. . . . I think that hurts their cause more than helps it. I personally feel that people like that are crackpots.
>
> Linda (after being pressed to be more specific about what groups she thought were doing a good job addressing problems of the environment): I don't really think in terms of groups, I think in terms of individuals.

Once the distinction between levels of politics is made, it becomes less surprising that, despite the critical treatment of government and business, both are essentially absent in discussions about how best to address environmental problems. The closest participants came to identifying this bias in television's treatment of environmental issues was in comments like those of Mark, who saw the potential for a docudrama like "Incident at Dark River" to mobilize political action "if we knew where to go . . . after watching [it]."

Summary and Conclusion

Opinions regarding complex political issues are dynamic, malleable constructs that emerge from the interaction of personal experience, the views of fellow citizens, and the views presented by the mass media. Both fictional and nonfictional television play a central role in this process, strongly influencing *what* people think and talk about and *how* they think and talk about it. In many ways television serves as a privileged member in public discourse, one to whom citizens feel an obligation to respond.

Citizens are active participants in this ongoing conversation, often demonstrating autonomy in selectively using, reinterpreting, or resisting media messages as they construct their opinions. This autonomy is limited, however. In many circumstances, television's images and information were less consciously used to construct and reinforce views that, under other circumstances, may have been expressed in very different ways.

The ability of citizens to critically identify some media biases, but not others, suggests that rather than simply asking what the bias of television is, a more fundamental question may be which biases viewers can identify and which they are unable to identify or resist. Systematically cataloging and empirically verifying the varieties of political uses of television requires a varied, subtle, and creative research design. We see focus groups as a useful piece of that design and believe the evidence presented here supports that view.

APPENDIX: FOCUS GROUP PROTOCOL

I. (Introduction): We're interested in finding out a little about what people think about a variety of issues, where they get their information from, and so forth.
   A. (Set them at ease, introduce coinvestigator, explain loose structure of discussion, break, and so on.)
   B. (Go around the room, ask each person his or her name, a little something about him- or herself.)
II. (If television present, introduce show as way of getting us to think about the topic of the environment. Tell them to relax, feel free to move about, talk during the video.)
III. (If television present): What did you think about the show?
IV. How concerned are you about environmental issues? Which ones? How often do you talk about it? With whom?
V. Do you ever act on your concerns? Get involved in any way? How?
VI. How good a job do you think (government, industry, public interest groups, the media, technical experts) are doing in regards to environmental problems?
VII. Do you think it is possible for us to adequately protect the environment in the United States today? Why? Why not?
VIII. What is the responsibility of corporations/industry in protecting the environment, the public?
IX. What should citizens do (what is their obligation)?

X. (If television present): Think back to the show. Do you think it was fair? Did it hold your attention? Did you learn anything? Would you watch it if it were on at home? Did you like or dislike the format (documentary magazine or fictional docudrama)?

XI. How often, if ever, do you talk about issues like the environment? With whom? Do you ever watch TV with others? Do you talk about what's on with them? Do you talk about what you've watched on TV with others later? Describe the circumstances. When watching alone, do you ever "talk back" to the TV? Out loud? Describe circumstances.

N O T E S

1. For a fuller critique of traditional models of opinion formation, see Delli Carpini and Williams 1994c, 782–85.

2. It should be noted, however, that the use of "900"-number telephone polls, the reading of viewer mail on the air, experiments with interactive television, and so forth serve to enhance this conversational aspect of television viewing.

3. For a fuller discussion of the utility of focus groups in social and psychological inquiry, see Delli Carpini and Williams 1994c.

4. Participants were residents of Lexington, Kentucky, and were recruited through a public notice placed in the local newspaper. The notice reported that two university professors were engaged in research about public opinion and asked for people interested in participating in small-group discussions about current issues. A twenty-dollar honorarium was offered, and no mention was made of either television or the particular issue to be discussed.

5. While the focus groups were conducted at the University of Kentucky, we attempted to make them as nonthreatening and natural as possible, holding them in rooms with comfortable furniture, allowing participants to sit where they wanted and to move about freely, serving pizza and other snack food, allowing people time before the focus groups to get used to each other, and so forth. Nonetheless, we readily acknowledge that these groups do not fully simulate the ways most people either watch television or talk about politics. However, focus groups are certainly *no less* realistic than are the techniques of survey research, experiments, or in-depth interviews (consider, for example, the dynamics of a telephone interview, in which one moment a person is sitting at dinner, watching TV, or conversing with family members, and the next is engaged in a formal interview with a stranger about a variety of issues he or she has had no time to think about). In addition, much (perhaps most) of the "real conversation" that takes place between a viewer and television is unspoken and thus unobservable except through some level of intrusion and artificiality. Focus groups, by stimulating both television viewing and conversation, attempt to make this conversation visible.

6. Three groups consisted of people in their late teens and twenties; three of people in their thirties and early forties; and three mainly of people in their mid-forties and fifties (though a few were older). This stratification was based on the assumption that people would be more comfortable talking with people roughly their own age.

7. For a detailed description and analysis of the messages contained in these broadcasts, see Delli Carpini and Williams 1994b.

8. Unless otherwise noted, all quotes are representative of broader patterns uncovered in our analysis of the transcripts. Also, note that all quotes are verbatim and that transcripts of the spoken word often appear awkward in print.

9. In a related point, aside from isolated comments about two government agencies (OSHA and EPA), when participants discussed solutions to environmental problems, they almost always talked about what individuals, not government, could do (i.e., recycling, talking to friends, getting more information, and so forth).

10. This notion was brought home to us in our pilot focus groups conducted with students on the University of Michigan campus. When asked what she thought the Michigan campus was like in the 1960s, one older participant replied apologetically: "It's not really fair to ask me, since I'm from Ann Arbor and lived here during the sixties . . ."

11. We found other suggestive examples of this kind of information processing regarding political activists: Rebecca's general references to "those kooks" mentioned earlier; the lumping of feminists, other political activists, even Al Sharpton into discussions of environmental activists, and so forth. As one discussant, trying to clarify who he meant by "environmental activists," said, "you know, extremists. . . . People who wear Birkenstocks."

CHAPTER 8

Perceptions and Conceptions of Political Media Impact: The Third-Person Effect and Beyond

Richard M. Perloff

This chapter examines the third-person effect: the view that a persuasive communication will exert stronger influence on other people than on the self. Importantly, Perloff argues that people—at both the mass and elite levels— may construct political meaning and behave in different ways because of their anticipation of others' reactions. In his review of the literature on the third-person effect, the author notes that individuals perceive and interpret others' views in relation to themselves. This process of perception is shaped by the kinds of media messages used, levels of personal involvement, issue importance, source bias, and demographic characteristics of the self and the other. Public and elite values, belief systems, and feelings about politics interact with perceptions of media effects in the construction of political views. Perceptions of mass media impact also play a part in the construction of political meaning and decision making on the elite level, as examples from presidential debates and Vietnam War news coverage suggest.

Americans think the underpinnings of society—from Congress to schools to neighborhoods—are collapsing, according to a survey conducted for the Massachusetts Mutual Life Insurance Company. Yet Americans generally profess themselves happy with their own representative in congress, their children's school, the safety of their own neighborhood. According to an Associated Press report, " 'The problem is with thee, not me. That's essentially what I keep hearing,' said Maureen Michaels, a New York City researcher who supervised the survey."

Comedian Dennis Miller had this to say during a 1991 performance on HBO:

I guess the other big problem confronting this country now is the specter, the dark presence, the imposing doom presented at us by the evil one, Satan's son, Andrew Dice Clay. Don't we look for things to bother ourselves about? Is anyone here that threatened by this man, is anyone in this

177

room so non-ego-formed as an adult that they're afraid listening to his record album will make them kill another human being? I mean, come on.

Don't you hate it when the liberal intelligentsia in this country comes down from this tête-à-tête they're having with the burning bush on the mountaintop and deigns to speak for what they construe to be the unwashed, stupid masses? Well, you know I can see through Andrew Dice Clay but then again I have Bachelor in Communication from Tallahassee Juko, but those people (the cattle), I don't think they get it; I best hip them to my personal wisdom.

These examples both call on the third-person effect, the perceptually oriented hypothesis articulated by W. Phillips Davison in 1983. The belief that events influence "thee" differently from "me" is consistent with the third-person effect hypothesis, and the perception that I will see through controversial comedian Andrew Dice Clay but others will fall prey to his nasty witticisms is central to Davison's approach to media effects. This chapter critically reviews research on the third-person effect, discusses its use in mass and elite contexts, and suggests ways of extending it to new political communication settings.

Conceptual Underpinnings

The third-person effect is the perception that a persuasive communication will exert a stronger impact on others than on the self. As Davison (1983, 3) noted, individuals exposed to a mediated message typically believe that the message will not have its greatest effect "on 'me' (the first person) or 'you' (the second person), but on 'them'—the third persons" (parentheses added). Thus, the third-person effect hypothesis contends that people are psychologically predisposed to overestimate the effects that communications have on others. Davison also maintained that these perceptions have an impact on behavior. He suggested that whatever effects persuasive messages have on attitudes and behaviors are not due to the direct persuasive impacts of the messages themselves. Instead, he asserted that the effects are due to the actions of those who anticipate some response on the part of others (the third persons), and act differently as a result. Thus, Davison argued that the perception that a communication exerts a stronger impact on others than the self can trigger behavioral responses.

The third-person effect hypothesis (if supported by empirical data) would seem to have important implications for a host of everyday events, ranging from bandwagon effects in elections that seem to be fueled by perceptions of powerful news media effects to attempts to censor media content (such as the 1988 film *The Last Temptation of Christ* or, more recently, Peter Arnett's controversial reporting from Baghdad) that, in the minds of some observers, seemed to exert a disproportionate impact on supposedly naive members of the media audience. The relevance of the third-person effect to these intriguing everyday phenomena has made it very attractive to communication researchers.

The third-person effect is a contemporary notion, rooted as it is in the relativity of perception (which will be discussed in greater detail subsequently) and committed as it is to the centrality of perceptions in public affairs. In our current era, the perception is the thing: politicians are concerned with how they are perceived, newscasters share the same concern when they hire audience consultants, and policymakers are forever wondering how an event will play in the media. By emphasizing perceptions, Davison placed the third-person effect in a decidedly contemporary light—it plays well with the idea, advanced by postmodern thinkers that (for better or worse) we are in an age in which facts are subjective, perceptions are relative, and texts are equivalent and interchangeable. What makes the third-person effect unique is its relational flavor: it emphasizes the discrepancy between perceptions of communication effects on others and on the self.

At the most basic level, though, the third-person effect hypothesis fits into, and grows out of, the literature on public opinion. Like pluralistic ignorance (Katz and Allport 1931), the looking glass perception (Fields and Schuman 1976), and the spiral of silence (Noelle-Neumann 1974, 1984), it emphasizes that people's perceptions and conceptions of public events are of central importance to the public opinion scholar. Like these other approaches, the third-person effect hypothesis assumes that much of our social and political behavior is guided by perceptions of reality, assumptions about the communications environment, and constructions of social and political events (Price and Roberts 1987).

In the next sections of this chapter, I review and synthesize research on the third-person effect. To organize the discussion, I draw on Zanna and Fazio's (1982) framework for reviewing research on attitude-behavior consistency. Zanna and Fazio noted that there have been three generations of research on attitude-behavior correspondence. The first generation focused on "what" questions (What is the relationship between attitudes and behavior?). The second generation examined "when" questions (under what conditions do attitudes predict behavior?). The third generation focused on "how" issues (How or through what processes do attitudes influence behavior?). Applying this scheme to the present context, first, I examine whether the research supports the third-person effect hypothesis; second, I discuss the factors that facilitate the operation of the third-person effect; and third, I discuss the processes that underlie the effect. The final section of the chapter outlines directions for future research.

Does the Evidence Support the Third-Person Effect Hypothesis?

A number of papers and articles have examined aspects of the third-person effect hypothesis as outlined by Davison. Both experiments and surveys have probed third-person issues. In the experiments, subjects typically read a message and then estimate the effects that the message will have on their attitudes toward the topic and the attitudes of others. In the surveys, respondents are typically asked to estimate the extent to which certain types of media content will influence their attitudes and those of others.

One way to determine the size and significance of these accumulated results is to conduct a meta-analysis (e.g., Hedges and Olkin 1985; Rosenthal 1984, 1991). However, after reviewing each of the studies in great detail, it was concluded that meta-analytic procedures would not yield particularly informative results. A number of studies did not report sufficient amounts of statistical information (e.g., means and standard deviations and results of post hoc tests from significant Fs). Thus, the author opted to examine the studies using the traditional literary review methodology.

Articles and papers were assembled by carefully reviewing journals for articles on the third-person effect and by employing what Mullen and Rosenthal (1985) called the "invisible college approach." That is, the author corresponded with scholars who were actively involved in third-person effect research and asked if they had done any studies in the third-person area. This enabled me to obtain some unpublished studies, which helped to eliminate the "file drawer problem"—the bias in favor of reviewing published articles, which are more likely to reject than accept the null hypothesis.

Sixteen papers tested the notion that individuals perceive that communications exert a stronger impact on others than on the self. As table 8.1 indicates, fifteen of the sixteen studies reported evidence consistent with the third-person effect hypothesis. Only Glynn and Ostman (1988) failed to support the third-person view. However, their study provided a somewhat indirect test of Davison's hypothesis in that their questions probed perceived conformity to group influence rather than perceptions of persuasive message effects.

Several of the studies summarized in table 8.1 (e.g., Atwood; Cohen and Davis; Gunther and Thorson) reported a "reverse third-person effect" or a "first-person effect"—that is, respondents perceived that they would be more influenced than others. However, these investigations also found a third-person effect for other messages or for other respondents. Confidence in the generality of the third-person effect is enhanced by the fact that the findings emerged in both surveys and experiments and in designs that employed a variety of different message types, including news, political advertising, advertising, debates, and dramatic television programs.

TABLE 8.1. Research on Third-Person Effect

Study	Message Topic	Did Findings Support Third-Person Effect?
Atwood (1994)	Information on earthquakes	Yes, third-person and first-person effects obtained, with effects linked to beliefs about others' susceptibility
Cohen and Davis (1991)	Negative political ads	Yes, for supporters of candidate attacked when judging effects on other supporters; reverse third-person effect among opponents of candidate attacked when judging effects on supporters of candidate
Cohen et al. (1988)	Defamatory news stories	Yes
Glynn and Ostman (1988)	Perceived influence of public opinion	No
Griswold (1992)	Messages about the economy delivered during 1992 U.S. presidential election campaign	Yes, for opinions of Bush, but not for beliefs about Republican and Democratic candidates
Gunther (1991)	Defamatory news stories	Yes
Gunther (1994)	Pornography	Yes, with magnitude of third-person effect related to support for restrictions on pornography
Gunther and Mundy (1993)	Messages that varied in personal benefit likelihood	Yes, for messages judged "not smart to be influenced by" or "not so good for me"
Gunther and Thorson (1992)	Neutral and emotional ads, and public service announcements (PSAs)	Yes, for neutral ads; reverse third-person effect for emotional ads; no effect for PSAs
Lasorsa (1989)	ABC's "Amerika"	Yes, and particularly for individuals who perceived themselves as politically knowledgeable
Mason (1990)	Ambiguous descriptions of hypothetical events	Yes
Mutz (1989)	News stories about controversial political issues	Yes, and stronger effect on those who perceived the issue as personally important
Perloff et al. (1992)	ABC's "Amerika"	Yes
Price and Tewksbury (1994)	News about Whitewater investigation	Yes
Rucinski and Salmon (1990)	Political ads, news, debates, and polls	Yes
Tiedge et al. (1991)	Effects of media on personal life (self-report measures)	Yes

Some authors have argued that third-person effects are an artifact of the order of questions about communication effects on others versus self. These scholars have contended that third-person effects have emerged because subjects have been asked to indicate their perceptions of communication effects on others prior to indicating their perceptions of communication effects on the self. According to this view, a primacy effect is operating such that individuals are willing to acknowledge large effects on the first question but not on the second. However, several studies have counterbalanced question ordering and have still found that a third-person effect emerged (e.g., Gunther 1994; Mason 1990; Price and Tewksbury 1994; Tiedge et al. 1991).

It is also possible that the third-person effect artifactually results from the practice of asking self-other questions in a back-to-back format. According to this view (Price and Tewksbury 1994), the question format encourages individuals to contrast responses to a media-effects-on-self question from a media-effects-on-others query. Stronger support for the third-person notion would emerge if the effect occurred among subjects who were asked to make only one estimate of media effects (either on themselves or on others). Price and Tewksbury obtained such support. They found that the third-person effect did not depend upon having the same subjects answer both items. Specifically, subjects who were asked to estimate media effects on others only perceived stronger media effects than those asked only to estimate media effects on the self.

Behavioral Effects

Davison (1983) argued that third-person perceptions influence behavior. However, only three studies have examined this notion, and they have provided mild support at best for the third-person view. Mutz (1989) found that perceived effects of media coverage of a campus protest involving divestment of university financial holdings in South Africa decreased willingness to engage in a public discussion on this issue. However, in a 1991 experiment, Gunther reported that degree of discrepancy between message effects on self and others was not significantly associated with amount of money awarded in damages to the subject of a defamatory news story. Griswold (1992) found that there was a negative correlation between the third-person effect and voting intentions; however, his findings are open to serious question in that he did not control for relevant demographic or political partisanship variables. Importantly, none of the aforementioned studies measured actual behavior. Thus, the behavioral component of the third-person effect hypothesis remains unsubstantiated at the present time.

Summary

As I have noted, all the studies that have directly tested the third-person effect hypothesis have obtained evidence that individuals perceive that communications will exert a stronger impact on others than on themselves. However, some studies have found that the effect emerged only under certain conditions, and others have reported a reverse third-person effect. In view of these findings, it is reasonable to inquire about the strength of the effect. Unfortunately, the present review does not permit a precise answer to this question. Lasorsa (1992) argued, based on an earlier review, that about 50 percent of the members of a particular sample are susceptible to a third-person effect. Thus, it stands to reason that the third-person effect is likely to vary as a function of the situation and is more likely to show up in certain situations than in others. In the next section, I will discuss the conditions that facilitate and impede the third-person effect.

What Conditions Facilitate the Third-Person Effect?

Message Topic

The overwhelming majority of third-person effect studies have employed messages that focused on negative (and in some cases socially undesirable) outcomes. Messages such as defamatory news coverage, negative political ads, and pornography are likely to cause an audience member to say "the effect of that message may not be so good for me" or "it is not smart to be influenced by" that message (Gunther and Mundy 1993). Gunther and Mundy argued that a third-person effect should be particularly likely to emerge in the case of such messages. On the other hand, these authors argued, the self-other discrepancy should be smaller in the case of messages that promised to benefit the individual or that advocated socially desirable outcomes. In support of this hypothesis, Gunther and Mundy found that when a message advocated recommendations that were not perceived to be personally beneficial or involved large risks (e.g., news of a protein lotion designed to "strengthen" hair), there was a significant third-person effect. However, when the message promised to benefit the individual (suggestions to include oat bran in a low-cholesterol diet), the third-person effect failed to emerge. In a similar vein, Gunther and Thorson (1992) found a third-person effect for advertisements, but not for public service announcements (PSAs), which presumably have more desirable effects. Thus, it appears that a third-person effect is particularly likely to emerge when the message advocates outcomes that are not perceived to be beneficial to the self or when it makes statements that give rise to the perception that "it is not smart to be influenced by that message."

Involvement

Based on Davison's (1983) speculations and social judgment theory, several researchers have examined the impact of ego involvement on perceptions of media effects on third persons (Perloff 1989; Perloff et al. 1992; Vallone, Ross, and Lepper 1985).

Perloff (1989) developed a videotape of televised news coverage of the 1982 War in Lebanon. He showed the thirteen-minute videotape to pro-Israeli partisans, pro-Palestinian partisans, and to a control group composed of individuals who did not have strong attitudes toward either side of the Middle East conflict. Pro-Israeli partisans were more likely than pro-Palestinian activists and control group members to perceive that the news coverage would cause a neutral audience to become less favorable toward Israel and more favorable toward the Palestine Liberation Organization (PLO). Conversely, pro-Palestinian partisans were more likely than pro-Israeli activists and control group members to believe that the news coverage would cause audience members to become less enchanted with the PLO and more positive toward Israel. Similar findings regarding the impact of ego involvement on third-person perceptions were reported by Vallone, Ross, and Lepper (1985).

The aforementioned studies on ego involvement focused on perceptions of message effects on third persons; they did not directly examine whether involvement magnified the gap between perceptions of effects on others and on the self. Using a related construct, importance (see Krosnick 1988 and Salmon 1986 for discussions of the importance and involvement constructs), Mutz (1989) found that perceptions that an issue was highly important magnified the tendency to perceive that media affected others more than the self.

Perceived Source Bias

There is a greater discrepancy between perceived message effects on others and the self when the source of the message is perceived to be negatively biased (Cohen et al. 1988; Gunther 1991) or when the audience attributes persuasive intent to the communicator (Gunther and Mundy 1993). Cohen and his colleagues asked some subjects to read a libelous news story that was attributed to a source who harbored a negative bias toward a public figure, whereas other subjects read the same story attributed to a source who had a positive bias; still other subjects read the story, but for them the source was unnamed. The third-person effect was significantly greater among negative-bias subjects than among subjects in the other conditions. Similarly, Gunther (1991) found that the gap between perceptions of message effects on self and others was larger when the story was attributed to a biased source (the *National Enquirer*) than to a more objective source (the *New York Times*).

These findings are, in one sense, counterintuitive. Persuasion research has found that communicators who are perceived to be credible and unbiased induce more attitude change than those who are seen as less credible or more biased (Hovland and Weiss 1951; Hass 1981). One would therefore expect subjects to indicate that a highly credible source would have a greater impact on others' opinions than a less credible source would. Such a finding would occur if people processed message effects on others in a way identical to how they processed message effects on the self. Clearly, people do not process the self and others in this way. As Lasorsa (1992) noted, people probably say to themselves: "I know how biased this message is, but others may not recognize its propagandistic nature and, therefore, they will 'fall for' what I 'see through.'"

It is important to emphasize that media credibility is not an objective factor but, instead, a dynamic variable that emerges through the interaction of source and receiver. Gunther (1992) has gone so far as to argue that credibility should be viewed as a relational variable, as an audience member's reaction to specific news media content. Gunther found that group involvement predicted more variance in credibility judgments than did media characteristics, audience demographics, and general skepticism toward media.

These findings, coupled with the aforementioned studies of involvement, suggest that when respondents are highly ego involved in the message (and/or have strong attitudes about the issue), they are likely to perceive a source as negatively biased; this perception should in turn increase the disparity between perceptions of media effects on self versus on others. Thus, two individuals may be exposed to the same message source but, by virtue of their different perceptions of the source's bias, be differentially susceptible to the third-person effect. And this, of course, is our experience in real life: one person (typically someone with a strong position on the issue in question) is convinced that the media are biased against his or her side and overestimates the extent of media effects, whereas another individual, who harbors a different set of beliefs and attributions about the world and a communicator's intentions, does not assume the media are quite so biased; the latter person is typically less inclined to assume that the media exert a disproportionate effect on others. Thus, there is a strong emphasis upon the relativity of perception in the third-person effect hypothesis.

Demographic and Other Correlates

Tiedge et al. (1991) found significant third-person effects among the better-educated and older members of their sample (see also Rucinski and Salmon 1990, Gunther 1994). Tiedge and his colleagues found that, for better-educated respondents, the third-person effect was due to the perception that mass media exerted a strong influence on others rather than to the belief that it had relatively few effects on the self. By contrast, for older respondents, the effect was due to the perception that mass media had relatively few effects on the self.

It is important to point out that demographic variables such as age and education reflect or indirectly point to underlying conceptual factors that actually are impacting on perceptions of media effects on others and the self. Education may be indicative of perceived expertise, which (as Lasorsa [1989] found) increases the strength of the third-person effect. Or, it may indicate political knowledge, which reduces estimates of personal vulnerability (Price and Tewksbury 1994). Age may be reflective of accessibility of social attitudes and confidence in one's ability to resist influence attempts.

Social Distance

Three studies have found that the discrepancy between perceived communication effects on others and on the self increases as the hypothetical others are defined in more broad and global terms (Cohen et al. 1988, Cohen and Davis 1991, Gunther 1991). For example, Cohen and associates found that subjects perceived that news stories would exert a greater impact on "other Stanford students" than on themselves and a larger effect on "other Californians" and a still larger impact on "public opinion at large."

The research on social distance raises several issues. First, it is not clear, as some scholars have implied, that there is a linear relationship between social distance and the third-person effect. Cohen et al. (1988) found evidence of linearity; however, Cohen and Davis (1991) did not, and Gunther (1991) did not report any statistical tests of the linearity assumption. Quite probably, the relationships are more complex than we third-person effect researchers have assumed. Second, none of the investigators employed any perceptual measures of social distance. Consequently, we don't know whether subjects actually believe that "other Californians" was a broader category than "other Stanford students." Part of the problem here lies with the concept of social distance; it is a complex variable that includes various components, such as perceived similarity, familiarity, and identification.

Indeed, it is possible to conceptualize social distance in at least two different ways. According to one view, social distance falls along a continuum going from "just like me" to "not at all like me." The category at one extreme includes the respondent, whereas the category at the other extreme would not. A second view is that social distance reflects the heterogeneity and size of the audience or group in question. According to this view, social distance is represented by a continuum that goes from "my closest group or community" to "my largest group or community." It is this second concept that Cohen et al. (1988)

and Gunther (1991) examined. The point is that social distance can be concep-
tualized and measured in different ways, and this has not been made explicit by
researchers studying this concept.

Summary

Several conditions facilitate the third-person effect. The effect is particularly
likely to emerge when the message advocates outcomes that are not perceived
to be beneficial for the self or when it makes statements that give rise to the
perception that "it is not smart to be influenced by that message." It remains an
empirical question whether a third-person effect would emerge for positive
messages that make recommendations that are perceived to benefit the self or
for messages that contain socially desirable recommendations. As for now, the
available evidence suggests that the effect may be limited to messages that
have negative consequences. Research also indicates that third-person effects
are magnified when the issue is personally important to the respondent, when
the source is perceived to be negatively biased, when the respondent is well
educated, and when the hypothetical others are defined in broad and global
terms.

Through What Processes Does the Third-Person Effect Operate?

In this section, I will discuss the processes that underlie the third-person effect.
First, though, I want to emphasize that the third-person effect diverges sharply
from two other contemporary approaches to social perception and public opinion: the looking glass self-view (Fields and Schuman 1976) and false consensus theory (Ross, Greene, and House 1977). Both these approaches assume
that people overestimate the proportion of others who share their views about
social and political issues. There is considerable evidence to support these
theoretical approaches. For example, Granberg and Brent (1983) found that
across ten presidential elections, voters assumed that the candidate they preferred would win election, and Van Der Pligt, Van Der Linden, and Ester
(1982) found that activists on both sides of the nuclear energy debate perceived
that their preferred position had more support in the population. On an anecdotal level, I recall a comment made to me by survey researcher John Robinson.
Robinson noted that during the 1960s, his radical students frequently assumed
that American blue-collar workers shared the students' disaffection with
American society and would join their protest activities. The workers, however, were far more conservative than students imagined, yet the students'
perception revealed that they held a looking-glass view of political reality.

These illustrations and findings indicate that people assimilate others' political views to their own. However, the third-person effect is an example of a judgmental contrast. Rather than assuming that other people will react as they will to a communication, they assume the opposite: "others will be strongly influenced by what they see, but I will not be swayed in the slightest."

Thus, a different perceptual dynamic seems to operate in the case of perceptions of communication effects than in the case of perceptions of public opinion. In the case of perceptions of communication effects, people assume that others do not process information in the same way as they do themselves.

More precisely, there are two explanations for the disparity between perceptions of communication effects on others and on the self. The first view is that people overestimate the effects that media have on others, the second emphasizes that individuals underestimate the impact that communications have on themselves. Turning to the first view, one might ask why individuals assume others are so influenced by mediated portrayals. One explanation is that individuals have acquired "media effects schema"—knowledge structures that include a number of beliefs about the media and the audience. These beliefs probably include the notion that televised messages exert strong impacts, that vivid messages are persuasive (Collins et al. 1988), that dramatic presentations of a message (as in a television miniseries) strongly influence attitudes, and that audience members are gullible and susceptible to persuasion (Atwood 1994).

The second (not necessarily incompatible) explanation is that individuals underestimate media effects on the self. Perceptions of minimal effects on the self can occur for several reasons and can work through several processes.

First, it is possible that unconscious psychodynamic processes are at work and individuals project their own beliefs that the media influence them onto others. Unwilling or unable to acknowledge that they are themselves affected by media, they find it more psychologically palatable to assume that it is others who are influenced. This interpretation is plausible, though difficult to test. It may have some truth to it, but it has trouble accounting for ego-involved partisans' perceptions that media exert negative effects on others. It seems unlikely that partisans assume that they are influenced by media reports (even on an unconscious level).

A second explanation is cognitive. According to this view, individuals have little insight into their own psychological functioning (Nisbett and Wilson 1977) and assume they are not influenced by media portrayals. Thus, they underestimate effects on the self because they are unaware of their own psychological vulnerabilities.

A third explanation, not unconnected with the first, emphasizes the need for control and self-esteem preservation. This viewpoint holds that receivers need to believe that they are invulnerable to negative life events in order to preserve control and self-esteem (Weinstein 1980). One aspect of the "illusion of invulnerability" is the notion that one is not susceptible to influence by persuasive mass communications. As Gunther and Thorson (1992, 580) note, "seeing oneself as less vulnerable than others apparently helps to maintain and enhance one's self-identity." Consistent with the self-enhancement view, Gunther and Mundy (1993) and Gunther and Thorson (1992) found that individuals were relatively unlikely to indicate that communications influenced their own attitudes when there was reason to believe that such an admission of media effects might reflect negatively on the self.

It is important to emphasize that the various processes discussed herein probably occur simultaneously. It is also likely that different processes are salient in different situations and for different people. Gunther and Mundy's research suggests that self-enhancement needs are particularly influential when the message advocates negative or socially desirable outcomes. Conceivably, media schemas may be more salient when individuals are estimating effects of ambiguous messages (Mason 1990). In addition, as Tiedge et al. (1991) found, different processes may be salient among different receivers. Thus, in their study, education produced a third-person effect by increasing beliefs that media exerted a strong impact on others, whereas age produced a disparity by virtue of respondents' perceptions that the media exerted a negligible impact on themselves.

Several studies have tried to determine whether the third-person effect has its roots in overestimation or underestimation tendencies (Cohen et al. 1988, Gunther 1991, Gunther and Thorson 1992, and Perloff et al. 1992). Generally, researchers have compared perceived effects on self and on others with the actual impacts that the message exerts on the self. There is evidence that individuals both overestimate communication effects on others (Cohen et al. 1988, Lasorsa 1989, Perloff et al. 1992, Gunther 1991) and underestimate effects on themselves (Cohen et al. 1988, Gunther and Thorson 1992). In any case, and even if simple projection is involved, the effect is noteworthy because of the inherently distorted nature of the perceptual dynamic. As Tiedge et al. (1991, 152) note: Widespread perceptions of strong media effects on others and weak effects on the self cannot both be accurate since there would be too few people left to comprise the "others" (people in general) thought to be affected. If the widely held perception of the media to influence others is accurate, then most people must simply be wrong about the media's inability to influence them personally. Conversely, if most people are correct in their assumption that the personal effects of the media are minimal, then they tend to exaggerate the effects on others. In either case, most people appear to be willing to subscribe to the logical inconsistency inherent in maintaining that the mass media influence others considerably more than themselves.

Summary

Several interpretations of the third-person effect have been advanced. The effect may be due to the operation of media schemas, inaccessibility of knowledge about media effects on the self, and a need to assume that the self is unaffected by communications in order to preserve self-esteem or control over the social environment.

It is likely to be difficult to definitively say whether individuals are over-estimating communication effects on others *or* underestimating effects on the self. Separating out these processes is not likely to be easy, and it is not likely to bear fruit since they are conceptually and methodologically intertwined.

Taking the Third-Person Effect into the Real World

In this section I will enlarge the discussion of the third-person effect by speculating on its relevance to real-world political situations at both the mass and elite levels.

Public's Perceptions and Constructions

If you listen to radio talk shows, you will hear people call in and rail about the powers of the media. Egged on by talk show hosts, who voice the same message, callers vent their feeling that the media in this country call the shots and exert great power over government and society at large. Some callers observe that when the media favor a course of action, it is certain to become reality because the media exert great control over what people think. I do not know how common such statements are—and that is, of course, a fertile ground for empirical research. But they do reflect a certain populist sentiment and, on a scholarly level, they are fully in keeping with the third-person effect. After all, we don't hear callers complaining that the media are having too much effect on what they themselves think about politics; nor do we hear talk show hosts or callers worrying that the media are exerting too great an impact on their own innermost feelings and thoughts.

Yet we make a mistake if we assume that these are neutral, value-free perceptions of media effects. They are more than that. When people make such statements, they are not saying, in a voice of political neutrality, that the media have a great effect on everyone else, but no effect on the self. These statements are strongly political, and highly partisan; in fact, when people talk about the powers of the media, they are more often than not arguing that the media are biased in a direction that they do not agree with and that media are swaying public opinion in this direction. For example, the other day a caller to the Rush

Limbaugh program complained about the power of the liberal media, and then went on to suggest that such media have minimal impact on his own attitudes ("When I see Connie Chung, I look at my watch," he said). Note that the caller did not claim the media had a powerful impact on others, but that the liberal media had this impact.

Statements like these reflect the kind of oppositional third-person effect that Perloff (1989) and Vallone, Ross, and Lepper (1985) reported; under conditions of high ego involvement, people typically assume that media cause the public to become more negative toward "their side."[1] I would argue that most of the time that people speak about "powerful media effects," they are expressing their values, as well as their cognitions about mass media. Conservatives who call Rush Limbaugh complain that "the media" are leading the country down the primrose path of liberalism, and liberals who criticize news media political content are invariably nervous that such content will lead people to become more sympathetic with the conservative, hegemonic status quo. People rarely observe that the media exert powerful effects on the body politic without having in mind a particular type of impact that they find objectionable.

This is an important point, because Davison (1983) implied that the third-person effect was value-neutral. He noted that there was a discrepancy between perceptions of media effects on others and on the self, but he did not give sufficient attention to the ways in which people's values, belief systems, and feelings about politics interacted with their perceptions of media effects. The third-person effects that matter in the real world are those that are tinged by political ideologies. These are the third-person perceptions that influence action. Indeed, conservative talk show hosts have been quite adept at mobilizing beliefs about powerful liberal media effects to their advantage. Callers who went the extra distance of contacting the White House to protest the nomination of Zoe Baird for attorney general may have been egged on by their belief that the liberal media were having a powerful effect in suppressing popular opposition to Baird's failure to make Social Security payments to her child's nanny.

Third-Person Perceptions at the Elite Level

The third-person effect also operates at the elite level, perhaps more powerfully because elites are so consumed by the press and its effects. Some authors (Baughman 1989, 15) have argued that American presidents and politicians have harbored third-person perceptions since the beginning of the Republic: Both Washington and Addison came to manifest the third-person effect. The *Aurora* (a Jeffersonian paper), Washington complained, was "preparing the public mind. . . . There seems to be no bounds to [the editor's] attempts to destroy all confidence that the people might and ought to have in their government." The harsh attacks on the Federalists, Addison declared in 1796, "abused [the people] in their information and perverted [them] in their judgments."

Washington was certainly not the only president who assumed an oppositional third-person effect. Throughout American history, presidents have held hostile media biases and have no doubt projected these onto the public or assumed that the public was unduly influenced by press coverage of events. Perhaps the most famous example of this is Lyndon Johnson, who is reported to have watched Walter Cronkite's critical documentary on the Tet Offensive and concluded, "It's all over" (Ranney 1983, 52). According to popular history and some scholarly accounts, Cronkite's broadcast sealed Johnson's decision not to run for reelection in 1968. I would argue instead that it was Johnson's perception that Cronkite's views exerted a powerful impact on public opinion that influenced his decision. Interestingly, that perception may not have been accurate. Hallin (1986) has argued that Johnson could have used the Tet Offensive—and media doubts about the war—as a vehicle to argue that an all-out war should be waged against Vietnam. It is possible that, given the U.S. victory in Tet, the power of the bully pulpit, and press subservience to Establishment sources, this policy might, at least temporarily, have positively swayed public and elite opinion in Johnson's direction.

Careful historical study would no doubt unearth more recent examples of presidential third-person perceptions, ranging from Richard Nixon's war against the press to Bill Clinton's concern that radio talk shows are filled with a "constant, unremitting drumbeat of negativism and cynicism" (Jehl 1994). While we will never know for sure, we can only assume that these presidents were not themselves influenced by press coverage, but were all too ready to assume that the public was irreparably damaged by the news.

A final application of the third-person effect to elite decision making can be gleaned from an empirical study conducted by Rothbart and Hallmark (1988). Their study suggests that third-person perceptions can operate at the international level as well.

In 1939, the United States received nightly broadcasts from London by the American journalist Edward R. Murrow, reporting on the psychological and physical consequences of the Nazi bombing of British cities . . . Contrary to Nazi intent, the bombing did not move the British toward surrender, but strengthened rather than diminished their resolve to resist German domination. Shortly after the United States entered World War II, the Americans joined the British in costly bombing raids over Germany, in part to decrease the Germans' "will to resist." Later research by the Office of Strategic Services comparing lightly and heavily bombed areas found only minimal differences in civilians' "will to resist" . . . It is interesting to reflect on why we would expect bombing to demoralize our enemies, while recognizing that it had diametrically opposite effects on our allies. (Rothbart and Hallmark 1988, 248)

Based on these observations and studies of in-group/out-group categorization, the authors hypothesized that coercion would be judged as a relatively more effective influence strategy than conciliation by out-group members than by in-group members. This hypothesis is theoretically similar to the third-person effect. If we view the in-group as an extension of self and the out-group as an example of a third person, then we can view the authors as suggesting that one type of social influence strategy (coercion) is more effective on others than on self. The authors tested the hypothesis by asking subjects to read a description of a conflict between two hypothetical countries. Subjects were asked to take the perspective of the defense minister of one of the nations. They were asked to evaluate a variety of behavior change strategies in terms of their effectiveness in influencing the actions of their own or the other country. As the authors predicted, when out-group members rather than in-group members were making the judgment, coercion was viewed as a more effective social influence strategy than was conciliation.

Thus, to the extent that in-group members assume that the out-group is more susceptible to coercion than is the in-group, they may be likely to recommend that punishment-type strategies be employed to "bring the out-group into line." This conclusion has disturbing implications for the resolution of intergroup conflict.

Beyond the Third-Person Effect: Perceptions of Media Effects

The third-person effect focuses on the perceived discrepancy between communication effects on others and on the self. On a more general level, it focuses on perceptions of media effects and in so doing calls research attention to another area of beliefs about media, one that is somewhat different from credibility (Gaziano 1988) and that complements the work of Kosicki and McLeod (1990) on media schemata. It seems appropriate that a chapter in a book on construction of political reality focuses at least briefly on the larger issue of the nature of people's beliefs about media impact. This section will discuss the ways in which such beliefs can make a difference in political communication.

Elsewhere I have explored the nature of political consultants' beliefs about political advertising and have shown that they differ rather dramatically from those of journalists (Perloff and Kinsey 1992). It is quite likely that consultants' beliefs about the political universe—their theories and the ways in which they construct political reality—influence their behavior and their approach to political campaigns. Much work needs to be done in this area, but an example from American political history may help us appreciate just how important political actors' theories of media effects are.

Consider the widely held belief that John Kennedy won the first presidential debate with Richard Nixon in 1960 because he came off as more visually preeminent, as more attractive and more in tune with the stylized nature of the television medium. It is now part of the political folklore that those who saw the debate on television thought Kennedy won and those who heard the debate on radio thought Nixon won. However, this belief is based on only one study, with a small sample size (Jamieson and Birdsell 1988). Yet in 1976, Richard Cheney, President Gerald Ford's chief of staff, was highly influenced by the notion that appearances were everything in the 1960 presidential debate.

> We were very much aware not only of the supposed impact on the viewer of the televised picture of Nixon's discomfort, but also of the statement that has often been made that the people who heard the first Kennedy-Nixon debate thought Nixon won, while the people who saw it thought Kennedy won. That kind of information was in all of our minds as we looked at it. (Cheney 1979, 148)

Cheney went on to note that he was not trying to make Ford look "Kennedyesque" rather than "Nixonesque" in Ford's upcoming debate against challenger Jimmy Carter. However, he and his advisers were sufficiently influenced by their beliefs about the visual effects of the 1960 debate that they watched reruns of the debate, made certain Ford watched it, and were concerned that both candidates' podiums be as close together as possible in order to make Ford's greater height stand out. The interesting thing is that when scholars have examined the first debate of 1960 closely, they have discovered that visuals were not the only factor—nor necessarily the major one—in Kennedy's success. In a thoughtful chapter on the Kennedy-Nixon debates, Windt (1994) argues that Kennedy outperformed Nixon verbally and made a more effective claim to leadership. Realizing that the debate was not really a debate, but an opportunity to make politician gains, Kennedy developed a strategic perspective on the debate that served him well. He developed a theme for the debate—presidential leadership in the 1960s—and articulated it effectively in his opening and closing statements. Nixon, by contrast, "seemed to have no positive purpose for the debate" (Windt 1994, 21), accepted Kennedy's agenda of moving ahead in his opening statement, and chose to debate Kennedy in a picayune point-by-point way that made him look less presidential and perhaps more defensive. Kennedy also answered questions in a more direct and forceful way and used colorful language to tell the public where he would take the country if elected.

Had Cheney and his advisers viewed the first debate in this manner, they might have given Ford different advice; for example, they might have been less concerned with visual issues than with how Ford spoke, the words he used, and the themes he developed. Such an emphasis might have helped Ford, particularly in the critical second presidential debate of 1976 (see Chaffee and Dennis 1979).

The theories of media effects that consultants and others active in politics bring to the table are important. Those who conclude that Ronald Reagan's media success was due to his ability to manipulate the visual side of the news (e.g., Hertsgaard 1988) will offer different advice to presidents like Bill Clinton than those who believe that Reagan's popularity stemmed from his ability to speak in terms that people understood or his skill in convincing people that he had improved economic conditions (e.g., encouraging voters to label economic conditions as better and give him credit for it).

Elite theories of media are especially important in the area of foreign affairs. Foreign affairs is no longer the realm of gray bureaucrats and private diplomacy (Bennett 1994), but instead is waged on the public plain, what Manheim (1994a,b) calls strategic public diplomacy. There is no question among military leaders that the media play a critical role in gaining public consensus to begin a war (Bennett 1994).

As an example, consider the now-famous argument advanced by conservatives during the Vietnam War. According to this view, television lost the war in Vietnam by portraying the war as unwinnable and by constantly showing graphic footage of American casualties. Guided by their belief that television had a direct and negative impact on public opinion toward the Vietnam War, many conservatives pushed for restricting press access during the Grenada conflict and the Persian Gulf War. Of course, one can question the accuracy of this belief about Vietnam news (see Hallin 1986), but the fact remains that it has strongly influenced military decision making. We see once again that ideology, this time a conservative value system, is inextricably linked with beliefs about media effects and that perceptions about media effects are themselves an important ingredient in modern policy-making; these perceptions are grounded in values and a perspective on political communication. In addition, they can be spun and used by adept policymakers to advance a particular cause or promote a particular frame in the political arena.

Finally, it should be noted that journalists also hold theories of media and media effects, and these may shape their coverage of politics. Increasingly, journalists believe that image making, selling, and conveying feelings are what matter in politics (Perloff and Kinsey 1992). Reporters may privately abhor these values but may perceive that attention to public relations is what separates good from mediocre from bad presidents. They may believe that adroit presidential performances are what influence the public. But this approach has its dangers, as Brace and Hinckley (1992, 2) note:

> If journalists believe that (the presidency) is one of public relations merely, then their reporting can change the future by its description of the present. Stories on the White House's attention to falling ratings not only condone but also encourage this attention. Soon, presidents who do not have daily strategy meetings on their public approval will not be doing their job.

Where to from Here?

It should be clear that the third-person effect, and beliefs about media impact, have much to say about public opinion phenomena in everyday life and in the realm of elite policy-making. In particular, the third-person effect helps us comprehend the many instances in which people complain that the media have strong effects on everyone else, but deny that they themselves are affected. It helps us understand the diverse protests of media by ego-involved activists, calls for censorship, even libel suits by outraged private citizens and public figures. There is much that is interesting in the third-person effect. Yet important questions remain.

In the first place, we need to know how the third-person effect links up with other relevant public opinion concepts, such as pluralistic ignorance (Katz and Allport 1931, O'Gorman with Garry 1976); the looking-glass self (Fields and Schuman 1976), and the spiral of silence (Noelle-Neuman 1974, 1984; Donsbach and Stevenson 1984). It would be especially useful to know how perceptions of communication effects on others and the self mediate the spiral-of-silence effect (Mutz 1989). We also need to know whether a third-person effect can be obtained for messages that make positive recommendations, ones that are perceived to benefit the respondent or with which the respondent agrees.[1] In addition, we need to learn more about the processes underlying the third-person effect. Although it will be difficult to tease out underestimation from overestimation and projection from cognitive mechanisms, process-oriented studies are always useful in political communication and can be especially helpful in determining the extent to which the third-person effect has its roots exclusively in self-preservational needs.

Perhaps the most important direction for future research is to link the third-person effect with relevant policy concerns. Many studies suggest themselves. We need to know if in fact perceptions of powerful media effects are driving calls for censorship, as Gunther (1994) has found, and whether pleas for politically correct speech (Andsager 1994) have their roots in perceptions of negative media effects, as opposed to beliefs that "false" or "wrong" information should not be printed, regardless of effects. It would also be important to explore whether perceptions of negative media effects fuel the fires of partisan radio talk show listeners, propelling them from thought and affect to action. On the prosocial front, it would be interesting to explore whether the third-person effect can be used for socially useful purposes. For instance, can we help people develop more tolerant attitudes toward the body politic and more realistic beliefs about their own vulnerability to media fare by teaching them about the third-person effect?

Finally, on the macro level, it is important to determine the extent to which policymakers' behavior vis-à-vis the media has its roots in third-person effects, the conditions under which politicians are more likely to assume hostile media biases, and the circumstances under which they are more inclined to assume the public is with them (assimilation). Interviews with policymakers such as those conducted by Linsky (1986) would be useful here. Moving beyond the third-person effect to the issue of perceptions of media impact, we need to learn more about how consultants, politicians, journalists, and others active in the political arena construct the world of media, media effects, and public opinion.

Third-person perceptions and lay theories of media impact undoubtedly play a part in how policymakers and interest group activists think, plan, and strategize. In our own day, it would seem as if knowledge of political communication and policy is incomplete without some consideration of the role played by perceptions and conceptions of political communication effects.

NOTE

1. One important exception to this tendency was the belief of nuclear freeze activists that "The Day After" would convince millions of Americans that something had to be done now to prevent nuclear war. Activists were convinced that the 1983 television docudrama of nuclear annihilation would "send Americans by the millions flocking to their cause" (Hogan 1994, 47). Perhaps partisans perceived that the show would have a great effect on their own attitudes and generalized from themselves to others. Perhaps other processes were at work. In any event, this example does suggest that there are cases in which ego involvement leads to perceptions of positive media effects on third persons. Note that this case is consistent with the third-person effect in that partisans probably assumed that the program would have a larger effect on others than on themselves.

CHAPTER 9

Media Dependency and Multiple Media Sources

August E. Grant

In this chapter, August Grant discusses the limitations of previous measures of media dependency and proposes an alternative based upon media system dependency theory. He reviews the literature on media system dependency theory and discusses the importance of dependency relations to people's understanding of politics as well as other personal and social conditions. Media system dependency theory is important to constructionism, because it takes into account the human motivations that surround media usage and affect the process of understanding. Grant focuses on developing a scale to measure individuals' dependencies on media systems as well as on particular media outlets. He argues that traditional media usage measures are not adequate for capturing the individual's interaction with media.

Traditionally, most media effects research shares a common independent variable: a quantitative measure of exposure to a medium or message. This measure has proven useful for a number of reasons: it can be uniform across studies, it is simple, and it can be operationalized at different levels of measurement, that is, dichotomous (exposure/nonexposure), categorical (high, medium, or low levels of exposure), or continuous (exposure in minutes, programs, pages, or some other quantity). Nevertheless, the use of media exposure as an independent variable suffers a number of drawbacks. In experimental research, it may ignore previous experience with the medium that may play a part in the decoding process. In survey research, it may ignore the context in which the exposure takes place, including environmental variables that constrain access to the media.

While this variable has also been used in the study of political communication, scholars in the field have long recognized limitations of the measure. Offering television as an example, Zukin (1981) suggests that, because certain media are so pervasive, an exposure saturation point may be reached. In this case, Zukin suggests that the key measure is whether a person is exposed at all and not how much exposure the person experiences.

Another set of researchers advocate the use of measures of dependency upon media as predictors of political variables (Becker, Sobowale, and Casey 1979, Becker and Whitney 1980, Miller and Reese 1982, Reese and Miller 1981). Zukin (1981), in discussing contradictory results using measures of dependency, indicates that a major problem in this area is the lack of a uniform measure of dependency. Indeed, the most uniform measure found in the literature is the simple question: "Which do you rely on most for information about politics and current events—newspapers or television?" (McLeod, Glynn, and McDonald 1983; McCombs and Poindexter 1983; Miller, Goldenberg, and Erbring 1979; Miller and Reese 1982; Reese and Miller 1981). While this measure is outstanding in its simplicity, it does not allow for any differentiation of degree of dependency either within or across media.

This chapter proposes an alternative measure of an individual's relationship with the media based upon media system dependency (MSD) theory (Ball-Rokeach 1989, 1985; Ball-Rokeach and DeFleur 1976; Ball-Rokeach, Rokeach, and Grube 1984). The proposed measure was designed to go beyond simple exposure by capturing the "relationship" that individuals develop with a medium over time. This chapter begins by exploring the roots of MSD theory and the theoretical importance of the dependency relationship, followed by a discussion of empirical studies of the dependency relationship. Factors influencing the scale development are discussed next, and the scale is presented in the context of an ongoing research project. Finally, the chapter discusses applications, limitations, and instructions for using the scale.

Media System Dependency Theory

Media system dependency theory attempts to explain the media-relevant behavior of actors (individuals, organizations, or social systems) by examining the dependency relationships among actors within and across levels of analysis. The media system is defined by Ball-Rokeach (1989, 9) as " an information system in control of three types of 'dependency-engendering' information resources . . . that others have to have access to in order to attain their goals." Ball-Rokeach identifies these three types of resources as (1) information gathering or information creating, (2) information processing, and (3) information dissemination.

A goal of media system dependency theory is to provide a media system and effects theory that can be applied across levels of analysis. According to Ball-Rokeach (1989), media system dependency is an ecological theory, focusing on relationships between the parts within and between small, medium, and large systems. She explains that

society is an organism that can only be understood by knowing the relationships between its parts. . . . The media system is assumed to be an important part of the social fabric in modern societies and it is conceived to have relationships with individuals, groups, organizations and other social systems. (8)

The focus of media system dependency theory upon dependency relationships does not change across levels of analysis, but the goals and resources engendering dependency relationships vary by the unit of analysis. At the personal level, the theory is concerned with the types and patterns of dependency that individuals have with the media system in general and specific media in particular. The theory has even been applied to analyze specific dependency relations for specialized audiences of a genre of television programming, television shopping (Grant, Guthrie, and Ball-Rokeach 1991).

Ball-Rokeach, Rokeach, and Grube (1984) begin their discussion of the types of dependency relationships that individuals have with the media system by stating that there are three primary dimensions of human motivation that implicate media dependency relations: understanding, orientation, and play. They state that the three dimensions are " equally essential to individual welfare, that they are exhaustive, but also that they are not mutually exclusive since any media message may serve more than one type of dependency." They go on to explore two subdimensions for each of the three primary dimensions, making a personal-social conceptual distinction between the subdimensions. These distinctions yield six types of personal media system relations: action orientation, interaction orientation, self-understanding, social understanding, solitary play, and social play.

Within the orientation dimension, *action orientation* dependency is personal, referring to the use of the information resources of a medium to pursue or attain goals regarding personal behavioral decisions, for example, finding out what new products are available or getting information to help make a voting decision. *Interaction orientation* is social, referring to the reliance on the information resources of the medium to pursue or attain goals relating to how to act or interact with other individuals.

Self-understanding dependency is personal, referring to goals involving the use of the information resources of the medium to increase understanding of who we are as individuals and how we grow or change. *Social understanding* is social, referring to the attainment of goals regarding the building, maintaining, or changing of understanding of the larger social environment.

Similarly, *solitary play* refers to the personal use of the medium to attain individual goals of pleasure, enjoyment, relaxation, or escape, while *social play* refers to the use of the medium as part of a shared play experience, where the presence of others is necessary for the attainment of goals, for example, establishing and maintaining relationships.

Again, it must be stressed that these six dimensions of the personal media system dependency relation are not independent, but may occur in combination with each other. For example, individuals might watch a television news program to increase their knowledge of political events (social understanding) as well as to find out what the weather will be so they will know what type of clothing to wear (action orientation). Similarly, a person might watch a particular situation comedy as a way of relaxing (solitary play), but choose the specific program because he or she identifies with the characters (self-understanding).

The next important aspect of personal media dependency is the manner in which people approach the media in the process of pursuing personal goals. While the goal-related nature of personal dependency relationships seems to suggest that the audience is "active" in exposing itself to the media, Ball-Rokeach (1989) indicates that casual ("passive") viewing may activate a goal-seeking behavior. A casual viewer, defined as one who is incidentally exposed while engaged in another activity, may have a dependency activated during the incidental exposure and thus continue to view. (If no dependencies are activated, viewing is likely to end.) These casual viewers then have the potential to become as involved in the viewing as viewers who "actively" decide to expose themselves to television as a means of achieving a personal goal.

The key variable in determining the degree of involvement is not whether the initial exposure was "active" or "casual"; it is the degree of arousal, both cognitive (attention level) and affective (liking or disliking). Arousal is a function of the intensity of the relevant dependencies, so the dependencies activated are ultimately more important than how exposure originally took place (Ball-Rokeach 1989).

The nature and importance of dependency relationships was explored by Emerson (1962) in an article relating the power of an actor (individual, organization) to the dependence of other actors upon resources controlled by the first actor. Put simply, he stated that "power resides implicitly in the other's dependency" (32). He goes on to state that dependence of actor B upon actor A is proportional to the importance of the goals of B mediated by the resources controlled by A and inversely proportional to the availability of other sources to provide those resources.

The power-dependence relationship was applied and extended to the media system by Ball-Rokeach (1974) in a paper discussing media effects as the product of media-audience relations. This approach was a significant departure from the traditional approach of treating the media as a constant in the effects equation, instead conceptualizing the media system as an information system in control of scarce and prized information resources. The article suggested an "information perspective" from which "the effects of mass communicated information are determined primarily by systemic interdependency whereby audience information dependencies are successfully or unsuccessfully met by the media's use of its information resources" (15).

Ball-Rokeach (1974) limited her discussion to the dependency of the audience upon the media, addressing the role of the media in attitude formation, agenda setting, issue formation, belief structure change, value change, and ambiguity creation and resolution. These concepts were refined and elaborated further by Ball-Rokeach and DeFleur (1976) in an explication of a dependency model of mass media effects.

Ball-Rokeach and DeFleur (1976) centered their discussion on the dependency relationship of individual audience members with the media from a media effects perspective, but they also proposed a general conceptual model that included the dependency relationships among the societal system, the media system and the audience.

Dependency theory was developed further at the macro level by DeFleur and Ball-Rokeach (1988) in successive editions of a text summarizing theories of mass communications. Each edition made advances at integrating effects studies using a variety of approaches into a single theoretical perspective using dependency relationships among actors as the prime focus.

The most important work to date on dependency theory was published by Ball-Rokeach, Rokeach, and Grube (1984) in *The Great American Values Test: Influencing Behavior and Belief through Television* (hereafter cited as *GAVT*). In this work, media system dependency theory was more fully explicated and tested at the individual level. The *GAVT* experiment demonstrated that strong media effects—that is, long-term attitude, value, and behavior change—are possible using the television medium. In the field experiment, a half-hour television program designed to activate self-confrontation leading to increases in egalitarian and proenvironmental beliefs and behavior was created and broadcast simultaneously by all commercial television stations in an experimental city. The program was successful in achieving a significant change in values and attitudes among viewers and had a significant, long-term effect upon behavior.

The contributions of *GAVT* to media system dependency theory included a detailed operationalization at the individual level, creation of instrumentation for measuring individual-level media dependency, and a demonstration of the relationship between television dependency and program selection. Specifically, Ball-Rokeach, Rokeach, and Grube (1984) found that viewers with higher self-understanding and social understanding dependencies were more likely to tune in the program. In a successful attempt at controlling selective exposure, the program was heavily promoted with appeals to these dependencies.

What *The Great American Values Test* did for media system dependency theory at the personal level, Ball-Rokeach's (1985) article "The Origins of Individual Media-System Dependency: A Sociological Framework" did for the theory at the system level. Following an explication of the theory at the individual level, she explores the interdependencies between the media system and the economic and political systems and how those relationships are determinants of personal media dependencies.

The most complete discussion of media system dependency theory is found in Ball-Rokeach (1989). This chapter on media system dependency theory discusses and expands upon all the previous ideas regarding media system dependency at the individual and structural level. The chapter also relates the theory to a cross section of media effects studies and frames the theory in relation to a variety of sociological, psychological, and social-psychological perspectives (i.e., structural functional analysis, conflict theory, and symbolic interactionism).

Empirical Tests of MSD Theory

The number of empirical tests of media system dependency theory has increased in the past few years through the work of the Media System Dependency Research Group, headed by Sandra Ball-Rokeach at the University of Southern California. Grant, Guthrie, and Ball-Rokeach (1991) provide one of the most comprehensive tests of the theory at the individual level in a study of television shopping viewers. This project provides a "quantity" versus "quality" test of exposure measures versus dependency measures to predict the buying behavior of television shopping viewers. The results indicate that each is important: While the number of hours of television shopping programming viewed was the best predictor of the number of items purchased from the shopping service, dependency upon the television shopping genre was the central variable in the model of television shopping behavior. This dependency measure was directly related to television exposure, television shopping exposure, parasocial interaction with the hosts of the shopping programs, buying behavior, and demographics.

Grant (1989a), in examining the diversity of program types offered by cable television, also examined the diversity of dependency relationships implicated in the viewing of cable television. The results of this project suggest that the diversity of dependencies offered within channel types (broadcast networks, basic cable, pay cable, and superstations) increases as the number of channels within each channel type increases.

Other empirical studies have tested a corollary of media system dependency explicated by Ball-Rokeach (1974, 1985a) stating that, when faced with threatening or ambiguous situations, individuals' dependency upon the media for information will increase. For example, Hirschburg, Dillman, and Ball-Rokeach (1986) confirmed the corollary in a survey of individuals' information-seeking behavior immediately after the eruption of Mount St. Helens in 1980, finding that dependency relations with the media for information intensified for virtually all individuals, with few significant differences across social groups. Nigg (1982) observed a similar relationship between uncertainty and media use in a study of a community threatened by earthquakes.

These studies of media dependency during natural disasters are complimented by analyses of the relationship between media use and media dependency in the everyday life of audience members. In one such analysis, Loges (1994) found that, regardless of external variables, when perceived threat increases, dependency upon the mass media for information also increases.

Cohen, Adoni, and Drori (1983) provided further empirical evidence of media dependency, suggesting "that people depend upon the mass media for information about social phenomena that are remote from their everyday life experiences to a greater extent than they depend upon the media for phenomena accessible to direct experience" (206).

Power (1988) provided additional insight into the relationship between dependency and threat, using specific dimensions of individual-level media dependency to perceived threat. His study examined media behavior in relation to the AIDS epidemic, relating the social understanding, self-understanding, action orientation, and interaction orientation dimensions of personal media dependency to measures of arousal and self-attributed knowledge about the AIDS epidemic, controlling for personal experience with the disease. Overall mass media dependency was a strong predictor of arousal, which led to higher levels of self-attributed knowledge. However, when the overall measure of dependency was broken down into the four subdimensions listed earlier, only social understanding dependency directly affected arousal, with the other three dimensions having an indirect effect (through their relationship to social understanding dependency).

Aydin, Ball-Rokeach, and Reardon (1991) also measured separate personal dependencies upon the electronic media, the print media, and interpersonal communication in an analysis of the influences of each upon breast cancer patients' responses to their illnesses. Their analysis integrated aspects of social comparison theory with aspects of media system dependency theory.

Development of the MSD Scale

Most of the studies mentioned earlier involve the development of the scale reported herein. The first attempt to measure individual-level media dependency was an eleven-item scale used by Ball-Rokeach, Rokeach, and Grube (1984). Because the primary interest of the researchers was in the understanding dimensions, this scale used three items each to measure social understanding and self-understanding, with two items for interaction orientation, and one item each for solitary play, social play, and action orientation. The instrument asked each respondent "How often do you use television to:" for the eleven items, using a three-point response scale of "often," "sometimes," and "never."

Grant, Guthrie, and Ball-Rokeach (1991) refined the scale for their research by increasing the number of items for each dimension to two, yielding a total of twelve items, and changing the question to "In your daily life, how *helpful* is television to:", with a five-point response scale from "not at all helpful" to "extremely helpful." The next step in the evolution of the scale was made by Grant (1989b), who increased the number of items for each dimension from two to three, using items created by Ball-Rokeach, Rokeach, and Grube (1984), Grant, Guthrie, and Ball-Rokeach (1991), Power and Ball-Rokeach (1988), and Aydin, Ball-Rokeach, and Reardon (1991).

The lack of a standard measure of individual-level media dependency used in these studies resulted in a desire by the researchers to work together to create a standard measure of media dependency that could be applied across media. As reported by Ball-Rokeach, Grant, and Horvath (1995), this effort began with a series of focus groups in which respondents talked about how and why they used a variety of media, with attention to commercial content as well as editorial or program content. Based upon these focus groups, it was determined that the six conceptual dimensions of media dependency were indeed unique, and scale construction began. A series of scales were constructed and tested on a demographically diverse population to determine discriminability of items and dimensions across media, wording effects, and overall scale reliability (alpha).

The eighteen items used in the scale are listed in table 9.1, sorted by dimension. An example of the final, eighteen-item version of the scale is reproduced in figure 9.1. (In this example, the scale is measuring television dependency with specific instructions oriented for that medium.) Ball-Rokeach, Grant, and Horvath (1995) report the initial test of the scale, which involved more than a thousand respondents in San Bernardino, California, and Austin, Texas. In this test, the scale was used to measure dependency upon four media: newspapers, radio, magazines, and television. The reliability measures (Cronbach's alpha) were .93 for the newspaper scale, .93 for the radio scale, .92 for the magazine scale, and .93 for the television scale. Over-time reliability of the scale was tested by administering the scale to a subsample at two points, one year apart. The test-retest correlations (Pearson) were .90 for newspapers ($p < .001$), .69 for radio ($p < .005$), .75 for magazines ($p < .005$), and .90 for television ($p < .001$). (Aydin, Ball-Rokeach, Grant, and Horvath [1995]) also report reliability measures for each of the six dimensions, as well as confirmatory factor analyses for application of the scale to four media.)

Although the scale is designed to measure the six dimensions of individual-level media dependency, each of the six dimensions is strongly correlated with the others, allowing the six to be summed to yield a global

TABLE 9.1. Eighteen-Item Individual Media Dependency Scale

Action Orientation
    Decide where to go for services such as health, financial, or household.
    Figure out what to buy.
    Plan where to go for evening and weekend activities.
Interaction Orientation
    Discover better ways to communicate with others.
    Think about how to act with friends, relatives, or people you work with.
    Get ideas about how to approach others in important or difficult situations.
Self-Understanding
    Gain insight into why you do some of the things that you do.
    Imagine what you'll be like as you grow older.
    Observe how others cope with problems or situations like yours.
Social Understanding
    Stay on top of what is happening in the community.
    Find out how the country is doing.
    Keep up with world events.
Solitary Play
    Unwind after a hard day or week.
    Relax when you are by yourself.
    Have something to do when nobody else is around.
Social Play
    Give you something to do with your friends.
    Have fun with family or friends.
    Be a part of events you enjoy without having to be there.

measure of "media dependency." This variable is the measure we propose as an alternative to measures of exposure as a predictor of media effects.

At this point, it is important to differentiate the individual media dependency scale from similar scales created for use in studies of the uses and gratifications of media use. Although the individual items in the media dependency scale are similar to those used in uses and gratifications research, it is both conceptually and operationally distinct. From a conceptual perspective, these items are proposed as a theoretically derived set of goals that may be implicated in any relationship an individual develops with a medium. The same eighteen items are therefore proposed for use in any study of media dependency (varying the medium used as a referent in the question), thus allowing greater comparability of research findings across media. Perhaps more important for political research, the media dependency scale is specifically designed so that all of the items can be combined to create the overall measure of intensity of the dependency relationship discussed previously. The creation of this aggregate measure, proposed subsequently as an alternative to measures of exposure, offers a distinct operational difference from measures in the uses-and-gratifications tradition.

1. We would like you to consider the ways that you use television in your daily life. Consider the commercials as well as the shows you watch. For each of the ways listed, please indicate how much you rely upon television by circling the number that best represents how helpful television is to you.

In your daily life, how helpful is television to:	Not at all helpful				Extremely helpful
a. Stay on top of what is happening in the community?	1	2	3	4	5
b. Unwind after a hard day or week?	1	2	3	4	5
c. Gain insight into why you do some of the things you do?	1	2	3	4	5
d. Discover better ways to communicate with others?	1	2	3	4	5
e. Decide where to go for services such as health, financial, or household?	1	2	3	4	5
f. Relax when you are by yourself?	1	2	3	4	5
g. Find out how the country is doing?	1	2	3	4	5
h. Imagine what you'll be like as you grow older?	1	2	3	4	5
i. Give you something to do with your friends?	1	2	3	4	5
j. Figure out what to buy?	1	2	3	4	5
k. Think about how to act with friends, relatives, or people you work with?	1	2	3	4	5
l. Have fun with family and friends?	1	2	3	4	5
m. Observe how others cope with problems or situations like yours?	1	2	3	4	5
n. Keep up with world events?	1	2	3	4	5
o. Be a part of events that you enjoy without having to be there?	1	2	3	4	5
p. Get ideas about how to approach others in important or difficult situations?	1	2	3	4	5
q. Plan where to go for evening and weekend activities?	1	2	3	4	5
r. Have something to do when nobody else is around?	1	2	3	4	5

Fig. 9.1. Television dependency scale

Application of the Scale

The individual media dependency scale was designed to serve as an alternative measure of media use to traditional measures of exposure. The scale was designed to capture multiple dimensions of a person's relationship with the medium, while allowing application across a variety of media. The use of this standard scale as a predictor of media effects offers the same comparability across studies as the use of exposure measures. While the scale is not as simple as exposure measures, the scale also helps capture many more dimensions of the relationship individuals have with the media.

Because media dependency is a primary predictor of exposure, a significant, positive relationship is expected between the two variables. Previous research on television dependency reported positive correlations ranging from .22 to .35 between the television dependency and the television exposure. In the pilot test of the measure reported herein, exposure and individual-level dependency were correlated at .34 for newspaper, .31 for magazines, .36 for radio, and .30 for television. However, the relatively small variance explained by these correlations indicates that the dependency measure is capturing a significantly different relationship with the medium than mere exposure.

There are two distinct ways in which the scale can be applied to the study of political communication. First, the scale can be used either along with or as a substitute for measures of exposure as a predictor of media effects. Alternatively, the scale can be used in a causal model as a predictor of exposure.

One important variant of the scale is the referent used. While the pilot study solicited responses for four media (newspaper, radio, magazines, and television), the typical referent for the scale has been television. Reasons for this choice include the ubiquity of the medium and the strong interest in its effects. Other possible referents include "the media" (in general) or specific types of content within a medium (television shopping programs, newspaper feature articles, radio news broadcasts, and so on).

The limitations of the scale must also be addressed in relation to its use. The most obvious limitation is the length of the scale—it is much longer and more complicated than simple measures of exposure or dependency and may not be appropriate unless the dependency relationship is an important part of the inquiry. Because the scale measures a relationship that is comparatively stable over time, it may not be sensitive to specific experimental or quasi-experimental treatments. The scale also subsumes the content of the media, putting the focus on the long-term relationship individuals have with a medium.

The individual media dependency scale has a number of potential advantages over other measures of dependency. As a standard instrument, it will allow greater comparison of results across studies. As a multidimensional instrument, it captures a broader extent of the relationship individuals have with the media than an instrument measuring only one dimension. Finally, tests of the instrument indicate consistency of responses, both within the instrument and across the scale over time.

In applying the scale, some consideration should also be given to the theory underlying the scale. One of the basic principles of media system dependency theory is that, in order to understand the role of media in society, dependency relationships must be examined across levels of analysis as well as within (Ball-Rokeach 1989). Thus, an exploration that includes a measure of an individual's relationship with a medium or media should also address the organizational and societal dependency relationships that both impact and are impacted by the individual-level relationship.

CHAPTER 10

Whither Research on the Psychology of Political Communication?

Doris A. Graber

In the concluding chapter of the book, Doris Graber looks to the future direc-tions that research on the psychology of political communication may take. Drawing on hundreds of contemporary publications as well as the history of the subdiscipline, four directions are presented: the construction of political images, information processing and the formation of impressions, processing messages in decision making, and psychological manipulation. The article places constructionism in a broad context by showing its relevance to different psychological approaches to political communication. After discussing recent developments in research methods and targets, Graber points to areas in need of further investigation. She argues that the scholarly community should ac-tively determine and pursue research priorities rather than drift into projects based on the "whims of researchers and funding agencies."

The psychological processes that trigger political thinking and action have been a perennial focus of analysis. Practitioners of the art of politics have been keenly interested in the subject because political actions are based on the beliefs that political leaders and followers hold about the political world. Moreover, in the body politic, as Karl Deutsch has pointed out, communication constitutes the "nerves" of government.

That is why political elites throughout recorded history have tried to control political communication. They have attempted to foster the construc-tion of favorable images in the minds of potential supporters through the symbolism of majestic architectural creations and elaborate public ceremonies. They have sought to mold human minds through propaganda and terror in internal struggles and external wars. They have used public relations tactics and political advertising as gentler forms of political persuasion. They have attempted to shape the flow of political communication through official secrecy and through controls over mass media. Controls have ranged from government ownership and operation to various degrees of explicit censorship of news media or censorship through informal social pressures.

Practitioners of the art of government and politics have not been the only ones interested in creation and manipulation of political information environments. Scholars from early times on have studied the process. Confucius (551–479 B.C.) and Aristotle (384–322 B.C.) taught about the psychological aspects of politics. Nicolò Machiavelli argued in *The Prince* (1513) that rulers must study human nature so that they can successfully manipulate their subjects' thoughts and emotions. He provided detailed suggestions about the manner in which princes might do so.

The quest for knowledge about the psychology of political communication has continued unabated. Where is it currently, and what pressing societal needs should guide the research agenda for the immediate future? This chapter attempts to provide some answers to these questions. To keep these answers manageable, only selected publications will be cited as illustrations of various research trends. The bibliography ranges more widely. But, though it presents over two hundred sources, it merely scratches the surface of published studies. That, in itself, is testimony to the vigor of the current research enterprise that spans several disciplines and includes many scholars who do not ordinarily consider themselves psychologically oriented political communication researchers.

Contemporary research on psychological aspects of political communication has followed four major directions. In line with this fourfold pattern, the construction and impact of political images will be examined first. Two aspects of information processing are discussed second and third. One deals with the transformation of information into perceptions, attitudes, and opinions. The other examines the uses of information for making political decisions, including voting decisions. Psychological manipulation is the fourth area of discussion. It includes political socialization and resocialization of children and adults, as well as political advertising and other propaganda and psychological strategies. A brief fifth section of the chapter deals with research methods and targets. It is followed by concluding remarks that point to basic weaknesses in current research patterns and suggest new directions.

Images: Their Construction and Impact

The study of images created by political messages, long a focus for political psychology research, continues to attract scholars. It encompasses the process of image construction, which may be intentional or unintended. When this aspect of political communication research focuses on the verbal output of politicians, it is often referred to as political linguistics or rhetoric. It is one of the earliest research areas in the psychological study of political communication, tracing back to Aristotle's *Rhetoric* (322 B.C.) and Machiavelli's *The Prince* (1513). In addition to providing practical advice for practitioners of the art of political talk, the study of political rhetoric and linguistics has several other payoffs. It sheds light on the nature of images employed in political messages and on the reactions that these images produce in elite and mass audiences (Heritage and Greatbatch 1986, Francesconi 1986, di Mare 1987). It also reveals the values and mores embedded in the social context in which the message is disseminated (Bennett and Edelman 1985, Hart et al. 1994). It can be used to provide data from which psychologically oriented social scientists can infer the psychological characteristics and motivations of political leaders (DeMause 1986, Levy 1986, Winter and Carlson 1988, Tetlock 1993).

Stable as well as changing images have been scrutinized. For example, in the 1990s, a number of scholars examined the changing images of the nations of Eastern Europe and Soviet Asia. That included the images of these nations as a whole as well as the images of their political leaders as depicted in local and foreign media and perceived by local and foreign audiences. Changing images of the American domestic scene have also been under scrutiny. Several chapters in this book provide examples of image studies. They explore the creation of media images of elected officials, images of public policies, and the reactions of American audiences to various types of images.

The *structure* of political images disseminated throughout American society has remained a neglected research area. There have been few systematic attempts to discern what features are depicted about foreign countries, about political leaders, or about public policies, and what features are omitted. For example, are the qualities stressed for various political leaders based on a Freudian perception of personality or on some other psychological model? How useful is this model in terms of the images that consumers of this information must formulate as a basis for electoral decisions? For instance, should the images of political candidates presented in the media during election campaigns include information about the candidate's childhood traumas? Is such information relevant to job performance? Do data about marital fidelity or use of illicit drugs during adolescence give clues to prospective ethical behavior and performance? What information might provide hints about the candidate's ability to perform well under conditions of stress? To what extent should information about the candidate be accompanied by scenarios of the conditions likely to shape the political and psychological context prevailing during the prospective term of office? Answers to such questions could lead to more politically relevant journalism and political decisions based on sounder data.

Images diffused through mass media have been of particular concern to researchers. In the 1950s, a group of scholars, including Harold Lasswell, Daniel Lerner, and Ithiel de Sola Pool, studied political images in editorials in leading newspapers in major countries as indicators of future revolutions or other major political upheavals (Lasswell, Lerner, and Pool 1952). These scholars recommended routine monitoring of image changes in newspapers because they might serve as warning signs of changing elite perceptions. The studies said little about whether image changes presented by the media merely reflected developing conditions or whether they also stimulated politically explosive behavior. They thus left open the still unanswered question about the scope of the media's impact on political happenings.

The extent to which images disseminated through the mass media have an impact on political events remains an area of much conjecture and little proof (Iyengar 1992, Combs and Nimmo 1993). For example, was the apparent domino effect of the collapse of Eastern Europe's communist governments in the 1990s a natural consequence of internal problems, or did the particular framing of mass media messages play a significant part in the development of these events, as some scholars have argued? (Gerbner 1993). More generally, to what extent, if any, do political elites attempt to construct media images deliberately to influence national and international politics? Are there master manipulators of the image scene? If the answer is yes, who are they?

While much image research has focused on major political entities such as nations, political parties, or political leaders, there are important exceptions. They include research on images of politically disadvantaged groups, like racial and ethnic minorities, the handicapped, women, the elderly, or perpetrators and victims of crime (Cohen and Young 1973, van Dijk 1988 a, b, Downing 1990, Kahn 1994). How these groups are perceived and depicted appears to have major psychological and political consequences for the perceivers and the perceived, including their respective self-images. The study of the mass media images of such groups constitutes the sort of policy-relevant research that deserves increasing attention because it may reveal serious social problems for which solutions are possible.

It would be useful to know, for example, whether American mass media foster racial and ethnic conflict through their choice of symbols and framing in telling stories that involve people of diverse races and ethnic groups (Landsman 1985, Merelman 1992). Would alternative framing help? Is it useful, for instance, to omit racial identifications from crime stories and to show members of disadvantaged groups in prominent positions? Answers to such questions may permit researchers to recommend appropriate political labels and appropriate symbolism to create the kind of society that most Americans claim to want. Currently, we know all too little about the psychological and political consequences of the many haphazard attempts at social engineering that are in vogue in American society.

For instance, is there a scientific basis for the demand that national anthems ought to be restructured to glorify peace, rather than war? Do children's toys and competitive sports inspire aggression because of the subtle messages they convey about the excitement of fighting battles, or do they help to sublimate aggressive urges? Do the images of violence and socially undesirable behaviors presented on television encourage imitation, counteracting the values that American political culture claims to foster? Are political elites using subtle psychological symbolism to keep the sense of outrage of mass publics dulled so that they can be governed more readily for the benefit of these elites, as various liberal and left-wing scholars have long contended (Edelman 1964, 1993; Parenti 1993)? Do commercial and political advertising produce major social and political distortions that harm society?

Such public policy issues have been widely debated, but most of them have received little recent attention from psychologically oriented political communication scholars. While the number of such unresolved and often neglected issues is daunting, this should not prevent research that at least addresses some aspects of these questions and their public policy implications. The body of work produced by a diverse array of individual scholars may then provide a solid scientific basis for public policy-making (Spitzer 1993).

When one proposes research that may facilitate deliberate efforts to use labels and symbols to influence the political process, the specter of fostering misleading propaganda, mind manipulation, and even brainwashing raises its ugly head. Where is the boundary line between ordinary image construction that is an essential part of all human communication, including political discourse, and propaganda and other forms of deliberate persuasion? These issues and their ethical implications need continued exploration, along with research that determines the degree of efficacy of psychological techniques.

Most image research has been done through more-or-less conventional content analysis that deals with denotation of words, phrases, and themes, rather than with connotations constructed by various audiences. Connotation research has been avoided because the construction of meaning is deemed idiosyncratic and therefore difficult to assess for different individuals and groups. Notwithstanding this difficulty, the problem of ascertaining connotational meanings cannot be skirted if scholars want to know what meanings are actually conveyed (Cohen 1989). To tackle the problem of connotational meanings, more research is needed on the factors responsible for connotational variability, including the diverse contexts in which images are received and interpreted.

Cross-cultural research, such as Tamar Liebes's (1986) analysis of the perception of the American television soap opera *Dallas* by people of vastly different cultures points the way. It shows how the same texts, offered in different cultural contexts, give rise to substantially different constructions. The fact that all texts are polysemic, conveying multiple meanings, does not mean that senders cannot transmit desired meanings. It merely means that they must know how their audiences are likely to interpret messages and tailor their messages accordingly (Dennis, Gerbner, and Zassoursky 1991). Of course, when unintended audiences receive the message, unintended images may flourish.

Processing Messages: Impression Formation

Another thriving subdisciplinary area in political psychology that promises major advances in understanding human behavior is information processing. Scholars are trying to fathom how people actually process complex political information to derive perceptions of the reality that constitutes their world and how they construct attitudes, opinions, and feelings based on these perceptions. Current information processing studies, such as the studies in the second section of this book, are a logical sequel to earlier works on learning pioneered by scholars such as N. E. Miller and J. Dollard (1941) and Clark Hull (1952).

While little progress has been made in measuring information processing directly, various experiments as well as computer simulations are shedding light on how the human brain functions. Work by Milton Lodge and G. R. Boynton is an example of some of the novel approaches made possible by new research tools. Lodge tested political decision making in the laboratory with human subjects, while Boynton simulated the identical situation through a computer program. A comparison of computer decisions with human decisions was designed to assess the extent to which human and machine thinking processes produced similar results and used similar step-wise progressions.

Research done thus far suggests that processing varies depending on the type of information that needs to be digested and on a multitude of factors related to the characteristics of the audience and the context in which exposure to information occurs. Examples of influential factors are cultural variables, context variables, and personality variables, as well as the processors' political memories, political sophistication, and interest in politics (Lodge and Stroh 1993, Ottati and Wyer 1993, Wyer and Ottati 1993). Because multiple, interacting audience variables must be considered, a great deal of research will be needed to explore information processing under various conditions. Given the fundamental importance of knowing precisely how people construct complex political images to give meanings to their political worlds, such research should receive high priority.

A number of recent information processing studies have focused on learning variations springing from differences in the media through which information is transmitted. Research by Robinson and Levy (1986b) and Neuman, Just, and Crigler (1992) are examples. Other studies seek to dissect the learning process when a single medium contains a combination of stimuli that may reinforce each other or that may lack coordination (Tiemens et al. 1988). Television, for example, combines visual images with various sounds, including spoken messages, and often some written messages as well. Studies that try to determine the interaction effects of such complex stimuli are still in their infancy. Much more needs to be done, therefore. Discovering how and what people learn from visual information is especially important in an age when exposure to visual media constitutes the most common form of contact with political information (Rosenberg et al. 1986, Keeter 1987, Graber 1993).

The role played by political communication in shaping public opinion remains a continuing interest, as shown by W. Lance Bennett and John D. Klockner's chapter in this volume. Scholars are still seeking answers to basic questions about the triggering mechanisms that arouse public attention to particular issues, produce stereotyped images, and lead to mass opinion trends (Iyengar and Kinder 1987; Page, Shapiro, and Dempsey 1987; Zaller 1987, 1992). Recently, attention has turned to public opinion polling as an opinion-shaping force, not only as a device to measure public opinion. Researchers now realize that the focus of poll questions and the way in which they are asked can shape the thinking of respondents. It may produce ill-considered answers about issues that they have not previously contemplated in any serious way, and it can shape their thinking by focusing on particular perspectives and facets of the issue in question (Ratzan 1989, Herbst 1993). When polls are publicized, the same opinion-shaping forces that affect the answers given by poll respondents ripple out to the public, possibly with enhanced force when certain views seem to be widely shared and therefore legitimized. This is the reverse side of the spiral-of-silence phenomenon that Elisabeth Noelle-Neuman (1984) has documented. Her research shows that people keep silent when they think that their views are unpopular. Silence, if widespread, then condemns these views to neglect and even scorn.

Recent studies have also been concerned with priming effects of information, with the role of memory in forming mental images of current situations, and with attention-catching devices. Priming studies have examined how concepts to which a respondent has been alerted through news stories influence processing of subsequently received information. The effects appear to be substantial (Iyengar and Kinder 1987, Iyengar 1992). In memory studies, the emphasis has been on the changing perceptions of collective experiences, such as wars and public leaders or the reputations of journalists, and on the differences in the political schemata that people are likely to hold about similar happenings stored in short-term and long-term memory (Lang and Lang 1993, Kosicki and McLeod 1990).

Researchers interested in attention-catching devices have investigated variations in attention arousal and subsequent processing of information when message content stirs emotions, elicits empathy, or presents conflict and violence. The impact of cues that may steer people away from rationally based choices has aroused concern. This is especially true when such cues form part of election rhetoric, when they occur during various phases of international bargaining and conflict, and during incidents of terrorism (Morello 1988, Rapport and Alexander 1989, Wieviorka 1993). However, they are also of concern when information is transmitted during various types of more ordinary political negotiations.

Processing Messages: Decision Making

Political leaders affect their nations and the world through the decisions that they make. These decisions are shaped by the organizational structures that regulate the flow of information that enters the decision-making process and by the stored information that underlies the leader's perceptions and attitudes (Tetlock 1983, Barner-Barry and Rosenwein 1985, Jervis 1993). Important studies of small-group communication during decision making shed light on psychological pressures that affect information processing and image construction in these contexts, especially during crises (Simon 1956, Janis and Mann 1977, George 1980, Etheredge 1985). Irving Janis (1983), for example, showed how U.S. policymakers bungled policies designed to overthrow Cuba's communist government because group-generated psychological pressures produced faulty images that supported flawed policy suggestions. Little new work has been done in this politically crucial area in recent years, although several authors have continued to refine their ideas (Janis 1989, Park 1990, Gastil 1993).

William Riker, in an essay written for *Political Science: The State of the Discipline, 1983,* recommended that political scientists should focus more on what he called "heresthetics"—the manipulation of the structure of preferences and alternatives within which decisions are made. More attention should be paid to strategies designed to construct situations that will create suitable environments for sound political negotiations and bargaining. This is not the same as political rhetoric, which seeks to persuade through its own force. Rather, it involves strategic maneuvers designed to alter the decision-making context in ways that strengthen one contender and weaken the opposition (Manheim 1994b). Studies that deal with the psychological considerations that underlie deterrence policies belong to this genre. Creating an impression of invincibility or impending doom for the opponent can lead to major political victories (Jervis, Lebow, and Stein 1985).

Judging from the vast share of research resources devoted to the field, one might expect that a firm body of knowledge about voting decision determinants had been established. Not so. While much has been learned, major debates continue about fundamental issues. The scope of information on which average voters base their voting decisions in presidential elections is one example (Popkin 1991, Ferejohn and Kuklinski 1992). Some scholars contend that

American voters are using a widening knowledge base for voting decisions (Nie and Verba 1976, Keeter and Zukin 1983). Others claim that voters cast uninformed votes and have not reached higher levels of political sophistication as argued by Nie and Verba (Smith 1989). Similarly, more general research on the nature of belief systems and political sophistication has been challenged by experimental works such as Shawn Rosenberg's *Reason, Ideology and Politics* (1988). With so much dust raised in a seemingly settled area, research must continue to resolve the various controversies. The use of a variety of previously slighted research methods, such as experimental work, Q-methodology, depth interviews, and focus groups may shed light where more traditional survey research methods have failed.

Psychologically grounded voting behavior research has suffered from its ties to democratic theories. These theories have posited visions of ideal voters that are totally out of sync with current psychological knowledge. Classical democratic theories postulate that individuals strive to base political decisions on a complex, altruism-driven, cognitive calculus grounded in extensive knowledge of a large and diverse array of public policy issues. Research then seeks to discover how closely actual behaviors match the ideal. The firm belief in the basic correctness of these assumptions has discouraged efforts to construct and test alternative models of making voting decisions in various types of elections. In fact, the assumptions about the nature of voting are so pervasive that survey respondents generally frame their answers about voting processes in terms of the expectations created by democratic theory, rather than examining their actual voting behaviors. The need for more open, explorative research, unshackled from unrealistic assumptions, is pressing. The payoff may be new paradigms that provide far more accurate explanations than those currently available.

Some new foci for election research seem to be emerging already. The fact that presidential votes in the television age rest heavily on perceptions of the personal images of candidates, rather than primarily on their issue positions, is receiving much-belated recognition (Miller, Wattenberg, and Malanchuk 1986). The disdain previously accorded to voting criteria that lacked a focus on issues is fading. Social scientists have also become much more interested in the feelings, such as love and hate, anxiety and fear, or altruism and selfishness, that may affect voting decisions (Mansbridge 1990). However, studies of the role of affect in political attitudes and the interplay of affect and cognition are still in their infancy (Granberg and Brown 1989, Conover and Feldman 1986a, Lanzetta et al. 1985, Marcus and MacKuen 1993).

In many recent elections, turnout has been the most crucial factor in the election outcome. A fresh look at the motivations that lead to election turnout is urgently needed. Earlier studies examined the relation of turnout to a number of psychological predispositions, such as a sense of efficacy (Campbell et al.

1960). What has been missing is a serious examination of the role played by news stories and advertisements in depressing turnout to historically low levels. Only a few scholars have pursued this line of inquiry (Teixeira 1992).

Closer connections between studies of voting decisions and more general studies of decision making also would undoubtedly be beneficial. Most of the latter have focused on decision making by political elites (George 1980, Janis 1983). They have been far richer than the voting decision studies in terms of assessing the psychological factors that impinge on decision making. Jonathan Roberts (1988), for example, in his study of decision making during international crises, examined the personalities of decision makers, their feelings and subjective perceptions, their levels of fatigue and stress, their mental and physical health, and their use of drugs and other mind-altering stimuli that might impinge on decision making. All these factors play a part in voting decisions and deserve examination in that important context.

Psychological Manipulations

Psychological manipulations of people's political beliefs and actions occur in many guises. Among these is political socialization. It involves communicating societal traditions, values, and beliefs to people at various stages of the life cycle so that they can function appropriately as citizens of a given society. Political socialization research has many facets, ranging from scrutiny of the contents of textbooks and mass media content to studying the work of public information and propaganda ministries in developing and developed societies (Pye 1963, Fagen 1966, Davies 1977, Dawson, Prewitt, and Dawson 1977).

In the closing decade of the twentieth century, scholars deemed it important to analyze the casual and formal political resocialization going on in countries switching from Marxist ideologies to various forms of Western-style democracy. Apparently, the concerted efforts made throughout much of the century to indoctrinate people into Marxist ideologies had met with questionable success (Bahry and Silver 1990). Did the psychological characteristics of the audience and the appropriateness of the stimuli play an important role in this failure? Could the campaigns leading toward democratization and economic development do any better? What psychological stimuli evoke resocialization? Do the principles guiding political socialization during periods of political calm apply under crisis conditions? In the 1930s, Harold Lasswell examined psychological adaptations to major political upheavals in *World Politics and Personal Insecurity* (1935a). But too few political psychologists have followed in his footsteps (Conover 1991).

Some promising work done in the 1960s to try to head off international conflict and produce peace also deserves sequels. For example, Charles Osgood, in *An Alternative to War or Surrender* (1962) suggested his GRIT plan designed to reduce international tensions through "Graduated Reciprocation in Tension Reduction." Since tensions are endemic in international affairs, the need for tension reduction is always present, even when no major wars loom, hence studies should continue to focus on prevalent psychological stimuli that may produce national and international violence and on ways to develop psychological defenses. They should not be discouraged by the fact that earlier studies of potentially damaging stimuli, such as violent entertainment shows, failed to lead to a more peaceful world. Yesterday's failures, given new contexts and tools, may become tomorrow's successes. Behavior modification is possible.

A number of scholars have focused their research on public information campaigns, mostly about important public health issues. Typically, such campaigns try to persuade the public to adopt behaviors that will lessen risks. Behavioral changes range from simple steps recommended in no-littering and Smokey the Bear fire prevention campaigns to very difficult behavior modifications required in antismoking or AIDS prevention campaigns. Psychological challenges range from devising messages that will arouse the attention of target audiences to behavior reinforcement after the suggested behavior has been adopted (Rice and Atkins 1989). Given the importance of such campaigns to public welfare, increased research attention should be encouraged so that the factors that translate into successful campaigns can be more fully understood.

Another area worth exploring concerns the training of various population groups to overcome resistance to learning new technologies. For example, a study by the Office of Technology Assessment, a congressional research agency, points to the danger of growing knowledge gaps between those able to access new technologies and those who cannot. Those most in need of new technologies—educationally disadvantaged and isolated individuals—are least likely to possess the needed motivations and skills to master the new communication technologies. Political communication researchers should give attention to developing new approaches to reach and teach these population groups and socialize them so that they can benefit from the new political information environment.

In the decades surrounding World Wars I and II, a great deal of attention was paid to propaganda, psychological warfare, and other types of persuasive communication (Wasburn 1992). There has been a lull in that kind of academic research. However, in the wake of the many controversies about political advertising, interest appears to be rising. Advertisers and scholars want to know what features attract attention to their messages and convey their intended meanings (Kern 1989, Nesbit 1988, West 1993). They try to fathom how much information can be conveyed through extremely brief messages (Just, Crigler, and Wallach 1990). Questions regarding political advertising impact have also come to the fore. Do advertisements constitute priming that shapes the political climate and guides the thinking and feeling that goes into decision making by the audience? The main concern underlying questions about impact is the dread of manipulation. Obviously, the fears articulated in George Orwell's *1984* still haunt Americans. If psychology can tell us how people form perceptions, can clever manipulators control public opinion? The knowledge that people are active, rather than passive, message receivers who construct their own meanings from messages and that there are ways to immunize publics against unwitting acceptance of persuasive messages may give some comfort (Pfau and Burgoon 1988).

An important side issue springing from the negative reactions of American audiences to persuasion attempts relates to trust and credibility in media and in the political system. Suspicion of manipulation destroys trust. In turn, audiences who lose trust in the media or the political system or both often opt out of the duties of citizenship. They become alienated and cynical and refuse to participate (Anderson 1989). Evidence of such alienation abounds among the American public. It is a serious malady in a democratic society. Ways must be found to alleviate the political conditions that caused it and to restore confidence and trust.

Research Methods and Targets

Is there anything new for political communication researchers on the methodological horizon? The answer seems to be that the basic research approaches used for the study of the psychology of political communication in recent decades have remained intact but that they are constantly being refined. For example, focus group interviews have joined surveys and one-on-one in-depth interviews when it comes to studying the effects of political messages. Electronic monitoring devices and computer simulations help in understanding brain functions. Human coders of political messages have been replaced, for some tasks, by machines. There is more multimethod research, some of it borrowing research approaches from disciplines that are not normally associated with political communication, such as anthropology. Previously loosely defined concepts, such as the meaning of "tolerance," are undergoing clarification (Wagner 1986). However, methodological leaps, giant or otherwise, have remained in the realm of wishful thinking.

Major methodological weaknesses in qualitative and quantitative research remain unresolved. For example, the well-known problems of survey research threaten the validity of many quantitative studies using large population samples. Question wording remains troublesome, and it is difficult to control the external and internal contexts of the interview so that they do not affect answers unduly. Differences in conceptualization between researchers and their subjects also are likely to impair the validity of answers. Better ways to ascertain meanings that respondents construct for questions and answers are urgently needed. But none seem currently in the offing. We also know that respondents' recall is often faulty (Markus 1986, Powell 1989). Despite more careful pretesting, more open-ended questions, and better interviewer training, we still have not overcome such major problems. Therefore, the information gleaned from surveys—as well as from other methodologies—remains seriously compromised.

In the realm of targeting, there has been a broadening of the communications scrutinized as potentially relevant for politics. The range of social problems viewed from a communications perspective has broadened. Increasingly, problems have been examined at various levels, ranging from the individual to the group to large political units viewed singly or comparatively. Researchers have also liberalized their definition of political messages. It now extends to politically relevant messages conveyed through entertainment media. Research scrutiny has been extended beyond a narrow focus on incitement of deviant behavior that copies the behavior of fictional characters to the behavior-shaping effects of a wide array of social, economic, and political issues raised by entertainment fare.

The current expansion of the research arena parallels earlier developments. For example, research into civic education in schools, as a form of political socialization, has been broadened from looking at the curriculum to include examination of internal governing mechanisms in schools. Researchers reasoned that authoritarian practices of governance in teacher-pupil relations, for example, could well counteract academic teaching about the value of democratic governance. Other research areas are likely to benefit in the future from broader perspectives. In reviewing existing research and mapping out research needs, the connectedness of the various areas is striking. The research foci form an almost seamless web. Political image research, for example, shades into research on election decision making and into research on persuasive communication.

New Visions

Though research has been burgeoning, the same basic questions continue to be asked. The slow and haphazard development of new research perspectives is best explained by drift approaches that are common in the social sciences. Research priorities are determined through the whims of researchers and funding agencies. Drift approaches may be contrasted with cybernetic approaches of disciplinary development in which the research community or groups within that community determine where their discipline ought to be going to reach well-defined goals.

The cybernetic approach, in my opinion, is preferable to the drift approach. The goal ought to be the production of policy-oriented research that facilitates the solution of societal problems. This is in the tradition of psychologists such as B. F. Skinner (1938, 1948) and political scientists such as Harold Lasswell (1951) and Robert Dahl and Charles Lindblom (1953), who proclaimed that human problems can be solved through social science. As Lasswell put it, the emphasis should be "upon the fundamental problems of man in society" (1951, 8). Likewise, Heinz Eulau (1963) stressed the human focus by noting that "The Root is Man . . . The Goal is Man." To motivate people to behave in ways that produce more satisfactory public policies, it is essential to know more about the wellsprings of human behavior. This does not mean that social scientists who are interested in political psychology should become social engineers bent on curing society's ills. Rather, it means that they should provide the information on which social engineering can be based (George 1994).

A switch to a cybernetic approach to the development of political communication research requires extensive discussions among researchers about the directions that the field ought to take. Steering always involves tough choices by the person or group or forces doing the steering. It always engenders controversy. My preferred guiding principle for these choices is the relevance of the research to the amelioration of major contemporary social problems. Among these, I would emphasize conflict among racial and ethnic groups that is likely to lead to domestic violence, to the breakup of nations, and to international wars.

To conduct such research successfully requires team efforts because the many facets of major research questions cannot be handled effectively by single researchers or tiny research groups. There is precedent for such collaboration in the physical sciences. Physical scientists have identified major ventures, such as eradication of particular diseases or exploration of outer space. They have then organized large teams of researchers who have focused on various aspects of these problems. Social scientists, eager for answers to major problems, such as understanding human information processing or controlling the psychological factors that encourage violence, could and should do the same. If there is sufficient will to do this, ways and means will be found.

References

Adams, William C., ed. 1981. *Television Coverage of the Middle East.* Norwood, N.J.: Ablex.

————. 1982. *Television Coverage of International Affairs.* Norwood, N.J.: Ablex.

Adams, William C. et al. 1986. Before and after the day after: The unexpected results of a televised drama. *Political Communication and Persuasion* 3:191–213.

Adatto, Kiku. 1990. Sound-bite democracy. Research paper, Joan Shorenstein Barone Center on the Press, Politics and Public Policy, Kennedy School of Government, Harvard University.

Alger, Dean E. 1995. *The Media and Politics.* Belmont, Calif.: Wadsworth.

————. 1991. Schizophrenia: The media and the incumbent reelection issue. *PS: Political Science and Politics* (June).

Allen, Richard L., Michael C. Dawson, and Ronald E. Brown. 1989. A schema-based approach to modelling an African-American racial belief system. *American Political Science Review* 83:421–41.

Althaus, Scott, Jill Edy, Robert M. Entman, and Patricia Phelan. 1994. Revising the indexing hypothesis: Officials, media, and the Libya crisis. Paper presented at the annual meeting of the American Political Science Association, New York.

Alwitt, L., and A. Mitchell. 1985. *Psychological Processes and Advertising Effects: Theory, Research, and Applications.* Hillsdale, N.J.: Erlbaum.

Anderson, Kenneth E. 1989. The politics of ethics and the ethics of politics. *American Behavioral Scientist* 32:479–92.

Anderson, Mark (Wellstone campaign director of communications). 1991. Interview by Dean Alger. Tape recording, July 29.

Andsager, Julie. 1994. Priming thought about expressive rights: The effects of general and specific messages. Paper presented at the annual meeting of the Association for Education in Journalism and Mass Communication, Atlanta.

Aristotle. [322 B.C.] 1952. *Rhetoric.* In *Great Books of the Western World,* edited by Robert M. Hutchins. Vol. 9. Chicago: Encyclopædia Britannica.

Armstrong, Scott. 1990. Iran-Contra: Was the press any match for all the president's men? *Columbia Journalism Review* (May/June): 27–35.

Arterton, F. Christopher. 1981. *Teledemocracy: Can Technology Protect Democracy?* Beverly Hills, Calif.: Sage.

————. 1984. *Media Politics: The News Strategies of Presidential Campaigns.* Lexington, Mass.: Lexington Books.

Atkin, Charles. 1980. Political campaigns: Mass communication and persuasion. In

Persuasion: New Directions in Theory and Research, edited by Michael E. Roloff and Gerald R. Miller. Beverly Hills, Calif.: Sage.

Atwood, L. Erwin. 1994. Illusions of media power: The third-person effect. *Journalism Quarterly* 71:269–81.

Axelrod, Robert. 1976. *Structure of Decision: The Cognitive Maps of Political Elites.* Princeton: Princeton University Press.

Aydin, C., S. J. Ball-Rokeach, and K. Reardon. 1991. Mass media resources for social comparison among breast cancer patients. Paper presented at the annual meeting of the International Communication Association, Chicago.

Bagdikian, Ben. 1992. *The Media Monopoly.* 4th ed. Boston: Beacon Press.

Bahry, Donna and Brian D. Silver. 1990. Soviet citizen participation on the eve of democratization. *American Political Science Review* 84:821–47.

Ball-Rokeach, S. J. 1974. The information perspective. Paper presented at the annual meeting of the American Sociological Association, Montreal.

———. 1985. The origins of individual media-system dependency—a sociological framework. *Communication Research* 12 (4):485–510.

———. 1989. Media system dependency theory. In *Theories of Mass Communication,* 5th ed, edited by M. L. DeFleur and S. J. Ball-Rokeach. New York: Longman.

Ball-Rokeach, S. J., and M. L. DeFleur. 1976. A dependency model of mass media effects. *Communication Research* 3:3–21.

Ball-Rokeach, S. J., A. E. Grant, and A. Horvath. 1995. A scale for measuring media dependency. Annenberg School of Communications, Los Angeles. Typescript.

Ball-Rokeach, S. J., M. Rokeach, and J. W. Grube. 1984. *The Great American Values Test: Influencing Behavior and Belief through Television.* New York: Free Press.

Ball-Rokeach, Sandra J. 1985. The origins of individual media system dependency: A sociological framework. *Communication Research* 12:485–510.

Bandura, Albert, and Richard Walters. 1963. *Social Learning and Personality Development.* New York: Holt, Rinehart and Winston.

Bantz, C. R. 1979. The critic and the computer: A multiple technique analysis of the *ABC Evening News. Communication Monographs* 46:27–39.

Barber, Benjamin. 1984. *Strong Democracy.* Berkeley: University of California Press.

Barner-Barry, Carol, and Robert Rosenwein. 1985. *Psychological Perspectives on Politics.* Englewood Cliffs, N.J.: Prentice Hall.

Barone, Michael, and Grant Ujifusa. 1987. *The Almanac of American Politics 1988.* Washington, D.C.: National Journal.

———. 1991. *The Almanac of American Politics 1992.* Washington, D.C.: National Journal.

Barrett, Laurence I. 1990. Housecleaning time? *Time,* October, 22, 29.

Bartels, Larry M. 1985. Expectations and preferences in presidential nominating campaigns. *American Political Science Review* 79:804–15.

———. 1987. Candidate choice and the dynamics of the presidential nominating process. *American Journal of Political Science* 31:1–30.

Barton, R. L., and R. B. Gregg. 1982. Middle East conflict as a TV news scenario: A formal analysis. *Journal of Communication* 32:177–85.

Baughman, James L. 1989. The world is ruled by those who holler the loudest: The third-person effect in American journalism history. *Journalism History* 16:12–19.

Becker, L., I. Sobowale, and W. Casey. (1979). Newspaper and television dependencies: effects on evaluations of public officials. *Journal of Broadcasting* 23:465–75.

Becker, L., and D. C. Whitney. 1980. Effects of media dependencies: Audience assessment of government. *Communication Research* 7:95–120.

Behr, Roy, and Shanto Iyengar. 1985. Television news, real-world cues, and changes in the public agenda. *Public Opinion Quarterly* 49:38–57.

Bennett, W. Lance. 1975. *The Political Mind and the Political Environment.* Lexington, Mass.: Lexington Books.

———. 1980. *Public Opinion in American Politics.* New York: Harcourt, Brace, Jovanovich.

———. 1981. Perception and cognition: An information-processing framework for politics. In *The Handbook of Political Behavior,* vol. 1, edited by Samuel E. Long. New York: Plenum Press.

———. 1982. Rethinking political perception and cognition. *Micropolitics* 2:175–202.

———. 1988. *News: The politics of illusion.* 2nd ed. New York: Longman.

———. 1989. Marginalizing the majority: conditioning public opinion to accept managerial democracy. In *Manipulating Public Opinion,* edited by Michael Margolis and Gary Mauser. New York, Dorsey Press, 321–62.

———. 1990. Toward a theory of press-state relations in the United States. *Journal of Communication* 40:103–25.

———. 1994. The news about foreign policy. In *Taken by Storm: The Media, Public Opinion, and U.S. Foreign Policy in the Gulf War.* Edited by W. Lance Bennett and David L. Paletz. Chicago: University of Chicago.

Bennett, W. Lance, and Murray Edelman. 1985. Toward a new political narrative. *Journal of Communication* 35:156–71.

Berelson, Bernard, Paul Lazarsfeld, and William McPhee. 1954. *Voting: A Study of Opinion Formation in a Presidential Campaign.* Chicago: University of Chicago Press.

Bishop, George F., Robert W. Oldendick, and Alfred J. Tuchfarber. 1984. Interest in political campaigns: The influence of question order and electoral context. *Political Behavior* 6:159–69.

Blodgett, Jeff (Minnesota Director for Sen. Wellstone). 1992. Conversation with Dean Alger, 20 August.

———. 1991. Interview by Dean Alger. Tape recording, 30 July.

Blumler, Jay, and Elihu Katz, eds. 1974. *The Uses of Mass Communications.* Newport Beach, Calif.: Sage.

Blumler, Jay G., and Michael Gurevitch. 1981. Politicians and the press: An essay on role relationships. In *Handbook of Political Communication,* edited by Dan D. Nimmo & Keith R. Sanders. Beverly Hills, Calif.: Sage, 467–93.

Bormann, E. 1982. A fantasy theme analysis of the television coverage of the hostage release and the Reagan inaugural. *Quarterly Journal of Speech* 68:33–145.

Brace, Paul, and Barbara Hinckley. 1992. *Follow the Leader: Opinion Polls and the Modern Presidents.* New York: Basic Books.

Broh, C. A. 1983. Polls, pols, and parties. *Journal of Politics* 45:732–44.

———. 1980. Horse-race journalism: Reporting the polls in the 1976 presidential election. *Public Opinion Quarterly* 44:514–29.

Brown, Steven R. 1980. *Political Subjectivity: Applications of Q Methodology in Political Science.* New Haven: Yale University Press.

Bruner, Jerome. 1986. *Actual Minds, Possible Worlds.* Cambridge: Harvard University Press.

Burke, K. 1969. *A Rhetoric of Motives.* Berkeley: University of California Press.

Campbell, Angus, Philip E. Converse, Warren E. Miller, and Donald E. Stokes. 1960. *The American Voter.* New York: Wiley.

———. 1966. *Elections and the Political Order.* New York: Wiley.

Campbell, Angus, Gerald Gurin, and Warren E. Miller. 1954. *The Voter Decides.* Evanston, Ill.: Row, Peterson and Company.

Cater, Douglass. 1959. *The Fourth Branch of Government.* Boston: Houghton Mifflin.

Chaffee, Steven H., and Jack Dennis. 1979. Presidential debates: an empirical assessment. In *The Past and Future of Presidential Debates,* edited by Austin Ranney. Washington, D.C.: American Enterprise Institute for Public Policy Research.

Chaffee, Steven H., and John L. Hochheimer. 1982. The beginnings of political communication research in the United States: Origins of the "limited effects" model. In *The Media Revolution in America and Western Europe,* edited by Everett M. Rogers and Francis Balle. Norwood, N.J.: Ablex, 263–83.

Cheney, Richard B. 1979. The 1976 presidential debates: a republican perspective. In *The Past and Future of Presidential Debates,* edited by Austin Ranney. Washington, D.C.: American Enterprise Institute for Public Policy Research.

Clayman, Steven. 1990. From talk to text: Newspaper accounts of reporter-source interactions. *Media, Culture and Society* 12:79–104.

Cohen, A. A., H. Adoni, and G. Drori. 1983. Adolescent's perceptions of social conflicts in television news and social reality. *Human Communication Research* 10:203–25.

Cohen, Akiba A. ed. 1989. Future directions in television news research. *American Behavioral Scientist* 33:131–268.

Cohen, Bernard C. 1963. *The Press and Foreign Policy.* Princeton: Princeton University Press.

Cohen, Jeremy, and Robert G. Davis. 1991. Third-person effects and the differential impact in negative political advertising. *Journalism Quarterly* 68:680–88.

Cohen, Jeremy, Diana Mutz, Vincent Price, and Albert Gunther. 1988. Perceived impact of defamation: An experiment on third-person effects. *Public Opinion Quarterly* 52:161–73.

Cohen, Stanley and Jock Young. 1973. *The Manufacture of News: Social Problems, Deviance and the Mass Media.* London: Constable.

Collins, Rebecca L., Shelley E. Taylor, Joanne V. Wood, and Suzanne C. Thompson. 1988. The vividness effect: Elusive or illusory? *Journal of Experimental Social Psychology* 24:1–18.

Combs, James E., and Dan Nimmo. 1993. *The New Propaganda: The Dictatorship of Palaver in Contemporary Politics.* New York: Longman.

Connolly, William E. 1983. *The Terms of Political Discourse.* 2nd ed. Princeton: Princeton University Press.

Conover, Pamela Johnston. 1991. Political socialization: where's the politics? In *Politi-*

cal Science: Looking to the Future, Political Behavior, vol. 3, edited by William Crotty. Evanston, Ill.: Northwestern University Press.

Conover, Pamela J., and Stanley Feldman. 1980. Belief system organization in the American electorate: An alternate approach. In *The Electorate Reconsidered,* edited by John C. Pierce and John A. Sullivan. Beverly Hills, Calif.: Sage.

———. 1984. How people organize the political world: A schematic model. *American Journal of Political Science* 28:95–126.

———. 1986a. Emotional reactions to the economy: I'm mad as hell and I'm not going to take it anymore. *American Journal of Political Science* 30:50–78.

———. 1986b. The role of inference in the perception of political candidates. In *Political Cognition,* edited by Richard R. Lau and David O. Sears. Hillsdale, N.J.: Erlbaum.

———. 1991. Where is the schema? Critiques. *American Political Science Review* 85 (4):1364–69.

Converse, Philip. 1964. The nature of belief systems in mass publics. In *Ideology and Discontent,* edited by David Apter. New York: Free Press.

Cook, Timothy. 1989. *Making Laws and Making News: Media Strategies in the U.S. House of Representatives.* Washington, D.C.: Brookings Institution.

———. 1994. Domesticating a crisis. In *Taken By Storm,* edited by W. Lance Bennett and David L. Paletz. Chicago: University of Chicago Press.

Crigler, Ann, Marion Just, W. Russell Neuman, D. Campbell, and J. O'Connell. 1988. Understanding issues in the news: 'I don't know much about this but . . . '. Paper presented at the annual American Association for Public Opinion Research Meeting, Toronto.

Crouse, Timothy. 1973. *The Boys on the Bus.* New York: Ballantine Books.

Cundy, Donald T. 1986. Political commercials and candidate image: The effect can be substantial. In *New Perspectives on Political Advertising,* edited by Lynda Lee Kaid, Dan Nimmo, and Keith R. Sanders. Beverly Hills, Calif.: Sage.

Dahl, Robert A., and Charles E. Lindblom. 1953. *Politics, Economics, and Welfare.* New York: Harper.

Dalton, Russell J. and Martin P. Wattenberg. 1993. The not so simple act of voting. In *Political Science: The State of the Discipline II,* edited by Ada W. Finifter. Washington, D.C.: APSA.

Darnton, Robert. 1975. Writing news and telling stories. *Daedalus* 104 (1):175–94.

Daves, Rob. 1990. Panel discussion on "What happened and what it means in the 1990 elections in Minnesota," Annual Meeting of the Minnesota Political Science Association, Minneapolis.

———. 1991. Interview by Dean Alger. Tape recording, 29 July.

Davies, James C. 1977. Political socialization: From womb to childhood. In *Handbook of Political Socialization,* edited by Stanley A. Renshon. New York: Free Press.

Davis, Richard. 1994. *Decisions and Images: The Supreme Court and the News Media.* Englewood Cliffs, N.J.: Prentice Hall.

Davison, W. Phillips. 1983. The third-person effect in communication. *Public Opinion Quarterly* 47:1–15.

Dawson, Richard E., Kenneth Prewitt, and Karen S. Dawson. 1977. *Political Socialization.* Boston: Little, Brown.

DeFleur, M. L., and S. J. Ball-Rokeach. 1988. *Theories of Mass Communication.* 5th ed. New York: Longman.

Delli Carpini, Michael, and Bruce Williams. 1994a. "Fictional" and "non-fictional" television celebrate earth day (or, politics is comedy plus pretense). *Cultural Studies* 8 (January): 74–98.

———— 1994b. Methods, metaphors, and media research: The uses of television in political conversation. *Communications Research* 21 (December): 782–812.

————. 1994c. The method is the message: Focus groups as a means of social, psychological, and political inquiry. In *Research in Micropolitics,* vol. 4, edited by Michael Delli Carpini, Leonie Huddy, and Robert Shapiro. Greenwich, Conn.: JAI Press, 57–114.

DeMause, Lloyd. 1986. Why did Reagan do it? *Journal of Psychohistory* 14:107–18.

Dennis, Everette E., George Gerbner, and Yassen N. Zassoursky. 1991. *Beyond the Cold War: Soviet and American Media Images.* Newbury Park, Calif.: Sage.

de Rivera, Joseph. 1968. *The Psychological Dimensions of Foreign Policy.* Columbus: Charles E. Merrill.

Deutsch, Karl W. 1963. *The Nerves of Government.* New York: Free Press.

Deutsch, Karl W., and Richard L. Merritt. 1965. Effects of events on national and international images. In *International Behavior,* edited by Herbert Kelman. New York: Holt, Rinehart and Winston.

Deutsch, Karl W. and others. 1957. *Political Community and the North Atlantic Area.* Princeton: Princeton University Press.

Dewey, John. 1974. *Democracy and Education.* Carbondale, Ill.: Southern Illinois University Press.

Diamond, Edwin, and Stephen Bates. 1984. *The Spot.* Cambridge: MIT Press.

Diamond, Edwin, Adrian Marin and Robert Silverman. 1990. Bush's first year: Mr. Nice Guy meets the press. *Washington Journalism Review* 12:42–44.

di Mare, Lesley A. 1987. Functionalizing conflict: Jesse Jackson's rhetorical strategy at the 1984 Democratic national convention. *Western Journal of Speech Communication,* 51:218–26.

Donsbach, Wolfgang, and Robert L. Stevenson. 1984. Challenges, problems, and empirical evidences of the theory of the spiral of silence. Paper presented at the annual meeting of the International Communication Association, San Francisco.

Doob, Leonard W. 1948. *Public Opinion and Propaganda.* New York: Holt.

Dorman, William A., and Steven Livingston. 1994. News and historical context: The establishing phase of the Persian Gulf policy debate. In *Taken By Storm,* edited by W. Lance Bennett and David L. Paletz. Chicago: University of Chicago Press, 63–81.

Downing, John D. H. 1990. U.S. media discourse on South Africa: The development of a situation model. *Discourse and Society* 1:39–60.

Drechsel, Robert. 1983. *News Making in the Trial Courts.* New York: Longman.

Druckman, Daniel. 1990. The social psychology of arms control and reciprocation. *Political Psychology* 11:553–81.

Dyer, Carolyn, and Oguz Nayman. 1978. Under the capitol dome. *Journalism Quarterly* 54:443–53.

Edelman, Murray. 1964. *The Symbolic Uses of Politics.* Urbana: University of Illinois Press.

———. 1988. *Constructing the Political Spectacle.* Chicago: University of Chicago Press.

———. 1993. Contestable categories and public opinion. *Political Communication* 10:231–42.

Emerson, R. M. 1962. Power-dependence relations. *American Sociological Review* 27:31–40.

Entman, Robert M. 1989. *Democracy Without Citizens: Media and the Decay of American Politics.* New York: Oxford University Press.

———. 1993. Framing: Toward clarification of a fractured paradigm. *Journal of Communication* 43 (4):51–58.

Entman, Robert M., and Benjamin I. 1994. The news before the storm: The limits to media autonomy in covering foreign policy. In *Taken By Storm,* edited by W. Lance Bennett and David L. Paletz. Chicago: University of Chicago Press, 82–104.

Entman, Robert M., and Andres Rojecki. 1993. Freezing out the public: Elite and media framing of the U.S. anti-nuclear movement. *Political Communication* 10:155–73.

Epstein, Edward Jay. 1973. *News From Nowhere.* New York: Random House.

Erber, Ralph, and Richard R. Lau. 1990. Political cynicism revisited: An information-processing reconciliation of policy-based and incumbency-based interpretations of changes in trust in government. *American Journal of Political Science* 34:236–53.

Erbring, Lutz, Edie N. Goldenberg, and Arthur H. Miller. 1980. Front-page news and real-world cues: A new look at agenda-setting by the media. *American Journal of Political Science* 24:16–49.

Erickson, K. 1989. Presidential leaks: Rhetoric and mediated political knowledge. *Communication Monographs* 56:199–214.

Ericson, Richard V., Patricia M. Baranek, and Janet B. L. Chan. 1989. *Negotiating Control: A Study of News Sources.* Toronto: University of Toronto Press.

Etheredge, Lloyd. 1985. *Can Governments Learn? American Foreign Policy and Central American Revolutions.* New York: Pergamon Press.

Ettema, James S., David L. Protess, Donna R. Leff, Peter V. Miller, James Doppelt, and F. L. Cook. 1991. Agenda-setting as politics: A case study of the press-public-policy connection. *Journal of Communication* 41:75–98.

Etzioni, Amitai. 1962. *The Hard Way to Peace.* New York: Collier Books.

Eulau, Heinz. 1963. *The Behavioral Persuasion in Politics.* New York: Random House.

Fagen, Richard R. 1966. *Politics and Communication.* Boston: Little, Brown.

———. 1969. *The Transformation of Political Culture in Cuba.* Stanford: Stanford University Press.

Farnham, Barbara. 1990. Political cognition and decision-making. *Political Psychology* 11:83–111.

Fedler, F., M. Meeske, and J. Hall. 1979. Time magazine revisited: Presidential stereotypes persist. *Journalism Quarterly* 56:353–59.

Feldman, Diane (Wellstone's pollster). 1990. Memo "To the political community," 20 July.

Feldman, Stanley, and Lee Sigelman. 1985. The political impact of prime-time television: "The day after." *Journal of Politics* 47:556–78.

Fenno, Richard. 1978. *Home Style*. Boston: Little, Brown.

Ferejohn, John A., and James H. Kuklinski, eds. 1992. *Information and Democratic Processes*. Urbana: University of Illinois Press.

Festinger, Leon. 1957. *A Theory of Cognitive Dissonance*. Palo Alto: Stanford University Press.

Fields, James M., and Howard Schuman. 1976. Public beliefs about the beliefs of the public. *Public Opinion Quarterly* 40:427–48.

Fishman, Mark. 1980. *Manufacturing the News*. Austin: University of Texas Press.

Fiske, J. 1987. *Television Culture*. London: Methuen.

———. 1988. *Introduction to Communication Studies*. New York: Routledge.

Fiske, Susan. 1986. Schema-based versus piecemeal politics: A patchwork quilt, but not a blanket of evidence. In *Political Cognition*, edited by R. Lau and D. Sears. Hillsdale, N.J.: Erlbaum.

Fiske, Susan, and Kinder, Donald. 1981. Involvement, expertise and schema use: Evidence from political cognition. In *Personality, Cognition, and Social Interaction*, edited by Nancy Cantor and John F. Kihlstrom. Hillsdale, N.J.: Erlbaum.

Forciea, Pat. 1991. Interview by Dean Alger. Tape recording, 6 August.

Forum, The (newspaper of Fargo, N.D.–Moorhead, MN). 1990. Poll shows Minnesotans cold toward Perpich, May 4, B3.

Francesconi, Robert. 1986. Implications of Habermas's theory of legitimation for rhetorical criticism. *Communication Monographs* 53:16–35.

Freedman, Jonathan, and David Sears. 1965. Selective exposure. In *Advances in Experimental Social Psychology*, edited by L. Berkowitz. Orlando: Academic Press, 41–80.

Gallie, W. B. 1955–56. Essentially contested concepts. *Proceedings of the Aristotelian Society* 56:167–98.

Gamson, William. 1992. *Talking Politics*. New York: Cambridge University Press.

Gamson, William A., and Andre Modigliani. 1989. Media discourse and public opinion on nuclear power: A constructionist approach. *American Journal of Sociology* 95:1–37.

Gans, Herbert G. 1979. *Deciding What's News*. New York: Vintage Books.

———. 1983. News media, news policy and democracy: Research for the future. *Journal of Communication* 33:3.

———. 1985. Are U.S. journalists dangerously liberal? *Columbia Journalism Review* (November/December) vol 24, no. 4:29–33.

Gastil, John, 1993. *Democracy in Small Groups*. Philadelphia: New Society Publishers.

Gaziano, Cecilie. 1988. How credible is the credibility crisis? *Journalism Quarterly* 65:267–78.

Geiger, Seth F., and Byron Reeves, 1991. The effects of visual structure and content emphasis on the evaluation and memory for political candidates. In *Television and Political Advertising*, vol. 1, edited by Frank Biocca. Hillsdale, N.J.: Erlbaum.

George, Alexander L. 1959. *Propaganda Analysis*. Evanston, Ill.: Row, Peterson.

———. 1980. *Presidential Decisionmaking in Foreign Policy: The Effective Use of Information and Advice*. Boulder, Colo.: Westview Press.

———. 1994. The two cultures of academia and policy-making: Bridging the gap. *Political Psychology* 15:143–72.

Gerbner, George. 1993. Instant history: The case of the Moscow coup. *Political Communication* 10:193–203.

Ginsberg, Benjamin. 1986. *The Captive Public: How Mass Opinion Promotes State Power.* New York: Basic Books.

Gitlin, T. 1980. *The Whole World is Watching: Mass Media in the Making and Unmaking of the New Left.* Berkeley: University of California Press.

Gleitman, Henry. 1986. *Psychology.* 2nd ed. New York: W. W. Norton.

Glynn, Carroll J., and Ronald E. Ostman. 1988. Public opinion about public opinion. *Journalism Quarterly* 65:299–306.

Goffman, Erving. 1974. *Frame Analysis.* Cambridge: Harvard University Press.

Graber, Doris A. 1984. *Mass Media and American Politics.* 2nd ed. Washington, D.C.: Congressional Quarterly Press.

———. 1986. Mass media and political images in elections. In *Research in Micropolitics,* vol. 1, edited by Samuel Long. New York: JAI Press.

———. 1987a. Framing election news broadcasts: News context and its impact on the 1984 presidential election. *Social Science Quarterly* 68:552–68.

———. 1987b. Kind pictures and harsh words. In *Elections in America,* edited by Kay L. Schlozman. Boston: Unwin-Hyman, 115–41.

———. 1988. *Processing the News.* 2nd ed. White Plains, N.Y.: Longman.

———. [1988] 1993. *Processing the News: How People Tame the Information Tide.* 2d ed. Reprint, Lanham, Md.: University Press of America.

Granberg, Donald, and Edward Brent. 1983. When prophecy bends: The preference expectation link in U.S. presidential elections, 1952–1980. *Journal of Personality and Social Psychology* 45:477–91.

Granberg, Donald, and Thomas A. Brown. 1989. On affect and cognition in politics. *Social Psychology Quarterly* 52:171–82.

Granberg, Donald, and Sven Holmberg. 1986. Political perception among voters in Sweden and the U.S.: Analysis of issues with explicit alternatives. *Western Political Quarterly* 39:7–28.

Grant, A. E. 1989a. The promise fulfilled? An empirical analysis of program diversity on television. Paper presented at the annual meeting of the International Communication Association, San Francisco.

———. 1989b. Seven audiences: an exploration of television viewing behavior. Paper presented at the annual meeting of the Broadcast Education Association, Las Vegas.

Grant, A. E., K. K. Guthrie, and S. J. Ball-Rokeach. 1991. Television shopping: A media system dependency perspective. *Communication Research* 18(6):773–98.

Greenwald, John, 1990. All shook up. *Time,* 15 October.

Griswold, William F. 1992. Third-person effects and voting intentions in a presidential primary election. Paper presented at the annual meeting of the Association for Education in Journalism and Mass Communication, Montreal.

Grossman, M. B., and M. J. Kumar. 1981. *Portraying the President: The White House and the News Media.* Baltimore: Johns Hopkins University Press.

Grossman, Michael Baruch, and Martha Joynt Kumar. 1979. The White House and the news media: The phases of their relationship. *Political Science Quarterly* 94:37–53.

Gulliver, P. H. 1979. *Disputes and Negotiations: A Cross-Cultural Perspective.* New York: Academic Press.

Gunther, Albert C. 1991. What we think others think: Cause and consequence in the third-person effect. *Communication Research* 18:355–72.

———. 1992. Biased press or biased public? Attitudes toward media coverage of social groups. *Public Opinion Quarterly* 56:147–67.

———. 1994. Overrating the X-rating: the third-person perception and support for censorship of pornography. *Journal of Communication* 45:28–39.

Gunther, Albert C., and Paul Mundy. 1993. Biased optimism and the third-person effect. *Journalism Quarterly* 70:2–11.

Gunther, Albert C., and Esther Thorson. 1992. Perceived persuasive effects of product commercials and public service announcements: Third-person effects in new domains. *Communication Research* 19:574–96.

Gustainis, J. J. 1989. Waist deep in the big muddy: Rhetorical dimensions of the Tet offensive. *Political Communication and Persuasion* 5:81–92.

Habermas, Jurgen. [1962] 1989. *The Structural Transformation of the Public Sphere.* Cambridge: MIT Press.

Hallin, Dan. 1986. *The Uncensored War: The Media and Vietnam.* Berkeley: University of California Press.

Hamill, Ruth, and Milton Lodge. 1986. Cognitive consequences of political sophistication. In *Political Cognition,* edited by Richard R. Lau and David O. Sears. Hillsdale, N.J.: Erlbaum.

Hart, R. 1987. *The Sound of Leadership: Presidential Communication in the Modern Age.* Chicago: University of Chicago Press.

Hart, R., P. Jerome, and K. McComb. 1984. Rhetorical features of newscasts about the president. *Critical Studies in Mass Communication* 1:260–86.

Hart, R., D. Smith-Howell, and J. Llewellyn. 1990. Evolution of presidential news coverage. *Political Communication and Persuasion* 7:213–30.

———. 1991. The mindscape of the presidency: *Time* magazine, 1945–1985. *Journal of Communication* 41:6–25.

Hart, Roderick P., Alison Regan, Vanessa Bowles Beasley, and Lisbeth Lipari. 1994. The Hill-Thomas hearings in rhetorical perspective. *Political Communication* 11:263–308.

Hass, R. Glenn. 1981. Effects of source characteristics on cognitive responses and persuasion. In *Cognitive Responses in Persuasion,* edited by Richard E. Petty, Thomas M. Ostrom, and Timothy C. Brock. Hillsdale, N.J.: Erlbaum.

Hedges, Larry V., and Ingrim Olkin. 1985. *Statistical methods for Meta-analysis.* Orlando: Academic Press.

Herbst, Susan. 1993. *Numbered Voices: How Opinion Polling Has Shaped American Politics.* Chicago: University of Chicago Press.

Heritage, John, and David Greatbatch. 1986. Generating applause: A study of rhetoric and response at party political conferences. *American Journal of Sociology* 92:110–57.

Herman, Edward. 1985. Diversity of news: Marginalizing the opposition. *Journal of Communication* 35:135–46.

Hershey, Marjorie. 1989. The campaign and the media. In *The Elections of 1988,* edited by Gerald Pomper. Chatham, N.J.: Chatham House, 73–102.

———. 1984. *Running for Office: The Political Education of Campaigners.* Chatham, N.J.: Chatham House.

Hertsgaard, Mark. 1988. *On Bended Knee: The Press and the Reagan Presidency.* New York: Farrar, Straus & Giroux.

Hess, Stephen. 1986. *The Ultimate Insiders: U.S. Senators in the National Media.* Washington, D.C.: Brookings Institution.

———. 1984. *The Government/Press Connection: Press Officers and Their Offices.* Washington, D.C.: Brookings Institution.

———. 1981. *The Washington Reporter.* Washington, D.C.: Brookings Institution.

Hillsman, Bill. 1990. Confidential memo to Wellstone for U.S. senate advertising committee, undated (circulated in July).

———. 1991. Interview by Dean Alger. Tape recording, 31 July.

Hirschburg, P. L., D. A. Dillman, and S. J. Ball-Rokeach. 1986. Media system dependency theory: Responses to the eruption of Mount St. Helens. In *Media, Audience, and Social Structure,* edited by S. J. Ball-Rokeach and M. G. Cantor. Beverly Hills, Calif.: Sage.

Hochberg, J. 1986. Representation of motion and space in video and cinematic displays. In *Handbook of Perception and Human Performance,* vol. 2, edited by K. R. Boff and J. P. Thomas. New York: John Wiley.

Hofstetter, C. Richard. 1976. *Bias in the News: Network Television Coverage of the 1972 Election Campaign.* Columbus: Ohio State University Press.

Hogan, J. Michael. 1994. *The Nuclear Freeze Campaign: Rhetoric and Foreign Policy in the Telepolitical Age.* East Lansing: Michigan State University Press.

Hovland, Carl I., and Walter Weiss. 1951. The influence of source credibility on communication effectiveness. *Public Opinion Quarterly* 15:635–50.

Hull, Clark L. 1952. *A Behavior System.* New Haven: Yale University Press.

Iyengar, S., and D. Kinder. 1986. More than meets the eye: TV news, priming, and public evaluations of the president. *Public Communication and Behavior* 1:135–71.

Iyengar, Shanto. 1989. Framing effects in politics: Television news and public opinion. In *Public Communication and Behavior,* vol. 3, edited by George Comstock. New York: Academic Press.

———. 1992. *Is Anyone Responsible? How Television News Frames Political Issues.* Chicago: University of Chicago Press.

Iyengar, Shanto, and D. Kinder. 1987a. *News that Matters: Television and American Opinion.* Chicago: University of Chicago Press.

———. 1987b. Television news and citizens' explanations of national affairs. *American Political Science Review* 81:815–31.

Iyengar, Shanto, and William J. McGuire, eds. 1993. *Explorations in Political Psychology.* Durham, N.C.: Duke University Press.

Iyengar, Shanto, Mark D. Peters, and Donald R. Kinder. 1982. Experimental demonstrations of the "not-so-minimal" consequences of television news programs. *American Political Science Review* 76:848–58.

Izard, Carroll. 1977. *Human Emotions.* New York: Plenum.

Jackson, Brooks. 1985. A senator's advice: Don't give consentive consent to reelection debate. *Wall Street Journal*, 2 May.

Jamieson, Kathleen Hall. 1988. *Eloquence in an Electronic Age*. New York: Oxford University Press.

———. 1992. *Dirty Politics*. New York: Oxford University Press.

Jamieson, Kathleen Hall, and David S. Birdsell. 1988. *Presidential Debates: The Challenge of Creating an Informed Electorate*. New York: Oxford University Press.

Jamieson, Kathleen Hall, and Karlyn Campbell. 1983. *The Interplay of Influence*. Belmont, Calif.: Wadsworth.

Janis, Irving L. 1983. *Groupthink: Psychological Studies of Policy Decisions and Fiascoes*. Boston: Houghton Mifflin.

———. 1989. *Crucial Decisions: Leadership in Policymaking and Crisis Management*. New York: Free Press.

Janis, Irving L., and Leon Mann. 1977. *Decision Making: A Psychological Analysis of Conflict, Choice, and Commitment*. New York: Free Press.

Jehl, Douglas. 1994. Clinton calls show to assail press, Falwell and Limbaugh. *New York Times*, 25 June.

Jervis, Robert. 1993. The drunkard's search. In *Explorations in Political Psychology*, edited by Shanto Iyengar and William J. McGuire. Durham, N.C.: Duke University Press.

Jervis, Robert, Richard Ned Lebow, and Janice Gross Stein. 1985. *Psychology and Deterrence*. Baltimore: Johns Hopkins University Press.

Johnson, K. S. 1985. The honeymoon period: Fact or fiction? *Journalism Quarterly* 62:869–76.

Johnson, S., and W. G. Christ 1987. Women through *Time:* Who gets covered? Paper presented to the annual convention of the Association for Education in Journalism and Mass Communication, San Antonio, Texas.

Johnson-Cartee, Karen S., and Gary A. Copeland. 1991. *Negative Political Advertising*. Hillsdale, N.J.: Erlbaum.

Just, Marion, Ann Crigler, Dean Alger, Timothy Cook, Montague Kern, and Darrell West. 1996. *Cross-Talk*. Chicago: University of Chicago Press.

Just, Marion, Ann Crigler, and Lori Wallach. 1990. Thirty seconds or thirty minutes: What viewers learn from spot advertisements and candidate debates. *Journal of Communication* 40:120–33.

Kahn, Kim Fridkin. 1994. The distorted mirror: Press coverage of women candidates for statewide office. *Journal of Politics* 56:154–73.

Kaid, Lynda Lee, Robert Gobetz, Jane Garner, Chris Leland and others. 1993. Television news and presidential campaigns: The legitimization of televised political advertising. *Social Science Quarterly* 74, no. 2.

Katz, Daniel, and Floyd H. Allport. 1931. *Students' Attitudes*. Syracuse, N.Y.: Craftsmen Press.

Katz, Elihu. 1987. Communications research since Lazarsfeld. *Public Opinion Quarterly* 51:S25–S45.

Katz, Elihu, and Paul Lazarsfeld. 1955. *Personal Influence: The Part Played by People in the Flow of Communications*. New York: Free Press.

Keeter, Scott. 1987. The illusion of intimacy: Television and the role of candidate personal qualities in voter choice. *Public Opinion Quarterly* 51:344–58.

Keeter, Scott, and Cliff Zukin. 1983. *Uninformed Choice: The Failure of the New Presidential Nominating System*. New York: Praeger.

Kerbel, Matthew. 1994. *Edited for Television*. Boulder, Colo.: Westview Press.

Kern, Montague. 1989. *30-Second Politics: Political Advertising in the Eighties*. New York: Praeger.

Kernell, S., and G. C. Jacobson. 1987. Congress and the presidency as news in the nineteenth century. *Journal of Politics* 49:1016–35.

Kernell, Samuel. 1986. *Going Public: News Strategies of Presidential Leadership*. Washington, D.C.: Congressional Quarterly Press.

Kessel, John. 1988. *Presidential Campaign Politics: Coalition Strategies and Citizen Response*. 3rd ed. Homewood, Ill.: Dorsey Press.

Kessler, Pat. 1991. Interview by Dean Alger. Tape recording, 30 October.

Kinder, Donald R. 1981. Presidents, prosperity and public opinion. *Public Opinion Quarterly* 45:1–21.

Kinder, Donald R., and R. Kieweit. 1981. Sociotropic politics: The American case. *British Journal of Political Science* 11:129–62.

Kingdon, John W. 1984. *Agendas, Alternatives and Public Policies*. Boston: Little Brown.

Klapper, Joseph T. 1960. *The Effects of Mass Communications*. New York: Free Press.

Kosicki, Gerald M., and Jack M. McLeod. 1990. Learning from political news: Effects of media images and information-processing strategies. In *Mass Communication and Political Information Processing*, edited by S. Kraus. Hillsdale, N.J.: Erlbaum.

Kraus, Sidney, and Richard Perloff, eds. 1985. *Mass Media and Political Thought*. Beverly Hills, Calif.: Sage.

Kressel, Neil J. 1987. Biased judgments of media bias: A case study of the Arab-Israel dispute. *Political Psychology* 8:11–226.

Krosnick, Jon. 1988. The role of attitude importance in social evaluations: A study of policy preferences, presidential candidate evaluations, and voting behavior. *Journal of Personality and Social Psychology* 55:196–210.

Krueger, Richard. 1988. *Focus Groups: A Practical Guide for Applied Research*. Newbury Park, Calif.: Sage.

Kubey, Robert, and Mihaly Csikszentmihalyi. 1990. *Television and the Quality of Life*. Hillsdale, N.J.: Erlbaum.

Kuklinski, James H., Robert Luskin, and John Bolland. 1991. Where is the schema? Going beyond the "S" word in political psychology. *American Political Science Review* 85 (4):1341–56.

Landsman, Gail. 1985. Ganienkeh: Symbol and politics in an Indian/white conflict. *American Anthropologist* 87:826–36.

Lane, Robert. 1962. *Political Ideology*. New York: Free Press.

Lang, Gladys Engel, and Kurt Lang. 1983. *The Battle for Public Opinion: The President, the Press, and the Polls during Watergate*. New York: Columbia University Press.

Lang, Kurt, and Gladys Engel Lang. 1959. Mass media and voting. In *American Voting Behavior,* edited by Eugene Burdick and Arthur J. Brodbeck. Glencoe, Ill.: Free Press, 217–35.

Lang, Kurt, Gladys Engel Lang, Hans-Mathias Kepplinger, and Simone Ehmig. 1993. Collective memory and political generations: A survey of German journalists. *Political Communication* 10:211–29.

Lanzetta, John T., Denis G. Sullivan, Roger D. Masters, Gregory J. McHugo. 1985. Emotional and cognitive responses to televised images of political leaders. In *Mass Media and Political Thought,* edited by Sidney Kraus and Richard M. Perloff. Beverly Hills, Calif.: Sage.

Larson, M. 1989. Presidential news coverage and "All Things Considered": National Public Radio and news bias. *Presidential Studies Quarterly* 19:347–53.

Lasorsa, Dominic L. 1989. Real and perceived effects of "Amerika." *Journalism Quarterly* 66:373–78, 529.

———. 1992. How media affect policymakers: The third-person effect. In *Public Opinion, the Press and Public Policy,* edited by J. D. Kennamer. New York: Praeger.

Lasswell, Harold. 1964. The structure and function of communication in society. In *Religion and Civilian Series: The Communication of Ideas,* edited by Lyman Bryson. New York: Cooper Square Publishers, Inc., 37–51.

Lasswell, Harold D. 1927. Theory of political propaganda. *American Political Science Review* 21:627–31.

———. 1935a. *World Politics and Personal Insecurity.* New York: Whittlesey House (McGraw Hill).

———. 1935b. The study and practice of propaganda. In *Propaganda and Promotional Activities: An Annotated Bibliography,* edited by Harold D. Laswell, Ralph D. Casey, and Bruce Lannes Smith. Minneapolis: University of Minnesota Press, 1–27.

———. 1951. The policy orientation. In *The Policy Sciences: Recent Developments in Scope and Method,* edited by Daniel Lerner and Harold D. Lasswell. Stanford: Stanford University Press.

———. 1969. The structure and function of communication in society. In *Mass Communications,* edited by Wilbur Schramm. Urbana: University of Illinois Press.

Lasswell, Harold D., Daniel Lerner, and Ithiel de Sola Pool. 1952. *The Comparative Study of Symbols.* Stanford: Stanford University Press.

Lasswell, Harold D., Daniel Lerner, and Hans Speir. 1980. *Propaganda and Communication in World History.* 3 vols. Honolulu: University of Hawaii Press.

Lau, Richard R., and Ralph Erber. 1985. Political sophistication: An information-processing perspective. In *Mass Media and Political Thought,* edited by Sidney Kraus and Richard M. Perloff. Beverly Hills, Calif.: Sage.

Lau, Richard, and David Sears, eds. 1986. *Political Cognition: The 19th Annual Symposium on Cognition.* Hillsdale, N.J.: Erlbaum.

Lazarsfeld, Paul F., Bernard Berelson, and Hazel Gaudet. 1944. *The People's Choice.* New York: Duell, Sloan and Pearce.

Lazarsfeld, Paul, Bernard Berelson, and William McPhee. 1954. *Voting.* Chicago: University of Chicago Press.

Lazarus, Richard. 1984. On the primacy of cognition. *American Psychologist* 35:124–29.

Lefcourt, Herbert M. 1976. *Locus of Control: Current Trends in Theory and Research.* Hillsdale, N.J.: Erlbaum.

Leonard, Thomas C. 1986. *The Power of the Press: The Birth of American Political Reporting.* New York: Oxford University Press.

Levenson, H. 1973. Multidimensional locus of control in psychiatric patients. *Journal of Consulting and Clinical Psychology* 41:397–404.

Levitin, Teresa E., and Warren E. Miller. 1979. Ideological interpretations of presidential elections. *American Political Science Review* 73:751–71.

Levy, Arnon. 1986. Mass media as intermediary of conscious and unconscious group-fantasy: The case of Sharon. *Journal of Psychohistory* 14:121–30.

Lichter, S. Robert, Stanley Rothman, and Linda S. Lichter. 1986. *The Media Elite.* Bethesda, Md.: Adler & Adler.

Liebes, Tamar. 1986. Cultural differences in the retelling of television fiction. *Critical Studies in Mass Communication* 5:277–92.

Liebes, Tamar, and A. Crigler. 1990. Defining "us" and "them": Frames of political discourse in the U.S.A. and Israel. Paper delivered at the annual meeting of the International Communication Association, Dublin, Ireland.

Liebes, Tamar, and Elihu Katz. 1990. *The Export of Meaning.* Oxford: Oxford University Press.

Linsky, Martin. 1986. *Impact: How the Press Affects Federal Policy Making.* New York: W. W. Norton Co.

Lippmann, Walter. 1965 [1922]. *Public Opinion.* New York: Free Press.

Liu, Alan P. L. 1971. *Communications and National Integration in Communist China.* Berkeley: University of California Press.

Lodge, Milton, and Ruth Hamill. 1986. A partisan schema for political information processing. *American Political Science Review* 80:505–19.

Lodge, Milton, and Kathleen M. McGraw. 1991. Where is the schema? Critiques. *American Political Science Review* 85 (4):1357–64.

Lodge, Milton, Kathleen M. McGraw, and Patrick Stroh. 1989. An impression-driven model of candidate evaluation. *American Political Science Review* 83, no. 2.

Lodge, Milton, and Patrick Stroh. 1993. Inside the mental voting booth: An impression-driven process model of candidate evaluation. In *Explorations in Political Psychology,* edited by Shanto Iyengar and William J. McGuire. Durham, N.C.: Duke University Press.

Lodge, Milton, and John C. Wahlke. 1982. Politicos, apoliticals, and the processing of political information. *International Political Science Review* 3:131–50.

Loges, W. E. 1994. Canaries in the coal mine: Perceptions of threat and media system dependency relations. *Communication Research* 21 (1):5–24.

Long, Samuel. 1981. *The Handbook of Political Behavior,* vol. 1. New York: Plenum Press.

Lule, J. 1988. The myth of my widow: A dramatistic analysis of news portrayals of a terrorist victim. *Political Communication and Persuasion* 5:101–20.

Machiavelli, Nicolò. [1513] 1952. *The Prince.* In *Great Books of the Western World,* vol. 23, edited by Robert M. Hutchins. Chicago: Encyclopædia Britannica Press.

MacKuen, Michael B., and Steven Lane Coombs. 1981. *More Than News: Media Power in Public Affairs.* Beverly Hills, Calif.: Sage.

Malaney, G. D., and T. F. Buss. 1979. AP wire reports vs. CBS TV news coverage of a presidential campaign. *Journalism Quarterly* 56:602–10.

Manheim, Jarol. 1979. The honeymoon's over: The news conference and the development of presidential style. *Journal of Politics* 41:55–74.

Manheim, Jarol B. 1994a. Strategic public diplomacy: Managing Kuwait's image during the Gulf conflict. In *Taken By Storm: The Media, Public Opinion, and U.S. Foreign Policy in the Gulf War,* edited by W. Lance Bennett and David L. Paletz. Chicago: University of Chicago Press.

———. 1994b. *Strategic Public Diplomacy and American Foreign Policy: The Evolution of Influence.* New York: Oxford University Press.

Manheim, Jarol B., and Robert B. Albritton. 1984. Changing national images: International public relations and media agenda-setting. *American Political Science Review* 78:641–57.

Mansbridge, Jane J., ed. 1990. *Beyond Self-Interest.* Chicago: University of Chicago Press.

March, James G., and Johan P. Olsen. 1989. *Rediscovering Institutions: The Organizational Basis of Politics.* New York: Free Press.

Marcus, George E., and Michael B. Mackuen. 1993. Anxiety, enthusiasm, and the vote: The emotional underpinnings of learning and involvement during presidential campaigns. *American Political Science Review* 87:672–85.

Marcus, George E., and Wendy Rahn. 1990. Emotions and democratic politics. In *Research in Micropolitics,* edited by Samuel Long. Greenwich, Conn.: JAI Press, 29–58.

Markus, Gregory B. 1986. Stability and change in political attitudes: Observed, recalled, and explained. *Political Behavior* 8:21–44.

Mason, Laurie. 1990. Faulty factfinders: The self-other bias in resolution of ambiguous messages. Ph.D., Stanford University.

Mason, Tom. 1991a. What went wrong. *Minnesota Monthly,* April.

———. 1991b. Interview by Dean Alger. Tape recording, 16 September.

Matthews, Donald R. 1960. *U.S. Senators and Their World.* Chapel Hill: University of North Carolina Press.

McClosky, Herbert. 1967. Personality and attitude correlates of foreign policy orientation. In *Domestic Sources of Foreign Policy,* edited by James Rosenau. New York: Free Press, 51–109.

McCombs, M., and P. Poindexter. 1983. The duty to keep informed: News exposure and civic obligation. *Journal of Communication* 33:88–96.

McCombs, Maxwell, and Donald Shaw. 1972. The agenda-setting function of the mass media. *Public Opinion Quarterly* 36:176–87.

McGerr, Michael. 1986. *The Decline of Popular Politics: The American North, 1865–1928.* New York: Oxford University Press.

McGrath, Dennis. 1990a. Caucuses likely to create front-runner among Boschwitz's DFL challengers. Minneapolis *Star Tribune,* 26 February.

———. 1990b. Boschwitz maintains big lead over DFLers. Minneapolis *Star Tribune,* 6 June.

McGuire, William. 1989. Theoretical foundations of campaigns. In *Public Communication Campaigns,* 2d ed, edited by Ronald E. Rice and Charles Atkin. Newbury Park, Calif.: Sage.

McLeod, J. M., C. J. Glynn, and D. G. McDonald. 1983. Issues and images: The influence of media reliance in voting decisions. *Communication Research* 10:37–58.

Mead, George Herbert. 1934. *Mind, Self and Society.* Chicago: University of Chicago Press.

Meadow, Robert G., and Sigelman, Lee. 1982. Some effects and noneffects of campaign commercials: An experimental study. *Political Behavior* 4:163–75.

Merelman, Richard M. 1992. Cultural imagery and racial conflict in the United States. *British Journal of Political Science* 22:315–42.

Merrill, J. C. 1965. How *Time* stereotyped three U.S. presidents. *Journalism Quarterly* 42:563–70.

Miller, Arthur. 1991. Where is the schema? Critiques. *American Political Science Review* 85 (4):1369–80.

Miller, Arthur H., Edie N. Goldenberg, and Lutz Erbring. 1979. Type-set politics: Impact of newspapers on public confidence. *American Political Science Review* 73:67–84.

Miller, Arthur H., Martin P. Wattenberg, and Oksana Malanchuk. 1985. Cognitive representations of candidate assessments. In *Communication Yearbook, 1984,* edited by Keith R. Sanders, Lynda Lee Kaid, and Dan Nimmo. Carbondale: Southern Illinois University Press.

———. 1986. Schematic assessments of presidential candidates. *American Political Science Review* 80:521–40.

Miller, Mark Crispin. 1988. *Boxed-In: The Culture of TV.* Evanston, Ill.: Northwestern University Press.

Miller, M. M., and S. Reese. 1982. Media dependency as interaction: Effects of exposure and reliance on political activity and efficacy. *Communication Research* 9:27–248.

Miller, N. E., and J. Dollard. 1941. *Social Learning and Imitation.* New Haven, Conn.: Yale University Press.

Miller, Warren E., and Teresa E. Levitin. 1976. *Leadership and Change.* Cambridge, Mass.: Winthrop.

Minneapolis *Star Tribune.* 1990a. 51 percent dissatisfied with way things are going. 25 July, 5D.

———. 1990b. Boschwitz agrees to hold debate in Washington. 11 October.

———. 1990c. Public satisfaction is lowest since early Reagan years. 17 October.

Mishler, Elliot G. 1986. *Research Interviewing: Context and Narrative.* Cambridge: Harvard University Press.

Molotch, Harvey, David L. Protess, and Margaret T. Gordon. 1987. The media-policy connection: Ecologies of news. In *Political Communication Research: Approaches, Studies, Assessments,* edited by David L. Paletz. Norwood, N.J.: Ablex, 26–48.

Morello, John T. 1988. Argument and visual structuring in the 1984 Mondale-Reagan debates: The medium's influence on the perception of clash. *Western Journal of Speech Communication* 52:277–90.

Morgan, David. 1988. *Focus Groups as Qualitative Research.* Newbury Park, Calif.: Sage.

Morganthau, Tom. 1990. The voters strike back. *Newsweek.* 1 October, 28.

Mullen, Brian, and Robert Rosenthal. 1985. Basic meta-analysis: Procedures and programs. Hillsdale, N.J.: Erlbaum.

Mutz, Diana C. 1989. The influence of perceptions of media influence: Third-person effects and the public expression of opinions. *International Journal of Public Opinion Research* 1:3–23.

National Journal. 1990. Opinion outlook: Views on the economy. 8 September.

Nelson, Barbara. 1984. *Making an Issue of Child Abuse: Political Agenda Setting for Social Problems.* Chicago: University of Chicago Press.

Nesbit, Dorothy Davidson. 1988. *Videostyle in U.S. Senate Campaigns.* Knoxville: University of Tennessee Press.

Neuman, W. Russell. 1986. *The Paradox of Mass Politics: Knowledge and Opinion in the American Electorate.* Cambridge: Harvard University Press.

Neuman, W. Russell, Marion Just, and Ann Crigler. 1992. *Common Knowledge: News and the Construction of Political Meaning.* Chicago: University of Chicago Press.

Nie, Norman H., Sidney Verba, and John R. Petrocik. 1976. *The Changing American Voter.* Cambridge: Harvard University Press.

Niemi, Richard J., and Larry M. Bartels. 1983. New measures of issue salience: An evaluation. *Journal of Politics* 47:1212–20.

Nigg, J. M. 1982. Communication under conditions of uncertainty: Understanding earthquake forecasting. *Journal of Communication* 32:27–36.

Nimmo, Dan, and James E. Combs. 1988. *Mediated Political Realities.* 2nd ed. New York: Longman.

Nimmo, Dan, and Robert Savage. 1976. *Candidates and Their Images.* Pacific Palisades, Calif.: Goodyear.

Nisbett, Richard E., and Timothy D. Wilson. 1977. Telling more than we can know: Verbal reports on mental processes. *Psychological Review* 84:231–59.

Noelle-Neumann, Elisabeth. 1974. The spiral of silence: a theory of public opinion. *Journal of Communication* 24:43–51.

———. 1984. *The Spiral of Silence.* Chicago: University of Chicago Press.

Novak, Jay. 1991. Interview by Dean Alger. Tape recording, 31 July.

Office of Technology Assessment. 1990. *Critical Connections: Communication for the Future.* Washington, D.C.: Government Printing Office.

O'Gorman, Hubert, with Stephen L. Garry. 1976. Pluralistic ignorance—a replication and extension. *Public Opinion Quarterly* 40:449–58.

Orman, J. 1984. Covering the American presidency: Valenced reporting in the periodical press, 1900–1982. *Presidential Studies Quarterly* 14:381–90.

Ortony, Andrew, G. Clore, and A. Collins. 1988. *The Cognitive Structure of Emotions.* Cambridge: Cambridge University Press.

Orwall, Bruce. 1990. Campaign ad watch. *St. Paul Pioneer Press,* 3 November.

———. 1991. Interview by Dean Alger. Tape recording, 7 August.

Osgood, Charles. 1962. *An Alternative to War or Surrender.* Urbana: University of Illinois Press.

Ottati, Victor C., and Robert S. Wyer Jr. 1993. Affect and political judgment. In *Explorations in Political Psychology,* edited by Shanto Iyengar and William J. McGuire. Durham, N.C.: Duke University Press.

Page, Benjamin I., and Robert Shapiro. 1992. *The Rational Public.* Chicago: University of Chicago Press.

Page, Benjamin I., Robert Y. Shapiro, and Glenn R. Dempsey. 1987. What moves public opinion? *American Political Science Review* 81:23–43.

Paletz, D., and R. Entman. 1981. *Media Power Politics.* New York: Free Press.

Paletz, D., and K. Guthrie. 1987. The three faces of Ronald Reagan. *Journal of Communication* 37:7–23.

Parenti, Michael. 1993. *Inventing Reality: The Politics of News Media.* 2nd ed. New York: St. Martin's Press.

Park, Won Woo. 1990. A review of research on groupthink. *Journal of Behavioral Decision Making* 3:229–45.

Patterson, Thomas E. 1980. *The Mass Media Election: How Americans Choose their President.* New York: Praeger.

———. 1992. Irony of the free press: Professional journalism and news diversity. Paper delivered at the annual meeting of the American Political Science Association, Chicago.

Peffley, Mark, Stanley Feldman, and Lee Sigelman. 1987. Economic conditions and party competence: Processes of belief revision. *Journal of Politics* 49:100–21.

Perloff, Richard M. 1989. Ego-involvement and the third-person effect of televised news coverage. *Communication Research* 16:236–62.

Perloff, Richard M., and Dennis Kinsey. 1992. Political advertising as seen by consultants and journalists. *Journal of Advertising Research* 32:53–60.

Perloff, Richard M., Kimberly Neuendorf, Dennis Giles, Tsan-Kuo Chang, and Leo W. Jeffres. 1992. Perceptions of "Amerika." *Mass Comm Review* 19:42–48.

Pfau, Michael, and Michael Burgoon. 1988. Inoculation in political campaign communication. *Human Communication Research* 15:91–111.

Plutchik, Robert. 1980. A general psychoevolutionary theory of emotion. In Vol. 1 of *Theories of Emotion, Emotion: Theory, Research, and Experience,* edited by R. Plutchik and H. Kellerman. New York: Academic Press, 3–31.

Pool, Ithiel de Sola. 1952. *The Prestige Papers: A Survey of Their Editorials.* Stanford: Stanford University Press.

———. 1959. *Symbols of Internationalism.* Stanford: Stanford University Press.

———. 1963. The mass media and politics in the modernization process. In *Communication and Political Development,* edited by Lucian W. Pye. Princeton: Princeton University Press.

Popkin, Samuel. 1991. *The Reasoning Voter.* Chicago: University of Chicago Press.

Powell, Lynda. 1989. Analyzing misinformation: Perception of congressional candidates' ideologies. *American Journal of Political Science* 33:272–93.

Power, G. and S. J. Ball-Rokeach. 1988. A media system dependency approach to the AIDS epidemic. Annenberg School of Communications, Los Angeles. Typescript.

Price, Vincent, and Donald F. Roberts. 1987. Public opinion processes. In *Handbook of Communication Science,* edited by Charles R. Berger and Steven H. Chaffee. Newbury Park, Calif.: Sage.

Price, Vincent, and David Tewksbury. 1994. The roles of question order, contrast, and knowledge in the third-person effect. Paper presented at the annual meeting of the Midwest Association for Public Opinion Research, Chicago.

Protess, David L., Donna R. Leff, Stephen C. Brooks, and Margaret Gordon. 1985. Uncovering rape: The watchdog press and the limits of agenda setting. *Public Opinion Quarterly* 49:19–37.

Pruitt, Dean G. and Peter J. Carnevale. 1993. *Negotiation in Social Conflict.* Pacific Grove, Calif.: Brooks/Cole.

Putnam, Robert D. 1973. *The Beliefs of Politicians: Ideology, Conflict, and Democracy in Britain and Italy.* New Haven, Conn.: Yale University Press.

Pye, Lucian W., ed. 1963. *Communications and Political Development.* Princeton: Princeton University Press.

Ranney, Austin. 1983. *Channels of Power: The Impact of Television on American Politics.* New York: Basic Books.

Rapport, David C., and Yonah Alexander, eds. 1989. *The Morality of Terrorism: Religious and Secular Justifications.* New York: Columbia University Press.

Ratzan, Scott C. 1989. The real agenda setters: Pollsters in the 1988 presidential campaign. *American Behavioral Scientist* 32:451–63.

Reese, S. D., and M. Miller. 1981. Political attitude holding and structure: The effects of newspaper and television news. *Communication Research* 8:167–88.

Ricci, David. 1984. *The Tragedy of Political Science: Politics, Scholarship, and Democracy.* New Haven, Conn.: Yale University Press.

Rice, Ronald E., and Atkins, Charles K., eds. 1989. *Public Communication Campaigns.* 2nd ed. Newbury Park, Calif.: Sage.

Riker, William H. 1983. Political theory and the art of heresthetics. In *Political Science: The State of the Discipline,* edited by Ada W. Finifter. Washington, D.C.: American Political Science Association.

Roberts, Jonathan M. 1988. *Decision-Making During International Crises.* New York: St. Martin's Press.

Robinson, John P., and Mark R. Levy. 1986a. Interpersonal communication and news comprehension. *Public Opinion Quarterly* 50:165–75.

———. 1986b. *The Main Source: Learning from Television.* Beverly Hills, Calif.: Sage.

Robinson, Michael J. 1976. Public affairs television and the growth of political malaise. *American Political Science Review* 70:409–42.

Rosenberg, Shawn W. 1988. *Reason, Ideology, and Politics.* Princeton: Princeton University Press.

Rosenberg, Shawn, Lisa Bohan, Patrick McCafferty, and Kevin Harris. 1986. The image and the vote: The effect of candidate presentation on voter preference. *American Journal of Political Science* 30:108–27.

Rosenberg, Shawn W., with Patrick McCafferty. 1987. The image and the vote: Manipulating voters' preferences. *Public Opinion Quarterly* 51:31–47.

Rosenberg, Shawn, D. Ward, and S. Chilton. 1988. *Political Reasoning and Cognition: A Piagetian View.* Durham, N.C.: Duke University Press.

Rosenthal, Robert. 1984. *Meta-Analytic Procedures for Social Research.* Newbury Park, Calif.: Sage.

———. 1991. *Meta-Analytic Procedures for Social Research,* rev. ed. Newbury Park, Calif.: Sage.

Ross, Lee. 1977. The intuitive psychologist and his shortcomings: Distortions in the attribution process. In *Advances in Experimental Social Psychology,* vol. 10, edited by Leonard Berkowitz. New York: Academic Press.

Ross, Lee, David Greene, and Pamela House. 1977. The "false consensus effect": An egocentric bias in social perception and attribution processes. *Journal of Experimental Social Psychology* 13:279–301.

Rothbart, Myron, and William Hallmark. 1988. In-group–out-group differences in the perceived efficacy of coercion and conciliation in resolving social conflict. *Journal of Personality and Social Psychology* 55:248–57.

Rothman, Stanley, and S. Robert Lichter. 1987. Elite ideology and risk perception in nuclear energy policy. *American Political Science Review* 81:383–404.

Rotter, Julian. 1966. *Generalized Expectancies for Internal versus External Control of Reinforcement.* Psychological Monographs: General and Applied, vol. 80, no. 1. Washington, D.C.: American Psychological Association.

Rucinski, Diana, and Charles T. Salmon. 1990. The "other" as the vulnerable voter: A study of the third-person effect in the 1988 U.S. presidential campaign. *International Journal of Public Opinion Research* 2:345–68.

Rudd, Robert. 1986. Issues as image in political campaign commercials. *Western Journal of Speech Communication* 50:102–13.

Salmon, Charles T. 1986. Perspectives on involvement in consumer and communication research. In *Progress in Communication Sciences,* vol. 7, edited by Brenda Dervin and Melvin Voigt. New York: Ablex.

Salwen, M. B. 1985. The reporting of public opinion polls during presidential years, 1968–1984. *Journalism Quarterly* 62:272–77.

Schattschneider, E. E. 1975. *The Semisovereign People.* Hinsdale, Ill.: Dryden Press.

Schudson, Michael. 1978. *Discovering the News: A Social History of American Newspapers.* New York: Basic Books.

Schwartz, Tony. 1974. *The Responsive Chord.* Garden City, N.Y.: Anchor Books.

Sears, David O. and Jack Citrin. 1982. *Tax Revolt: Something for Nothing in California.* Cambridge: Harvard University Press.

Senese, Dick. 1991. Interview by Dean Alger. Tape recording, 30 July.

Sentor, F., L. Reynolds, and D. Gruenenfelder. 1986. The presidency and the print media: Who controls the news? *Sociological Quarterly* 27:91–105.

Shaw, Donald L., and Maxwell E. McCombs. 1977. *The Emergence of American Political Issues: The Agenda-Setting Function of the Press.* St. Paul: West.

Sigal, Leon V. 1973. *Reporters and Officials.* Lexington, Mass.: D. C. Heath.

———. 1986. Who? Sources make the news. In *Reading the News,* edited by Michael Schudson and Robert Karl Manoff. New York: Pantheon, 9–37.

Sigel, Roberta S., ed. 1989. *Political Learning in Adulthood: A Sourcebook of Theory and Research.* Chicago: University of Chicago Press.

Simon, Herbert A. 1956. *Administrative Behavior: A Study of Decision Making Processes in Administrative Organizations.* 2nd ed. New York: Macmillan.

————. 1982. Affect and cognition: Comments. In *Affect and Cognition,* edited by Margaret Clark and Susan Fiske. Hillsdale, N.J.: Erlbaum.

Skinner, B. F. 1938. *The Behavior of Organisms.* New York: Appleton, Century, Crofts.

————. 1948. *Walden Two.* New York: Macmillan.

————. 1953. *Science and Human Behavior.* New York: Macmillan.

Smith, C. R. 1977. Television news as rhetoric. *Western Journal of Speech Communication* 41:147–59.

Smith, Dane. 1990a. Are we simply smug? Minneapolis *Star Tribune,* 27 July .

————. 1990b. Wellstone seeks to fan anti-incumbent fires in debate. Minneapolis *Star Tribune,* 15 October.

————. 1990c. Senate race ads have been mainly positive. Minneapolis *Star Tribune,* 27 October.

————. 1990d. Walter Mondale criticizes Boschwitz's ads. Minneapolis *Star Tribune,* 5 November.

————. 1991. Interview by Dean Alger. Tape recording, 29 July.

Smith, Dane, and Dennis McGrath. 1991. Interview by Dean Alger. Tape recording, 30 July.

Smith, Eric R. A. N. 1989. *The Unchanging American Voter.* Berkeley: University of California Press.

Smoller, F. 1986. The six o'clock presidency: Patterns of network news coverage of the president. *Presidential Studies Quarterly* 16:31–49.

————. 1988. Presidents and their critics: The structure of television news coverage. *Congress and the Presidency* 1:75–89.

Smoller, Fred. 1990. *The Six O'Clock Presidency.* New York: Praeger.

Sniderman, Paul, Richard Brody, and Philip Tetlock. 1991. *Reasoning and Choice: Explorations in Political Psychology.* New York: Cambridge University Press.

Spitzer, Robert J., ed. 1993. *Media and Public Policy.* Westport, Conn.: Praeger.

St. Paul Pioneer Press. 1990a. Editorial: Wellstone our choice to face Boschwitz, 2 September.

————. 1990b. Editorial: In the 1990s, Paul Wellstone better for the state and nation, 28 October.

Stovall, J. 1988. Coverage of 1984 presidential campaign. *Journalism Quarterly* 65:443–49.

Streitmatter, R. 1985. The impact of presidential personality on news coverage in major newspapers. *Journalism Quarterly* 62:66–73.

Swanson, D. L. 1977. And that's the way it was? Television covers the 1976 presidential campaign. *Quarterly Journal of Speech* 63:239–48.

Sylvan, Donald A., Ashok Goel, and B. Chandrasekaran. 1990. Analyzing political decision making from an information-processing perspective: JESSE. *American Journal of Political Science* 34:74–123.

Taylor, Paul. 1990. Senate races go begging: Incumbents well financed, job not attractive. *St. Paul Pioneer Press,* 8 August.

Teixeira, R. A. 1992. *The Disappearing American Voter.* Washington, D.C.: Brookings Institution.

Tetlock, Philip E. 1983. Policy-makers' images of international conflict. *Journal of Social Issues* 39:67–86.

———. 1993. Cognitive structural analysis of political rhetoric: Methodological and theoretical issues. In *Explorations in Political Psychology,* edited by Shanto Iyengar and William J. McGuire. Durham, N.C.: Duke University Press.

Tetlock, Philip E., and Richard Boettger. 1989. Cognitive and rhetorical styles of traditionalist and reformist Soviet politicians: A content analysis study. *Political Psychology* 10:209–32.

Tiedge, James T., Arthur Silverblatt, Michael J. Havice, and Richard Rosenfeld. 1991. Discrepancy between perceived first-person and perceived third-person mass media effects. *Journalism Quarterly* 68:141–54.

Tiemens, Robert K., Malcolm O. Sillars, Dennis C. Alexander, and Dennis C. Werling. 1988. Television coverage of Jesse Jackson's speech to the 1984 democratic national convention. *Journal of Broadcasting and Electronic Media* 32:1–22.

Times Mirror. 1989. *The People, the Press and Economics.* Washington, D.C.: Times Mirror Center for The People and The Press.

———. 1990. *The People, The Press & Politics 1990: A Times Mirror Typology.* Washington, D.C.: Times Mirror Center for The People and The Press.

Toner, Robin. 1990. Poll: Discontent looms large in voters' pre-election mood. Minneapolis *Star Tribune,* October.

Tuchman, Gaye. 1973. Making news by doing work: Routinizing the unexpected. *American Journal of Sociology* 79 (1):110–31.

———. 1978. *Making News: A Study in the Construction of Reality.* New York: Free Press.

Tulis, Jeffrey. 1987. *The Rhetorical Presidency.* Princeton: Princeton University Press.

Turk, J. V. 1987. Between president and press: White House public information and its influence on the mass media. Paper presented to the annual convention of the Association for Education in Journalism and Mass Communication, San Antonio, Texas.

Turner, K. 1985. *Lyndon Johnson's Dual War: Vietnam and the Press.* Chicago: University of Chicago Press.

United States Government. 1968. *Report of the National Advisory Commission on Civil Disorders.* New York: Bantam Books.

Vallone, Robert P., Lee Ross, and Mark R. Lepper. 1985. The hostile media phenomenon: Biased perceptions and perceptions of media bias in coverage of the Beirut massacre. *Journal of Personality and Social Psychology* 49:577–88.

Van Der Pligt, J., J. Van Der Linden, and P. Ester. 1982. Attitudes to nuclear energy, beliefs, values, and a false consensus. *Journal of Environmental Psychology* 2:221–31.

van Dijk, T. 1988a. *News Analysis: Case Studies of International and National News in the Press.* Hillsdale, N.J.: Erlbaum.

van Dijk, Teun A. 1988b. *News as Discourse.* Hillsdale, N.J.: Erlbaum.

Wagner, Joseph. 1986. Political tolerance and stages of moral development: A conceptual and empirical alternative. *Political Behavior* 8:45–80.

Wasburn, Philo C. 1992. *Broadcasting Propaganda: International Radio Broadcasting and the Construction of Political Reality.* Westport, Conn.: Praeger.

Weaver, David H., Doris A. Graber, Maxwell E. McCombs, and Chaim H. Eyal. 1981.

Media Agenda-setting in a Presidential Election: Issues, Images, and Interest. New York: Praeger. 1981.

Weinstein, Neil. 1980. Unrealistic optimism about future life events. _Journal of Personality and Social Psychology_ 39:806–20.

West, Darrell. 1988. Activists and economic policymaking in Congress. _American Journal of Political Science_ 32:662–80.

———. 1993. _Air Wars._ Washington, D.C.: Congressional Quarterly Press.

Wieviorka, Michel. 1993. _The Making of Terrorism._ Translated by David Gordon White. Chicago: University of Chicago Press.

Williams, Bruce, and Albert Matheny. 1995. _Democracy, Dialogue, and Social Regulation._ New Haven, Conn.: Yale University Press.

Wilson, Woodrow. 1885. _Congressional Government._ Boston: Houghton Mifflin.

Windt, Theodore O. 1994. The 1960 Kennedy-Nixon presidential debates. In _Rhetorical Studies of National Political Debates 1960–1992,_ 2nd ed, edited by Robert V. Friedenberg. Westport, Conn.: Praeger.

Winter, David G., and Leslie A. Carlson. 1988. Using motive scores in the psychobiographical study of an individual: The case of Richard Nixon. _Journal of Personality_ 56:75–103.

Wyer, Robert S. Jr., and Victor C. Ottati. 1993. Political information processing. In _Explorations in Political Psychology,_ edited by Shanto Iyengar and William J. McGuire. Durham, N.C.: Duke University Press.

Zajonc, R. B. 1980. Feeling and thinking: Preferences need no inferences. _American Psychologist_ 35:151–75.

———. 1984. On the primacy of affect. _American Psychologist_ 39:117–23.

Zaller, John R. 1987. Diffusion of political attitudes. _Journal of Personality and Social Psychology_ 53:821–33.

———. 1992. _The Nature and Origins of Mass Opinion._ New York: Cambridge University Press.

Zaller, John, Dennis Chiu, and Mark Hunt. 1994. Press rules and news content: Two contrasting case studies. Paper presented at the annual meeting of the American Political Science Association, New York.

Zaller, John, and Stanley Feldman. 1992. A simple theory of the survey response. _American Journal of Political Science_ 36:579–616.

Zaller, John, with Mark Hunt. 1994. The rise and fall of candidate Perot: Unmediated versus mediated politics—part 1. _Political Communication_ 11:357–90.

Zanna, Mark P., and Russell H. Fazio. 1982. The attitude-behavior relation: moving toward a third generation of research. In _Consistency in Social Behavior_ (The Ontario Symposium), vol. 2, edited by Mark P. Zanna, E. Tory Higgins, and C. Peter Herman. Hillsdale, N.J.: Erlbaum.

Zeidenstein, H. 1984. News media perceptions of White House news management. _Presidential Studies Quarterly_ 14:391–98.

Zukin, C. 1981. Mass communication and public opinion. In _Handbook of Political Communication,_ edited by D. D. Nimmo and K. R. Sanders. Beverly Hills, Calif.: Sage.

Contributors

Dean Alger, Independent author and consultant, Moorhead, Minnesota

W. Lance Bennett, Professor of political science, University of Washington

Timothy E. Cook, Professor of political science, Williams College

Ann N. Crigler, Associate professor of political science, University of Southern California

Michael X. Delli Carpini, Associate professor of political science, Barnard College

William A. Gamson, Professor of sociology, Boston College

Doris A. Graber, Professor of political science, University of Illinois at Chicago

August E. Grant, Associate professor of radio/TV/film, University of Texas at Austin

Roderick P. Hart, Liddell Professor of Communication and professor of government, University of Texas at Austin

Marion R. Just, Professor of political science, Wellesley College

John D. Klockner, Ph.D. candidate in political science, University of Washington

John Llewellyn, Assistant professor of speech communication, Wake Forest University

W. Russell Neuman, Edward R. Murrow Professor of International Communications, The Fletcher School, Tufts University

Richard M. Perloff, Professor of communication, Cleveland State University

Deborah Smith-Howell, Assistant professor of communication, University of Nebraska at Omaha

Bruce A. Williams, Associate professor of urban and regional planning, University of Illinois at Urbana-Champaign

Index

DATE DUE

HIGHSMITH #45115